Literacy Instruction for Students Who Are Deaf and Hard of Hearing

PROFESSIONAL PERSPECTIVES ON DEAFNESS: EVIDENCE AND APPLICATIONS

Series Editors Patricia Elizabeth Spencer, Marc Marschark

Evidence-Based Practice in Educating Deaf and Hard-of-Hearing Students

Patricia Elizabeth Spencer and Marc Marschark

Introduction to American Deaf Culture

Thomas K. Holcomb

Literacy Instruction for Students Who Are Deaf and Hard of Hearing

Susan R. Easterbrooks and Jennifer Beal-Alvarez

Literacy Instruction for Students Who Are Deaf and Hard of Hearing

Susan R. Easterbrooks and
Jennifer Beal-Alvarez

OXFORD
UNIVERSITY PRESS

OXFORD
UNIVERSITY PRESS

Oxford University Press is a department of the University of Oxford.
It furthers the University's objective of excellence in research, scholarship,
and education by publishing worldwide.

Oxford   New York
Auckland   Cape Town   Dar es Salaam   Hong Kong   Karachi
Kuala Lumpur   Madrid   Melbourne   Mexico City   Nairobi
New Delhi   Shanghai   Taipei   Toronto

With offices in
Argentina   Austria   Brazil   Chile   Czech Republic   France   Greece
Guatemala   Hungary   Italy   Japan   Poland   Portugal   Singapore
South Korea   Switzerland   Thailand   Turkey   Ukraine   Vietnam

Oxford is a registered trademark of Oxford University Press in the UK and certain other
countries.

Published in the United States of America by
Oxford University Press
198 Madison Avenue, New York, NY 10016

Library of Congress Cataloging-in-Publication Data
Easterbrooks, Susan R.
  Literacy instruction for students who are deaf and hard of hearing /
by Susan R. Easterbrooks and Jennifer Beal-Alvarez.
  p. cm.—(Professional perspectives on deafness: evidence and applications)
  Includes bibliographical references and index.
  ISBN 978–0–19–983855–4
  1. Deaf—Education.   2. Hearing impaired—Education.   3. Reading.   4. Literacy.
  I. Beal-Alvarez, Jennifer.   II. Title.
  HV2469.R4E27 2013
  371.91′246—dc23
  2012036484

ISBN 978–0–19–983855–4

9 8 7 6 5 4 3 2 1
Printed in the United States of America
on acid-free paper

CONTENTS

Literacy Instruction for Students Who Are Deaf and Hard of Hearing

1 Introduction and Overview

PURPOSE

This book focuses on instructional practices for teaching reading to children who are deaf or hard of hearing (DHH) in the current research, political, administrative, and practical environments. The Common Core Standards movement and No Child Left Behind call for practitioners to use evidence-based practices that are supported by research during instruction for all students. Current administrative preference for educating all children and youth in inclusive environments with their peers has changed the nature of instruction received and the methods by which it is imparted. Advances in technology, such as early identification of hearing loss, cochlear implants, and digital hearing aids, have increased the diversity of the student population, compelling teachers to view each child as "a population of one." By "diversity" we refer not only to ethnic and cultural diversity but to sensory, linguistic, cognitive, and communicative differences as well. It is within this confluence of circumstances that teachers must teach their state's standard curriculum, use the embedded materials, and implement the practices and strategies presented in upcoming chapters. We begin with an overview of the DHH population and literacy in general and then focus on challenges in literacy that face DHH students.

A portion of DHH students do not graduate high school, which is unfortunate because college education generally enhances a person's employment prospects and increases his or her earning potential (Dohm & Wyatt, 2002). In 2004 in the United States, 17 percent of DHH students from 14 to 22 years of age dropped out of high school (U.S. Department of Education, 2009), whereas 4.7 percent of the total student population of the same age dropped out (Chapman, Laird, & KewalRamani, 2010). While approximately 72 percent of DHH students graduated with a high school diploma and continued on to college (U.S. Department of Education, 2009a), only 25 percent of that number continued on to graduate from college (Boutin, 2008). Students without complete educations still must find jobs, apply for loans, pay their bills, pay taxes, read a prescription bottle, fill out a check, and read ingredients on a soup can. This is why it is critical for teachers of DHH students to utilize evidence-based practices in the classroom. As an alternative, educators might consider Causal Factors (described below) when practices with an evidence base are not available. We must do everything we can to improve literacy outcomes.

Students with hearing loss struggle with printed material in two ways: 1) they struggle to learn to read, and 2) they struggle to read printed material associated with content area classes. That is, in addition to problems learning to read, they may then have problems reading to learn! Teachers of DHH students must teach students to read, and they must teach students ways to handle print material that is more difficult than their current skills can support. For example, students may not be able to read material needed to do their school assignments. Both basic literacy skills and facility with print material associated with academic subjects require attention. In addition, teachers must now accomplish this within the context of evidence-based practices (EBPs) for instruction as mandated by the Individuals with Disabilities Education Improvement Act

(IDEIA, 2004) and No Child Left Behind Act (NCLB, 2001, 2002). Due to the lack of evidence-based practices in deaf education and the diversity within the population, this is a challenging task.

But before we begin, let's meet Tammy (pseudonym). Tammy is a real teacher in a small suburban school system south of a major metropolitan area. She serves all of the DHH children in her elementary school. Her morning reading instruction group includes a kindergartener who uses only ASL; two first graders who use bilateral cochlear implants, one of whom communicates orally and whose parents speak primarily Mandarin in the home, and the other who received a cochlear implant at four years of age and uses both signs and speech for communication, with spoken Spanish as the primary home language; and a second grader and a third grader who both wear hearing aids and communicate using ASL, although their parents do not use it at home. During instruction, Tammy pairs her spoken instruction with English-based signs, repeating the instructions orally and then in ASL to meet the needs of all of her students. Tammy's group of students is representative of that of many teachers of the deaf in local school districts. Because literacy is a complex and multifaceted process that must be taught to a range of students like Tammy's, one single perspective on instruction would fail to meet the needs of students like hers. This textbook presents literacy instructional practices and strategies for students like those in Tammy's classroom.

THE DIVERSITY OF THE DHH POPULATION

Historically, DHH students were educated in separate schools for the deaf, and they tended to present a more homogeneous pattern of needs. Today, most are taught in the general education environment and are more heterogeneous in their needs (U.S. Department of Education [USDOE], 2009; Gallaudet Research Institute [GRI], 2008) as a result of early identification and intervention, the type of listening technology available, the absence or presence of additional learning challenges, and the increase in homes where English may not be the first language to which the child is exposed. This means that learners who are DHH bring unique patterns of strengths and weaknesses to the process of learning to read. When a teacher like Tammy has to determine the best ways to provide reading instruction, she must consider each child's hearing loss and its effect on literacy and learning.[1] There is no one-size-fits-all solution. Those students who have functional access to sound can benefit from instructional practices used with hearing children, albeit modified, while those without functional access to sound will need adaptations and modifications ranging from minimal to maximal.

Children who are DHH may use assistive listening devices such as hearing aids, FM systems, or cochlear implants. A cochlear implant (CI) is a surgically implanted amplification device with internal and external components that amplifies and transmits sound electronically. In contrast, hearing aids are listening devices that are only external, worn behind or in the ear. Approximately 14 percent of DHH children in a Gallaudet Research Institute (2008) sample had a CI, and while data for only half of the sample were reported, 15 percent had bilateral CIs. About 59 percent of DHH students used hearing aids for instructional purposes. Other students may use a combination of cochlear implants, hearing aids, or FM systems. FM systems are portable amplification devices that reduce the noise-to-distance ratio between the teacher and student. The amount of comprehensible amplification provided by these devices varies by child. For example, while one child with an unaided severe hearing loss may respond to sound in a manner similar to a child with a mild hearing loss when he or she wears hearing aids, another child may be unable to respond to sound from an amplification system in a usable manner. Children's varying levels of hearing loss and individual benefit from amplification create two populations of DHH students: those who can learn through spoken communication and thus read through that channel and those who primarily rely on visual communication. Children who can benefit

---

[1] Degree of hearing loss is classified in decibels (dB) into five categories: mild (26–40dB), moderate (41–55dB), moderate-to-severe (56–70dB), severe (71–90dB), and profound (greater than 91dB) (University of Rochester Medical Center, 2010). This means that a student will not hear sounds softer than the minimum dB indicated in each range. For example, conversational speech falls within 50–60dB (University of Rochester Medical Center), so students with a moderate-to-severe hearing loss will not have access to speech within a classroom without amplification of the sound through devices such as cochlear implants or hearing aids.

from spoken communication appear to be in the majority (70 percent) during the preschool years (Easterbrooks, Lederberg, Miller, Bergeron, & Connor, 2008), but that pattern changes as the population becomes older (Musselman & Akamatsu, 1999).

TWO POPULATIONS

The field of deaf education currently serves two populations: children who learn spoken communication via cochlear implants and hearing aids, and those who need alternative supports for communication, such as a natural sign language (e.g., American Sign Language) or a hybrid sign language (discussed below),[2] which may or may not be accompanied by some degree of verbal speech. These two primary avenues to learning exist within a spectrum, with children who use only oral communication at one end, those who use only sign language at the other end, and those who use each form of communication to varying extents in the middle. Further, students may change their communication preferences over time. For example, students who do not fully acquire spoken communication when younger frequently switch to a signing mode in elementary and middle school (Musselman & Akamatsu, 1999). How a teacher instructs students in the many elements of literacy depends on the individual needs of the students, from auditory instruction in letter-sound correspondences on one end of the spectrum to the use of Visual Phonics on the other end, and from spoken conversation surrounding books as a means to promote vocabulary knowledge to explicit instruction using manipulatives. In this textbook we attempt to provide a broad range of resources to meet the varying communication styles and learning styles of DHH children. After getting to know a student's unique needs and abilities, the teacher can choose which options will probably

---

[2] In sign-supported speech, the communicator supports his or her spoken language with signs, but the spoken language has primacy in conveying the message. In speech-supported sign, signs have primacy in conveying the message and are accompanied by the individual's best approximation of the spoken counterpart of the sign. Depending on the individual's skills and the communicative demands of the situation, a signer may use speech-supported sign in one situation and sign-supported speech in another.

work best for that child. Not all children will need the same options, but at least one option (or an individualized combination of them) can be expected to support success for each child. We do not presume to prescribe instruction but to make all reasonable options available to the prepared practitioner.

COMMUNICATION APPROACHES

Given the nature of the DHH population, the teacher of the deaf must have knowledge of multiple strategies, multiple languages, and multiple ways to meet the needs of his or her students. In this textbook, we refer to spoken languages and signed. The former may include spoken English, Spanish, Mandarin, etc. The latter includes the use of American Sign Language (ASL) or a hybrid form of sign language, such as a combination of ASL and English elements paired with spoken communication. ASL is a natural language with its own syntax and grammar, distinctly different from spoken language. In addition to signs presented on the hands, the use of space and nonmanual markers such as facial expression, head nod, body tilt, and eye gaze are used to express semantic and syntactic information (Neidle, Kegl, MacLaughlin, Bahan, & Lee, 2000; Wilbur, 2000).

In contrast to native users of ASL, some parents, teachers, and students use hybrid forms of signing. In hybrid forms, spoken English[3] is paired with signs ranging from strict adherence to ASL to invented systems such as Signing Exact English (Gustason & Zowolkow, 2006) to more relaxed applications that do not contain all of the grammatical morphemes[4] of either ASL or English (Maxwell & Bernstein, 1985). Nonmanual markers (e.g., "cha" mouth movement) are not incorporated

---

[3.] Although we refer to English in this context, similar challenges are found across all spoken languages. Most cultures have a signed version of their spoken language in addition to an indigenous version of the country's sign language, such as Signed Swedish or Swedish Sign Language, Signed South African or South African Sign Language, and Signed Chinese or Chinese Sign Language.

[4.] Grammatical morphemes in English are words or parts of words that cannot be divided into smaller parts, such as -ed or -ly, that contain meaning. ASL morphemes include such elements as mouth movements and use of space, among others.

into hybrid sign because they interfere with the presentation of words on the mouth (Wilbur, 2000). Hybrid sign may also incorporate initialized signs by replacing the handshape of an ASL sign with the handshape for the first letter in the word, such as "K" for "kitchen" (Lucas, Bayley, & Valli, 2001; McKee & Kennedy, 2006). According to the Gallaudet Research Institute (GRI; 2008), 92.5 percent of families with DHH children use spoken English in the home, 21.9 percent use spoken Spanish, and only 3.8 percent of families use ASL. Of parents who use some form of sign language, 24 percent reported that they used it "regularly" in the home across the DHH student population (GRI, 2008), while one-third of DHH children and families who received early intervention services used sign with their children (Mayne, Yoshinaga Itano, Sedey, & Carey, 2000). While the majority of parents used speech in the home, about 21 percent of DHH students used sign language interpreting services in school, 35 percent of teachers[5] used a combination of sign language and speech for instruction, and 11 percent of teachers used sign only (GRI). This means that 52 percent of teachers use only speech for instruction, reflecting teachers' responses to the diversity of instructional needs of DHH students. Because of these multiple communication approaches, teachers may instruct groups of students similar to Tammy's class described at the outset of the chapter.

READING OUTCOMES AMONG THE HEARING POPULATION

Not only must children learn to read, they must also read to learn information across content areas in school and throughout life, from instructions and recipes to daily news and magazines. Poor reading ability is associated with increased retention, school failure, and dropout rates, as well as unemployment and even incarceration (Florida Literacy Coalition, n.d.). Educators, politicians, scientists, and parents have spent countless

---

[5.] The reference to a "teacher" does not imply a job title but an activity description. One who teaches a child might be a speech therapist, an aide, or in some cases even a parent. The focus of this book is on how to teach regardless of who specifically is doing the teaching. We attempt to refer to this individual alternatively as he or she, intending no gender bias.

time, effort, and money investigating the necessary components to create readers of all children.[6]

LITERACY LEVELS OF DHH LEARNERS

The literacy abilities of some DHH students fall within the basic to below-basic range along with approximately 35 percent of all Americans. Whereas many DHH students graduate high school reading somewhere around a fourth-grade level (Allen, 1986; Traxler, 2000), as many as 30 percent of those who were deaf prior to the age of 3 years may leave school functionally illiterate, with a reading level below grade 2.9 on standardized tests (Vernon, Rafiman, Greenberg, & Monteiror, 2001). While large, national samples may provide a bleak outlook (Marschark, Lang, & Albertini, 2002), smaller samples of specific subgroups present a more hopeful picture (Connor & Zwolan, 2004; Geers, 2002; Pakulski & Kaderavek, 2001), and some states are beginning to report large numbers of DHH children meeting expectations on state tests of literacy (Easterbrooks & Beal-Alvarez, 2012).

LEARNING ENVIRONMENTS

The reason we must be concerned with the learning environment in which children are educated is that different environments pose different challenges to the effective acquisition of receptive and expressive communication. The auditory environment occurs in 360 degrees, permitting sound localization, especially when the listener turns his or her head to receive additional information; however, the visual environment is constrained to 120 degrees (Tasker & Schmidt, 2008). Visual constraints may limit how

---

[6.] Looking at illiteracy rates in a broader world context, we find that 774 million adults, or approximately one-fifth of the world's population, have been deemed illiterate (United Nations Educational, Scientific and Cultural Organization [UNESCO], 2008). According to the National Assessment of Adult Literacy (NAAL) report to the National Center for Education Statistics (NCES) of the Institute for Education Sciences (Baer, Kutner, Sabatini, & White, 2009), 30 million adult Americans have below-basic prose literacy (i.e., the skills to search, comprehend, and use continuous texts in editorials, news stories, brochures, and instructional materials), and of these 11 million (3.6%) are illiterate.

the child receives communication to a face-to-face line of sight with the teacher or classmates, though peripheral vision may be useful for picking up some meaning. The visual environment has an influence on the availability of speechreading, a factor associated with positive reading outcomes in both oral and signing children (Harris & Moreno, 2006; Scherer, 1969). Further, about 80 percent of deaf students attend their local public schools and spend the majority of their school day in the general education classroom (United States Department of Education, 2009a), where only 1–2 percent of teachers are deaf. This may result in lack of exposure to adequate adult models of sign language. Currently, only three states in the United States require teachers of deaf children to pass a proficiency exam for sign language skills. Interpreter abilities vary as well. A study of interpreters found expert interpreters (i.e., those with 25 years of experience, a deaf parent, and national certification) to be the most effective at accurately representing spoken information, while those with fewer credential were less so (Schick, Williams, & Kupermintz, 2006).

Participation in early intervention also affects children's language and therefore literacy abilities. DHH children whose parents had "ideal" or "good" involvement in early intervention had language scores comparable to their hearing peers, while children whose parents' participation was rated as "average" to "limited" had smaller lexicons; language scores across the sample were not related to the mode of communication families used (Moeller, 2000). Further, for deaf toddlers with hearing mothers, the strongest predictors of their language development were a mother's acceptance of the hearing loss and her motivation to compensate for her child's communication needs (Pressman, Pipp-Siegel, Yoshinaga-Itano, & Deas, 1999). From early intervention to classroom designs, DHH children face challenges among all aspects of the reading instructional process.

CURRENTLY DEBATED PERSPECTIVES ON READING INSTRUCTION

Bottom-Up, Top-Down, or Balanced Literacy Models

During the middle part of the 20th century, phonics and other bottom-up objectives appeared to be the preferred perspective on reading instruction.

A bottom-up approach to reading focuses on decoding, phonics, and analysis of words, phrases, and sentences (Flesch, 1955; LaBerge & Samuels, 1974). The philosophy was that once students knew enough of the discrete pieces and could put them all together, they would be able to read. Around the 1970s and 1980s a switch in perspective to more holistic approaches, called top-down approaches, took place (Goodman, 1986; Nunan, 1991), and students were taught strategies for unlocking the meaning of printed material even if they had not mastered earlier foundational skills. In top-down approaches, children constructed meaning by activating and applying prior knowledge. The argument was that readers would learn decoding skills more easily within the context of known information. The concern was that it was difficult to document actual growth in discrete skills; taken too far, we would be asking children to work at a level so high that they would not have sufficient supportive skills. As a result, the idea of balanced literacy became prominent in the 1990s because it combined instruction in discrete skills within cognitively engaging literacy activities focused on better comprehension (Cunningham & Stanovich, 1998; Stainthorp, 1989). Taylor, Pearson, Peterson, and Rodriguez (2003) identified four evidence-based dimensions of literacy instruction necessary to maximize student engagement: 1) supporting higher-level thinking, 2) encouraging independent application of skills learned, 3) being student-directed rather than teacher-directed, and 4) active rather than passive involvement in literacy activities. In 2000, the National Reading Panel redirected the discussion of literacy models once more.

General Education Model

In 1999, 14 experts from around the United States, called the *National Reading Panel* (NRP), convened to determine whether there was sufficient evidence in the available literacy research to support the use of bottom-up, top-down, or balanced literacy approaches. The members of the panel examined thousands of research articles on literacy development and concluded that both perspectives (bottom-up and top-down) provided their own unique contributions to the literacy process. The panelists identified six key factors that all teachers should address when designing instruction: phonemic awareness, alphabetics (letter knowledge, phonological awareness, and phonics), vocabulary, text comprehension, fluency, and motivation (National Institute of Child Health and Human Development, 2000). Many years have passed since the publication of these findings, and the list of critical skills has been reduced to five; the category of "motivation" seems to have received little attention. However, there remains a clearly distinct relationship between motivation and one's ability to read (Gottfried, 1985, 1990; Guthrie et al., 1996; Turner, 1995). Students who are internally motivated, for the most part, *will* learn to read. We see this often with deaf students who are of high school age. Suddenly they realize that they will be leaving school and will have to depend on reading and writing as a way to communicate with the world. Some researchers noted a marked increase in the skills of deaf students who were 17 or 18 years of age (Nover, Andrews, Baker, Everhart, & Bradford, 2002) that, we speculate, may be the result of students' sudden awareness of the future importance of reading in their lives. However, for the most part, one rarely sees reference to motivation in textbooks and research articles because it is hard to define and we cannot identify the steps needed to teach or assess it. The question is whether it is a teachable skill or an internal state. Because we know so little about how to teach motivation (and perhaps we cannot), it has been dropped from much of the discussion surrounding what we should teach and how we should teach it. Yet, because motivation appears to be individualized, teachers will want to identify successful motivators for their students during instruction.

Subsequent chapters in this book present a discussion of practices with varying levels of research support that address specific literacy skills. While these are foundational skills necessary to the reading process, they do not represent the whole picture, and the role of top-down versus bottom-up practices remains under discussion. It is more likely that, as with all strong differences of opinion, the truth varies by individual needs and lies somewhere in the middle of the argument.

In summary, literacy is a multifaceted process that is too complex to be addressed by a single perspective. Those instructing DHH children to read must incorporate those aspects of top-down and bottom-up instruction most beneficial to each learner. Some writers argue that literacy acquisition in deaf children is qualitatively the same but quantitatively delayed (Trezek, Wang & Paul, 2010) in comparison to hearing children. If this is the case, then teachers of the deaf must address all of the elements identified by the NRP (2000). If not, then we must expand our definitions of reading instruction to incorporate a broader perspective. We maintain that those who are teaching reading to DHH children must have as broad a perspective as possible, addressing individual needs along multiple continuums, recognizing the influence of all underlying aspects of language proficiency (i.e., phonology, morphology, syntax, semantics, and pragmatics) on reading, and respecting that children's languages will fall along a continuum from spoken language through hybrid signs to ASL.

CHALLENGES FACING TEACHERS OF DHH LEARNERS

In this section we describe some of the abiding issues that practitioners face when instructing DHH students to read. Recall the description of Tammy's class from the beginning of the chapter. Yin, a first grader in Tammy's class who uses bilateral cochlear implants and whose parents speak Mandarin, communicates orally in the classroom and at home. While Tammy will likely use English as the language of instruction in her classroom, she might take advantage of Yin's developing literacy skills by making connections between printed English and printed Mandarin, similar to Schleper's (2000b) writing activity in which a student mediated between both languages while writing a language experience story. Tammy might also highlight any similarities and differences between spoken English and spoken Mandarin, such as phonemes, to solidify Yin's listening and oral communication skills in both the classroom and the home environment. Keep Yin in mind as you read through the next section.

Multiple Languages for Instruction. Many DHH children struggle to master a first language (L1), no matter if that language is spoken or signed, often because their parents and caregivers are novice communicators. Nearly all (95 percent) of DHH children are born to hearing parents (Mitchell & Karchmer, 2004), and language use in the home may vary among spoken languages or signed languages. Children's access to language is affected by their uptake, which is their active recognition, interaction, and response to the communicative interactions to which they are exposed (Harris, 1992). Language acquisition involves more than just input. One can make information available to a child over and over, but simple input is insufficient; the materials used and the process undertaken must actively engage the child's full attention. Many parents of children who use sign language do not learn it at a level sufficient for fluent communication (Lederberg & Mobley, 1990). Similar to hearing children, whose vocabulary growth is directly related to how much language their mothers use with them (Huttenlocher, Haight, Bryk, Sletzer, & Lyons, 1991), the vocabularies of those DHH children who used sign language was predicted by the number of signs used by their hearing mothers (Lederberg & Everhart, 1998; Spencer, 1993). Most hearing mothers sign only a small amount of what they actually say (Lederberg & Everhart, 1998; Spencer, 1993). These factors result in the slow growth of a first language within an impoverished language environment (Lederberg & Beal-Alvarez, 2011).

To this we add the fact that the immigrant population of the United States increased dramatically in the 10 years up to 2000, from 19.7 million, or 7.9 percent of the total U.S. population, to 31.3 million, or 11.1 percent, an increase of 57 percent (Malone, Baluja, Costanzo, & Davis, 2003). This means that we must address the following questions: When do we use English? For students who sign, when do we use ASL? When do we use hybrid forms like Signed English? How and when do we show a connection between English, whether spoken or signed, and ASL? What are the predominant home languages that our students must master? When and how do we incorporate home language into reading instruction? How do we connect each language to print? Researchers have only begun to grapple with the pervasive nature of the above questions.

Multiple Locations Where Students Are Taught. It is approaching 40 years since the first special education legislation (P.L. 94–142) pronounced that all children had the right to a free, appropriate, public education, preferably in the school nearest their place of residence. Until that time, most

DHH children attended special schools. Today most DHH children attend school locally (USDOE, 2009a), and placements of DHH students vary greatly from school system to school system. Less than 47 percent of DHH students spend more than 21 percent of their educational day outside of their regular classroom, and less than 19 percent spend between 21 and 61 percent of the day in another setting. This trend has increased annually since 1995 (USDOE). The type of educational placement for DHH students will necessarily affect their opportunities for instructional choices.

General Education Influences on DHH Learners. Around the turn of the century, teachers faced several changes as a result of the field's movement away from balanced literacy to a focus first on fluency and then on phonological awareness; advice from the No Child Left Behind (NCLB) mandate that all children would be reading on grade level by 2013–2014 (United States Department of Education, 2005); and the assumption that the National Reading Panel's five areas of instruction would be sufficient to teach all children to read. While research is emerging for particular reading practices and strategies with DHH students, much more individual, child-based research that has practical applications for instruction in the classroom is needed.

In addition, the general education standards movement created profound changes to how and where DHH children receive their literacy instruction. The Standards Movement crystallized with the publication of a report from the U.S. Department of Education's National Commission on Excellence in Education (1983) titled *A Nation at Risk*. In this treatise, parents, educators, administrators, and legislators were dramatically warned: "If an unfriendly power had attempted to impose on America the mediocre educational performance that exists today, we might well have viewed it as an act of war" (p. 5). The Commission recommended a return to a focus on the basics of English, mathematics, science, social studies, and computer science; enhanced time engaged in learning; and a strengthening of standards at both the level of the curriculum and the level of teacher preparation (Easterbrooks & Putney, 2008). Standardization led further to large-scale, high-stakes assessments (Cawthon, 2007; International Reading Association, 1999; Luckner & Bowen, 2006). Today DHH children are frequently incorporated into the regular education classroom, where they receive instruction in their states' standard curriculum. Reading instruction may be conducted by a teacher qualified to work with DHH children or by a special education teacher, general education teacher, speech-language pathologist, parent, or other practitioner. For example, Sally is a third grader in Tammy's class who uses ASL and receives daily reading instruction in the general education classroom from the general education teacher and an educational interpreter. To maintain Sally's reading progress in general education, Tammy supplements Sally's reading instruction every day in a small group setting by providing additional vocabulary and reading strategy instruction after collaborative planning with the general education teacher. She also assists the teacher in maintaining proper functioning of Sally's hearing aids

All practitioners must make the effort to ensure that DHH learners receive a) access to needed amplification, b) careful coordination between curricula and student needs, c) collaboration among all service providers, and d) supportive modifications during instruction and assessment in the general education setting. Those serving DHH children must make themselves aware of practices that are valid and reliable in order to bring about the most effective and efficient growth in student learning.

RESULTING CHALLENGES OF LITERACY INSTRUCTION FOR DHH STUDENTS

Considering all of the factors above, practitioners serving DHH children, whether a teacher of the deaf (TOD), a general educator, a speech-language pathologist, a parent, or any other service provider, must address the following challenges in order to teach all DHH children to read and to learn through reading:

1. Listening devices are a key to instructional success for most DHH children. Effective teachers and practitioners know how to use the equipment effectively, when to use the student's personal aid and when to use the FM microphone, how to charge the FM system daily, how to change hearing aid and cochlear implant batteries, and how to monitor equipment for failure. If a hearing

aid, FM system, or cochlear implant is not working right, then the child cannot learn effectively. It would be like asking the child to close his or her eyes and then read. For those who use it, listening technology is not just assistive in nature; it forms a key instructional element that must be working maximally at all times. Effective teachers must learn how to troubleshoot technology problems and know who to ask to get them resolved.

2. Most children will receive instruction from their states' mandated curricula. Effective teachers and practitioners document the choice of an alternative curriculum when necessary. They know how to pre-test, teach, and post-test student outcomes while also integrating the child's individual language and reading goals into general education instruction. Effective teachers consider appropriate assessments for progress monitoring and benchmarking in reading and language, and modify assessments in a manner that maintains their validity.

3. Not all DHH children will be able to maintain the pace of the standard curriculum. Effective teachers and practitioners ensure that children are mastering not only an adequate breadth of skills but an adequate depth as well. This requires collaborating with the general education teacher on essential vocabulary, skills, and concepts that may need to be pre-taught in preparation for instruction (Burns, Dean, & Foley, 2004; Cannon, Fredrick, & Easterbrooks, 2010). Effective teachers must use pre-assessment to determine additional instruction the student may need. They must also negotiate how much of the curriculum (for example, how many vocabulary words) the student must master to achieve his or her performance goals, both on the Individualized Education Program (IEP) and to meet general education goals.

4. Most DHH students will take their states' required tests of literacy; in some instances, modifications are permitted. Effective teachers must know what modifications are allowed and learn how to advocate for appropriate modifications to the instructions, the format, and the form of response.

5. Learning through an interpreter is very challenging for even the best learner; students must know how to divide their attention among teacher(s), interpreter, material, comments of other students, and environmental signals. Further, qualified educational interpreters are not always readily available. For example, of 2,100 educational interpreters across the United States, 60 percent had inadequate skills to provide full access to the general education classroom (Schick et al., 2006). Effective teachers must understand the challenges students face when instruction is mediated through an interpreter. They must advocate when needed for sufficient classroom interpreting support.

6. Most students will need instructional modification in the classroom. For example, if the teacher is using the scripted SRA reading program, the child may struggle to keep up if he or she is using an interpreter. Effective teachers must permit alternative responses. DHH learners will need sufficient time to receive a message from the interpreter, think about the message, think about the answer, and then formulate the answer. When using audio materials such as audiobooks or videotapes with sound in the general classroom, teachers must make arrangements for the student to have access to the information that other students receive (e.g., closed captioning, interpretation).

7. Finally, effective teachers and practitioners will pay extra attention to the visual and auditory environments. The room should be arranged so that the student can see the teacher, the interpreter (if appropriate), the board, and some of his or her classmates at all times. Children who use speechreading will need visual access to those cues. New and previous vocabulary words and organizers should be easy to see. Students should have sufficient time to finish reading a passage before answering a question; DHH readers cannot read the text and watch the teacher or interpreter simultaneously. If a classmate says something of instructional importance and the student is still looking at her book, effective teachers must repeat this necessary information to her. Regarding the auditory environment,

effective practitioners assess the level of background noise within the classroom. He or she should also seat the student away from additional noise sources, such as heating or air conditioning vents and windows, and provide absorption of reflected noise through alternatives such as carpeting.

Teachers and other education practitioners will need to keep these and many more instructional issues in mind when teaching reading to a DHH child.

EVIDENCE-BASED PRACTICES, CAUSAL FACTORS, AND POSITIVE STUDENT OUTCOMES

Walking down the halls of any elementary school, one sees good reading instruction taking place, including the use of language experience activities, bulletin boards, classroom routine charts, special events charts, word walls, and labels posted throughout classrooms, among other strategies. While these "tried and true" methods are common, they do not necessarily have strong evidence in their support. NCLB obligates us to use scientifically proven practices, or evidence-based practices (EBPs), that are supported by research that is both valid and compelling (Graham, 2005). However, instructional decisions continue to be made based on colleague opinion and personal experience (Brackenbury, Burroughs, & Hewitt, 2008) because the evidence base in deaf education is lacking in depth and breadth (Easterbrooks & Stephenson, 2006; Luckner, Sebald, Cooney, Young, & Muir, 2005/2006). The compelling purpose behind the EBP movement is to ensure that practitioners are using practices, materials, strategies, and interventions that *cause* positive learning outcomes in students. We are obligated to engage in practices for which there is proof of effectiveness in causing positive change. Said differently, we search for a causal relationship between an intervention (e.g., a specific instructional strategy) and an outcome (e.g., increases in student vocabulary). Causal evidence usually comes from an empirical study that compares results from an intervention group with results from a control group (i.e.,

one that did not have the intervention) and generally involves large par-
ticipant pools. More often, the evidence base in deaf education comprises
quasi-experimental results where there was no control group and/or
where a correlation was identified rather than a cause. It is important to
note that a correlation (i.e., two sets of results are related to each other in
some way) is *not* a cause. When only correlational data are available, it is
important to consider multiple examples in the literature that document
the correlation. When choosing a practice, material, strategy, or intervention, practitioners should consider its evidence base. The following
guidelines (see Figure 1.1) may help practitioners make appropriate decisions about the evidentiary base of a practice.

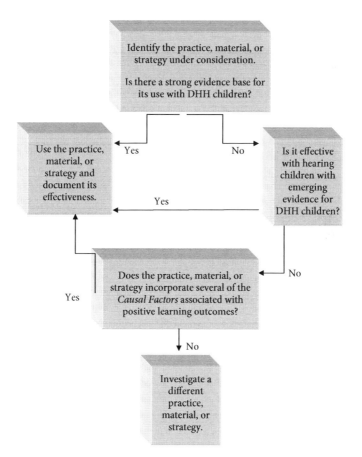

FIGURE 1.1. Flowchart of Decision Making to Determine Evidence for a Practice, Material,
Strategy, or Intervention. Created and contributed by S. Easterbrooks

Step 1   Causal Evidence for Use with DHH Students. Choose the instructional practice, material, strategy, or intervention for potential use. Is there evidence in the literature providing strong empirical support that this will *cause* positive learning outcomes in DHH students? If there is no documented causal relationship between a practice, material, strategy, or intervention among DHH learners, then are there multiple sources of research showing a correlation between the practice and positive outcomes with other learners? Are there any single-case design (SCD) or qualitative studies in its support? If not, then is there expert opinion available on its usefulness? Have any blue ribbon panels (e.g., What Works Clearinghouse) reviewed the materials? Has a joint committee of stakeholders (e.g., the Conference of Educational Administrators of Schools and Programs for the Deaf, Inc.) met and documented its support of the practice? If not, see Step 2.

Step 2.   Causal Evidence for Use with Hearing Students and Emerging Evidence for DHH Students. Ask the same questions as were asked above about EBPs for hearing students. Is there evidence in the literature of a strongly persuasive nature that the practice under consideration causes positive learning outcomes in hearing children? If there is, and if emerging evidence is also available in the deaf education literature, then one might build a case for use of the practice. If there is no evidence available, then practitioners will need to gather their own evidence in the classroom (e.g., action research,[7] other data collection) to document effectiveness and include evidence from Step 3.

Step 3.   Evidence That the Practice Incorporates Factors Known to Have a Causal Relationship with Positive Outcomes. If

---

[7] Action research refers to participatory research by the individual (e.g., teacher) using an identified practice. It requires implementation of a standard set of procedures for problem identification, data collection, and reflection and may be conducted in the classroom.

there is no persuasive evidence for the use of a particular practice, material, strategy, or intervention, then determine whether or not the practice incorporates sociological, cognitive, or psychological factors known to have a causal relationship with good reading outcomes (see Table 1.1). If the practice incorporates Causal Factors, then it might be worth investigating, and at a minimum, practitioners should document its effectiveness in the classroom through action research and data collection in the classroom itself. We address options for data collection throughout this book.

What Are the Positive Causal Factors Associated with Good Instruction in General and Reading Instruction in Particular?

Based on evidence from previous reviews of the knowledge base for DHH literacy (Easterbrooks & Stephenson, 2006; Luckner et al., 2005/2006), the evidence base in deaf education is still developing. We have very few empirical studies of interventions comparing experimental versus control groups that document a cause-effect (i.e., causal) relationship between different methods, materials, approaches, or strategies; for the most part we must rely on quasi-experimental or SCD studies or common sense about what to do. However, that does not give us license to say, "I'll just keep doing what I am doing until we have better data." Rather, educators are compelled to establish alternatives.

Another way of looking at the issue of EBPs is from the perspective of the psychological, social, or instructional factors known to have a causal relationship with positive child outcomes. A *Causal Factor* is a good general teaching practice, as opposed to a specific intervention, method, material, or strategy that has been shown to lead to positive learning outcomes. Causal Factors may be used for considering an EBP based on the Transitive Property of Equality (i.e., If A = B and B = C, then A = C). For example, there is only one published empirical study of the popular *Fairview* materials (Ausbrooks-Rusher, Schimmel, & Edwards, 2012). However, these materials address language needs of

Table 1.1. *Causal Factors Underlying Good Reading Instructional Practice for DHH Students (HOTS & CoVES)*

Causal Factors	Description
HOTS = Higher-Order Thinking Skills	Instruction that has as its focus higher-order, critical thinking, and problem-solving skills, including the ability to draw inferences, leads to better outcomes for students. Thinking about reading and thinking about thinking (metacognition) are components of this area as well.
Co = Communication	Instruction presented through comprehensible communication leads to better outcomes. Students learn better when their teachers are competent communicators in the modalities and languages used by their students or when materials account for communication challenges; communication provides a social context, which fosters motivation.
V = Visual Support (visual imagery, organization, and memory)	Instruction that supports the development of visual imagery and visual memory to aid comprehension and recall leads to better outcomes. Visualization and visual organizers are important components of this category.
E = Explicit Instruction	Some skills are more efficiently learned if taught directly (i.e., systematic, direct, engaging, outcome-oriented) rather than implicitly.
S = Scaffolding and Mediation	Based in sufficient learning supports, scaffolded instruction leads students to expanded views of information and to mastery of information that is difficult to grasp and leads to better outcomes. Depends on guidance from a more knowledgeable other (MKO).

Modified from: Easterbrooks, S. R. (2010).

the deaf child, and better language skills lead to better reading outcomes, and so the Transitive Property allows speculation that these materials may cause positive reading outcomes. A primary assumption of this approach is that good teaching influences good learning. To investigate the factors that support good teaching, Easterbrooks (2010) reviewed the literature on sociology, cognition, and psychology and identified factors that correlated with or had a causal relationship with good teaching and learning in DHH students. This resulted in the development of a list of five factors that correlated with positive outcomes. In this book we present additional links to the literature that go beyond simple correlation and identify those that have a causal nature, that is, they are known to cause positive learning outcomes in DHH students.

When an evidence base is unavailable, we suggest the use of practices that incorporate most or all of the five Causal Factors described below within a good teaching paradigm. This, paired with adequate documentation of the effectiveness of the practice, would form a type of evidence that is useful during an IEP meeting. Table 1.1 identifies five Causal Factors that are known to support learning in DHH students. Throughout this book, we present practices that have a research base, and we also describe practices that incorporate Causal Factors in their approach to instruction. We suggest the mnemonics *HOTS* and *CoVES* as a way to remember these important Causal Factors.

Causal Factor 1 = **HOTS**

The first component of good instruction that causes positive outcomes in learners is a focus on Higher-Order Thinking Skills (HOTS). In reading, most of the important questions about a passage (e.g., What was the turning point in the story? Why did the character change his mind?) require higher-order thinking skills. DHH students who received HOTS training thought of more than one solution to a problem, thought before responding, and were able to organize information sequentially (Martin & Jonas, 1986). Successful teaching that promoted higher-order language use and critical thinking skills, such as the ability to draw an inference or predict outcomes in a story, resulted in positive learning gains in students (Brigham & Hartman, 2010). This is especially important in literacy acquisition because much of what we read requires us to draw inferences. This skill depends upon accessing prior knowledge, which taxes the DHH student's knowledge reservoir (Strassman, 1997). Practices that promote higher-order language and critical thinking skills are important correlates of thinking and learning, and these skills can be taught (Fritschmann, Deshler, & Schumaker, 2007).

Causal Factor 2 – Communication

The second Causal Factor of good instruction is a communication match between teacher and students. Those teachers who use language that the child can understand have students who learn better (Hermans, Ormel, Knoors, & Verhoeven, 2008). This is just common sense. Parent communication predicts child communication whether the child is hearing, uses spoken language, or uses sign language (Huttenlocher et al., 1991; Lederberg & Everhart, 1998; Spencer, 1993). Levy, Rodriguez, and Wubbles (1993) examined outcomes for typically hearing middle-school students and found that, discounting the significant influence of socioeconomic factors and previous achievement, teacher communication style accounted for the majority of variance in malleable outcomes, that is, in the outcomes open to teacher influence. Language and learning have a social context (Partington & Galloway, 2005/2006). When children and teachers mutually understand each other, learning can occur (Hartman, 1996). Teachers should be skilled in using the language of their students, whether spoken or signed.

Clearly, whether in the spoken mode or the signed mode, communication has an influence on literacy acquisition. For example, Fung, Chow, and McBride-Chang (2005) studied the emergent literacy skills of deaf children who communicated orally and whose parents were taught how to converse with their children about information in storybooks, also known as dialogic reading. The authors found better emergent literacy outcomes in children whose parents communicated with them using dialogic conversations than those whose parents did not. On the other hand, teachers who are skilled signers directly influence a child's learning (Lane, Hoffmeister, & Bahan, 1996; Reeves, Newell, Holcomb, & Stinson, 2000), and there is a strong positive relationship between students' signing abilities and literacy levels (Hermans et al., 2008; Padden & Ramsey, 2000; Singleton, Supalla, Litchfield, & Schley, 1998; Strong & Prinz, 1997). College students at the National Technical Institute for the Deaf identified "fluency in sign communication as the most important characteristic of an effective teacher" (Goodman, 2006, p. 6). Unfortunately, only 38 percent of deaf education teachers judged their ability to produce signs to be as good as their expression in English (Lane et al., 1996). Teachers of DHH students must possess superior communication skills whether they use spoken English, hybrid sign systems (with or without speech support), or ASL.

Causal Factor 3 = Visualization

A third factor that causes positive learning outcomes in DHH students is that of making information visually available, including visualization, visual organization, or other visual enhancements. Instructional strategies that support visualization or use of visuospatial strategies for comprehension, retention, and memory are based in this Causal Factor and, therefore, might be considered to have an evidence base. The use of visual supports is a time-honored strategy for assisting students with typical hearing (Clarke, 1991) and improving reading outcomes in DHH children (Scherer, 1969). The use of programs based on developing visual imagery has been shown to increase gray matter volume (GMV) (i.e., in those parts of the brain associated with visual imagery and learning) and reading outcomes (i.e., comprehension, phonics, and vocabulary) in students with dyslexia (Ecalle, Bouchafa, Potocki, & Magnan, 2011). Imagery is one of the cognitive tools by which all children, hearing or deaf, code information when they store it in their memory (Paivio, 2008). DHH students, no matter their mode of communication, tend to be visually oriented and may even have special strengths in visuospatial abilities (Hauser, Lukomski, & Hillman, 2008). The use of visual organizers supports the use of written language in DHH students (Stoner & Easterbrooks, 2006). When researchers (Mousley & Kelly, 1998) asked students to visualize the solution to a complex, three-dimensional puzzle before attempting to solve the puzzle, students who visualized the solution first performed better than those who did not. Teachers of DHH students must incorporate visual support into their reading instruction.

Causal Factor 4 = Explicit Instruction

The next Causal Factor associated with positive learning outcomes is the use of explicit instruction instead of implicit instruction. In explicit instruction, teachers present a clear goal to the student, demonstrate an example of expected performance, guide the student to implement and practice the goal, and then provide sufficient opportunities for student practice until mastery (Hall, 2002). Like many hearing children with hearing parents, deaf children of deaf parents may acquire vocabulary in ASL incidentally (Brackenbury, Ryan, & Messenheimer, 2006; Hauser et al., 2008). Yet even these children require explicit instruction in order to acquire more complex vocabulary (Paatsch, Blamey, Sarant, & Bow, 2006). Explicit instruction has proven effective in vocabulary instruction (MacGregor & Thomas, 1988), reading comprehension (Banks, Gray, & Fyfe, 1990; Walker, Munro, & Rickards, 1998a, 1998b), and instruction in the use of morphologic, keyword, and context clues (Calvert, 1981), and may be even more important for children with delayed language. Andrews (1988) found that reciprocal teaching, a strategy that employs explicit instruction, produced significantly better prereading outcomes for an experimental group of DHH children than those found in a matched control group.

Causal Factor 5 = Scaffolding and Mediation

Causal Factor 5 is the presence of a strong teacher/mentor who understands how to scaffold instruction and help the student go beyond the information given (Bruner, 1973). Bruner, Goodnow, and Austin (1956) introduced the term "scaffolding" to educators in the 1950s in relation to how parents teach their children to talk. Two decades later, Vygotsky (1978) expanded that concept to include *instructional scaffolding*. Scaffolding refers to bridging the student's current ability level to an incrementally higher ability level through instruction in his or her zone of proximal development (ZPD) by a more knowledgeable other (MKO), or someone whose knowledge and skills in the instructional area exceed those of the student (Vygotsky, 1978). This differs from other definitions of mediated learning, such as learning through signed mediation or real-time text mediation (Marschark & Wauters, 2008). The role of the MKO is to provide multiple perspectives on meaning (Feuerstein, Hoffman, & Miller, 1980; Kozulin & Presseisen, 1995) whereby the "mediator" has the intentional purpose of selecting and calling up prior knowledge that contributes to drawing inferences (Strassman, 1997) as well as integrating information from previous parts of the text (Richardson, MacLeod-Gallinger, McKee, & Long,

2000). The ZPD refers to the area between the student's current ability level and the needed skills to attain the next level of knowledge. When receiving support within his or her ZPD, a student is ready and able to grow cognitively with appropriate guidance and support, or scaffolding. Skills above the ZPD are in the learner's *frustration* level. Skills within the ZPD are in the learner's *instructional* level, and skills below the ZPD are in the learner's *independent* level. Instructional strategies that are related to this Causal Factor include scaffolding, teacher modeling, explanation, verifying and clarifying student knowledge, hints and cues, and a careful de-escalation of support toward independent mastery (Byrnes, 2001). Because DHH students tend to have difficulties coordinating ideas across material (Marschark & Hauser, 2008), mediation strategies are needed to help them see relationships across content and to develop strategies for retention and recall of information.

If direct evidence from research is not available on a curriculum, intervention, strategy, material, or practice, then an alternative for evaluating that practice is to decide if factors known to cause positive outcomes (Causal Factors) are inherent in the product or practice. In summary, good teaching practices that cause positive learning outcomes are 1) promotion of higher-order language and critical thinking; 2) a good match between teacher/child communication; 3) visual representation and organization of ideas, concepts, and processes; 4) explicit instruction; and 5) scaffolding and mediation by a more knowledgeable person.

CURRENTLY AVAILABLE CURRICULA FOR DHH LEARNERS

If we were to agree with the position that DHH children read qualitatively the same as hearing children but are just delayed, then the use of general education materials with appropriate modifications would make sense. However, the previously mentioned national reading results would suggest that we need to do something more than simply putting standard reading textbooks in front of DHH children. What that "something more" is will vary from child to child. To meet the instructional needs of individual DHH students, teachers and practitioners will want to look closely at the information from the *What Works Clearinghouse* (WWC) (http://ies.ed.gov/ncee/wwc), which is a registry of practices, products, and packages that have undergone careful scrutiny for research rigor (including randomized, controlled research trials) by a panel of highly qualified individuals who are experts in the process of determining scientific rigor. The WWC is referred to as a "research synthesis organization" (Odom et al., 2005, p. 143). The publication landscape changes rapidly, and the reader is encouraged to frequent the WWC routinely. Be sure to review all curricula on the WWC when searching for those with an evidence base.

Only a handful of curriculum guides have been developed specifically for children who are DHH. Table 1.2 presents a sampling of curricula that are available and provides information relative to the evidence base and associated Causal Factors in their support. Very few curricula have an actual evidence base. We present these in this chapter because most curricula address multiple aspects of literacy acquisition, whereas we have attempted to break out some of the important pieces for more intensive scrutiny throughout the remainder of this book.

Our goal in this book is the presentation of comprehensive strategies, materials, and practices from which the teacher may pull for the needs of each individual child in his or her classroom. In this text we present a vast selection of literacy practices and strategies that teachers of DHH students may find appropriate for one or more of their students. Not all teachers will use everything in this book, but every child will benefit from at least some strategy or practice presented. While we comprehensively describe these reading tactics, we do not advocate one approach over another. All elements presented are components of a comprehensive reading curriculum. Some elements may require more adaptations than others, while others may be more necessary for particular DHH students to meet their diverse communication and instructional needs.

MAKING APPROPRIATE CHOICES

The list of options for curricula, methods, materials, and interventions for teaching reading to DHH students is seemingly endless, leaving the

Table 1.2. *Available Curricula or Extensive Materials for DHH Students*

Curriculum or Product	Developed for DHH or Hearing	Evidence Base	Causal Factors
Foundations for Literacy	DHH	Developing evidence base Lederberg, Miller, Easterbrooks, & Connor, 2011	Co, V, E, S
Fairview Reading Program	DHH	Developing evidence base Schimmel & Edwards, 2003; Schimmel, Edwards, & Prickett, 1999	Co, V, E
Children's Early Intervention for Speech-Language-Reading	Both	Author recommends use with DHH, but no evidence available Tade & Vitali, 1994	V, E
Reading Bridges Quigley, McAnally, Rose, & Payne (2003)	DHH	Developed for DHH. Indirect evidence base available Rose, McAnally, Barkmeier, Virnig, & Long, 2006;	Co, E, S
Reading Milestones Quigley, McAnally, Rose, & King (2002)	DHH	Developed for DHH. Indirect evidence base available Quigley, McAnally, Rose, & King, 2002	Co, E, S
Interactive Shared Book Reading	Both	http://ies.ed.gov/ncee/wwc/reports/early_ed/isbr/ Lamb, 1986; Mautte, 1991; McCormick & Mason, 1989; Schleper, 1995	HOTS Co, V, E, S
Reading Recovery	Both	Limited evidence base available Charlesworth, 2006; Heenan, 2007	E

teacher the task of making appropriate choices. Two related concepts may help practitioners make appropriate choices: universal design for learning (UDL) and differentiated instruction (DI). The concept of universal design began with the recognition that physical structures (i.e., buildings, sidewalks, etc.) should be architecturally designed from their inception to allow access for all individuals, with or without disabilities.

When applied to learning, universal design has three primary goals (Rose & Meyer, 2002, 2006): to provide students with multiple means of *representation*, multiple means of *engagement*, and multiple means of *expression*. The primary means by which we represent information is through language; in other words, we tell people things. When struggles with language occur, alternatives for representation are necessary, including enactive representation and iconic representation (Bruner, 1973). Enactive representation involves the enactment of the concept, whether through demonstration, simulation, three-dimensional modeling, or other manipulative means. Iconic representation involves the use of visual imagery including but not limited to pictures, visual organizers, thinking maps, charts, graphs, and maps. By engagement we mean the interactive process among teachers, students, and materials. Levels of scaffolding, or support provided to the learner, play an important role in the engagement process along with the use of stimulating, learner-appropriate materials. For example, the teacher can follow the approach of "I do, we do, you do" to demonstrate modeling of the concept, followed by guided practice with the student and independent practice conducted by the student alone. *Expression* refers to variations in the way students demonstrate their knowledge, such as through performance, written response, spoken or signed response, etc. When initiating a universal design approach, these three goals of representation, engagement, and expression allow teachers to differentiate instruction in three distinct areas: content, process, and product. *Content* concerns curriculum, that is, what is taught or what teachers want students to learn, know, and do. For some students the content will be exactly the same as the content for hearing children; for others it will be very different, depending on the current needs and levels of performance of each student. Differentiation of content requires teachers to understand the content of their state's learning objectives or standards, what to do when a student is not able to master the state standards, and what instructional materials (e.g., textbooks) are approved by the state's curriculum committee. *Process* concerns how students go about making sense of what they are learning. Levels of representation, levels of scaffolding, and instructional modality are important elements of the process for DHH students. *Product* concerns how students demonstrate what they learned (Tomlinson, 1995, 2001). Decisions regarding product cut across modalities (i.e., spoken, signed, or a combination), languages (i.e., English, ASL, Spanish, etc.), and types and levels of representation. Differentiation of process requires teachers to create multiple means for student engagement, such as didactic instruction or demonstration. Differentiation of product requires teachers to encourage students to use multiple means for expressing what they have learned. In addition to the knowledge teachers can gain from universal design goals and differentiated instruction principles, they must be aware of the continuum of specific challenges that the DHH population may face, including a child's cognitive capacity and his or her language(s) and modality to determine the best fit for instruction. Figure 1.2 presents four continua along which UDL and DI may fall when applied to the needs of DHH students. These continua range from most similar to what happens in the general education classroom (least differentiated) to least similar to what happens in the general education classroom (most differentiated).

When making decisions about any instructional material, strategy, or practice (in addition to determining whether it has an evidence base), teachers and practitioners will need to consider these continua carefully. A student may need less differentiation along some of the continua but more differentiation along others. There are no hard and fast rules. This is where one's professional training, experience, and discretion must be applied. For example, Juan, Tammy's second grader, may need an interpreter (most differentiated along the modality continuum) but may be perfectly capable of handling all other materials and goals in the general classroom (least differentiated on the other continua). However, Eva, a new student to the school district, may need to work on an alternative curriculum altogether that does not include age-appropriate state standards (most differentiated) because of her cognitive and physical disabilities but may use sign-supported English (mid-range differentiation) because her hearing loss is in the mild-moderate range and was acquired after she learned spoken English. Still other children may require a closed set of answer options (e.g., three choices) in reading and language arts

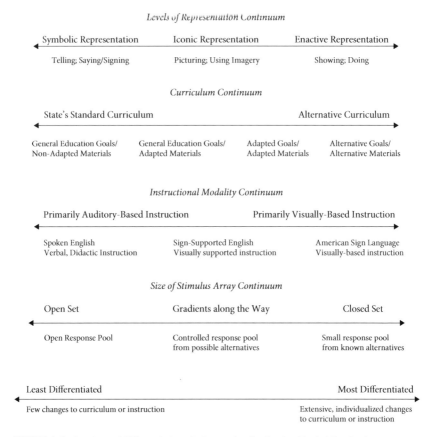

FIGURE 1.2. Continua of Differentiations in Instruction for Deaf or Hard-of-Hearing Learners from Least Differentiated to Most Differentiated. Created and contributed by S. Easterbrooks

with no restrictions in math (i.e., open set). Every child's pattern will be different, may change as the child matures, and may differ from subject to subject and environment to environment. In this book we present a range of possible instructional strategies, materials, and procedures and leave it up to the professional to choose whether or not these meet the needs of an individual child.

SUMMARY

This chapter provided the reader with an orientation to the complexities associated with the DHH population, the various languages and communication modes through which reading may be taught and learned, and the nature of the evidence base. We related these to the reading instructional process as found in today's complex service venues. In the remainder of the book we present facets of reading and instructional strategies supported by evidence or Causal Factors along the entire continuum of communication, from spoken language to the use of sign language in some manner, in the following chapters: Current practices (Chapter 2), assessment (Chapter 3), vocabulary (Chapter 4), decoding (Chapter 5), grammar and text comprehension (Chapter 6), fluency (Chapter 7), and future challenges (Chapter 8). In conclusion, the needs of DHH learners are as broad as the individual members of the population are different. There is no single strategy that will serve all children. Teachers, support service providers, clinicians, researchers, and other practitioners must call upon their professional training, discernment of appropriate strategies suggested herein, and the individual needs of their students to determine which practices are instructionally sound and educationally warranted to provide maximum instructional benefit for their students.

RESOURCES

Laurent Clerc National Deaf Education Center http://www.gallaudet.edu/clerc_center/information_and_resources/info_to_go.html
National Center for Special Education Research www.ies.ed.gov/ncser
What Works Clearinghouse www.whatworks.ed.gov

2 Current Practices

PURPOSE

Chapter 1 presented an overview of the topic of evidence-based practices (EBPs) and stressed the importance of identifying evidence of a causal relationship between a curriculum, set of materials, strategy, or intervention and positive learning outcomes. (Note: From this point forward we refer collectively to curriculum, materials, strategy, and intervention as "practices.") We also introduced the notion that the evidence base on literacy in deaf education is emerging. We proposed the use of research synthesis organizations (i.e., What Works Clearinghouse) and provided a chart of Causal Factors to guide decision making. But another alternative when searching for practices that work is locating evidence from the field, defined as an "expert committee report, consensus conference, and clinical experience of respected authorities" (Odom et al., 2005, p. 144). In this chapter, we identify the pioneers in general education on whose work current literacy practices were built, cite the recommendations of an expert organization (the Laurent Clerc National Deaf Education Center), and discuss additional evidence from numerous researchers on the effectiveness of the practices identified. The succeeding chapters address the evidence base as it relates to the specific literacy skills of phonological awareness, vocabulary, fluency, and text comprehension.

READING INSTRUCTIONAL PRACTICES

Teacher-supported, student-interactive models of learning to read came into their own around the 1980s and 1990s, promulgated by pioneering work such as Reading Recovery (Clay, 1972, 1975, 1993); independent, shared, and guided reading (Fountas & Pinnell, 1996, who were colleagues of Clay); and interactive reading (Rumelhart, 1985); as well as renewed interest in fluency (Rasinski, 1999), among other work. These literacy practices have gained the stature of "business as usual" in today's schools. With impetus from the Laurent Clerc National Deaf Education Center (http://clerccenter.gallaudet.edu), shared, guided, and independent reading was adapted for use with children who are DHH. Extensive reviews of these practices are available on the program's website. These practices are useful with DHH children whether they use spoken English, ASL, or a hybrid form of signing. Guided reading and independent reading are based on the works of Fountas and Pinnell (1996, 2005) and incorporate the use of materials at the reader's independent and instructional levels. If the student can read 95–98 percent of the words in the passage, this material is at the student's *independent* reading level. If the student can read less than 90 percent of the words, the material is at the student's *frustration* level. Material at the *instructional* level requires the child to know 90–95 percent of the words in a passage. Teachers can use leveled readers, such as those by Fountas and Pinnell (2009), which have been examined using a formula to determine their level of difficulty. Teachers can determine the level of reading materials that is appropriate for individual students by using readability formulas that look at sentence length, vocabulary difficulty, and the number of syllables in words (Chall & Dale, 1995; Flesch, 1948; Fry, 1989). Teachers can also read the text themselves and compare the demands of the text to their knowledge of their students' abilities (Schirmer & Schaffer, 2010) or have a student do a trial reading of the text. If a school uses basal readers, teachers can assess students' reading levels through the application of the formerly mentioned formulas or Fountas and Pinnell's leveling factors. For DHH readers, keep in mind the level of contextual support provided by leveled reading passages (Schirmer & Schaffer) and strategies to approach unknown words within text for those students who cannot "sound them out."

Shared reading, guided reading, and independent reading provide a solid foundation for moving children from reading with others to reading to others and by themselves. Although the evidence base for DHH children is small, we present these practices because they are so well known and relied upon in schools. For example, Tammy often groups Juan, Eva, and Millie during guided reading so she can scaffold instruction to meet their individual needs. At the same time she assigns Yin and Sally to practice independent reading. Later she works with Yin and Sally on guided reading, has Juan engage in independent reading, and encourages Eva and Millie to do a paired reading activity. She culminates her literacy instruction segment by conducting a shared reading activity with the group, where she engages them in vocabulary development and a deeper understanding of narrative structure.

Shared Reading

Shared reading occurs between an adult, such as a parent or teacher, and one to several children, in the home or school environment. Shared reading is a process of "reading a book over and over again on successive days" (Schleper, 1998, p. 5) with varied activities for student engagement. Books for shared reading contain elements that capture students' attention, such as predictability, repetition, cumulative or known sequence, rhythm, rhyme, and familiar patterns from children's environments (Schleper, 1998). During shared reading, children frequently comment on the story, ask questions, and focus on different aspects of the story across readings, resulting in deeper understanding and multiple opportunities to build language (Martinez & Roser, 1985; Schleper, 1998). When a shared book is read in sign language, the experience serves as an early bridge to English print (Erting & Pfau, 1997), as the teacher (i.e., more knowledgeable other) mediates visible text from a big book to a signed rendition. This practice is consistent with the Causal Factors of communication and scaffolding presented in Chapter 1.

Six basic steps occur during the shared reading process. First, the practitioner picks a book he or she likes because the reader's enthusiasm for the book will likely be contagious (Schleper, 1998). On the first day, the teacher introduces the book to students, beginning with an introduction of the cover, title, author, and student predictions for the book (Schleper, 1998). Then the teacher reads the story through to the end (Schleper, 1998), with both illustrations and print visible to students (Schleper, 2006). The teacher then reads the book a second time and asks students to join in when they like (Schleper, 1998). Afterwards, the teacher and students can discuss interesting vocabulary words, illustrations, connections between printed English and sign language, story content, main ideas, sequence, and facts and opinions about the story, as the teacher tailors the discussion to the students' developmental levels (Schleper, 1998). We also suggest discussions about the conventions of print (i.e., left to right), letter–sound relationships, and sight words, depending on the individual needs of each student.

On successive days, the teacher reads the story again, followed by discussions or student engagement in relevant activities, such as pointing to the print while reading, creating a classroom version of the story for the classroom library, or role-playing the story (Schleper, 1998). Depending on communication needs, other students may enact the story with manipulatives (puppets, dolls, etc.). Remember that the discussions and activities should be tailored to the developmental levels of each student. The teacher continues rereading the storybook as long as students are engaged and forming new knowledge, possibly up to two weeks. Schleper also suggests returning to shared reading stories across the school year by rereading a favorite book before beginning a new shared reading book. (For the specific details on Schleper's steps of shared reading, see Schleper, 2006.)

The teacher explicitly models language during shared reading through four strategies identified by Bowe (2002). First, he or she provides specific vocabulary for an activity in which a student in the class (Dunst, Herter, Shields, & Bennis, 2001) or a character in the shared book engages, such as making a cake with a focus on "make, bake, oven, stir, pour." Next, the teacher provides additional details on student responses or story elements (Bowe, 2000) (e.g., "Yes, the red hen stirred the cake with a spatula!"). Additionally, the teacher can engage in self-talk to model "thinking aloud" and decision making (Bowe). For example, the teacher might say, "I wonder who will eat the cake. I would like to eat a piece!" Finally, he or she can engage in parallel talk (Bowe) with students to provide a running record of words that describe what a character or student is doing as he or she engages in the shared reading activity (e.g., "You saw the chick say no. You saw the kitten say no. Who will eat the cake?").

Another approach to shared reading is the *Partner Reading and Content, Too* approach (Ogle & Correa-Kovtun, 2010). After a teacher models the reading process for content-related material (including identification of certain parts of the textbook, text structure, pictures and captions, headings, diagrams, thinking aloud, etc.), he or she pairs students with similar independent or instructional reading levels for additional practice. Students engage in a 20- to 30-minute partnered reading session using the content-specific text. Partners begin by previewing the entire book during their first exposure to the text. Next, each partner reads the first two adjacent pages silently, followed by a reread to "prepare for their performance read and select a question to ask their partner either from a prepared question sheet" or a self-generated question (Ogle & Correa-Kovtun, p. 535). Each partner alternates reading his or her page aloud, presenting the generated question, engaging in a discussion about the text, and gaining ownership of the concepts and vocabulary from the text. Finally, partners switch roles and repeat the process, making their way through the entire text. They can also add new vocabulary words to their personal notebooks at the end of the reading session. If needed, the teacher can conduct mini-sessions after partnered reading to expand or reinforce student knowledge.

Guided Reading

Guided reading is a process through which children move from teacher-led instruction to student-led instruction within the student's *zone of proximal development* (Vygotsky, 1978) while using high-quality literature (Schirmer & Shaffer, 2010) at the student's instructional level. Effective teachers scaffold new reading concepts, vocabulary, language, and connections to the student's life and other texts at the reader's individual pace. Effective teachers ask the student to read parts of a story aloud, retell the story, or answer comprehension questions. This is generally done within small group instruction of children who are all on the same reading level (Tompkins, 2000). During a guided reading session, the teacher has a specific skill (e.g., fluency) or strategy (e.g., summarizing) in mind that he or she hopes to impart to the child. Two types of guided reading are common in schools. The first is observational, in which the teacher asks students to make predictions as she monitors their progress. The second is interactive, in which the teacher is more like a coach, prompting the child to read, asking and answering questions, and reflecting both on the passage and on the skills mastered (Cooper, 2000). A key element is that the teacher uses materials within the child's *instructional* level. Guided reading is based on all five of the Causal Factors (i.e., HOTS & CoVES).

Independent Reading

Independent reading is the process whereby students practice fluency with reading materials at their *independent* level rather than their instructional level. DHH students must have access to strategies for identification of unfamiliar words they may encounter during independent reading. Strategies include asking a peer or the teacher for the meaning, referring to a high-frequency word wall, using an online sign language dictionary, etc. For students to successfully read independently, they must have adequate time to engage in independent reading in a non-distracting environment (Dry & Earle, 1988). Teachers can give students opportunities to interact with and share their independent reading through standard book reports where they share the story line and their opinion of the book, or through retelling of their favorite part of the book (Gárate, 2000). Teachers can also provide opportunities for literature circle book discussions with peers or response cards with various prompts or questions to which students can respond (Schleper, 2002). Students can write about a story in a literacy journal or refer to their story during Writer's

Workshop. Independent reading gives students opportunities to select their own text, make personal connections to it, and share it with others.

Parental Involvement in Literacy Acquisition

Although not an instructional methodology in and of itself, one more topic requires attention in a book on teaching reading to DHH learners: the involvement of parents in their children's education. Hart and Risley (1995) demonstrated incontrovertibly that the amount of communication a child hears from his or her mother has a significant influence on language and literacy outcomes. This relates directly to the Causal Factor of communication, as parents are children's primary teachers, even through middle and high school. Mothers who talk and read to their children for the most part have children who communicate and are readers. Because of all the communication issues, concerns, and barriers that hearing parents of deaf children face, they tend not to interact with their children in the same manner as deaf mothers. From a cultural context, this affects a child's sense of himself or herself as a literate person and can have a self-fulfilling prophecy effect on reading achievement.

Interactive shared reading between parents and their children improves reading skills in both hearing (Arnold, Lonigan, Whitehurst, & Epstein, 1994; Whitehurst et al., 1994) and deaf children (Fung, Chow, & McBride-Chang, 2005). During the storybook interactions examined in these studies, mothers asked different types of questions, modeled language, expanded their children's language, and gave appropriate feedback. Deaf children ages 5 to 9 years with hearing parents increased their vocabulary across an 8-week period when their parents created dialogue about shared stories using prompts and picture cards (Fung et al., 2005). When hearing mothers used techniques such as recast, open-ended questions, parallel talk, and expansion during shared reading, their children with CIs scored higher on language assessments than the children of mothers who simply used labeling, imitation, directives, and yes/no questions (DesJardin, Ambrose, & Eisenberg, 2008). When mothers read for over an hour weekly with their deaf children, they asked more than twice as many questions during the shared reading experiences as mothers who read with their children less than an hour weekly (Kaderavek & Pakulski,

2007). For children who use sign language, engagement in storybook reading is enhanced by eye contact and signing space, including signing on the child and on the storybook page, and providing additional information during reading (Swanwick & Watson, 2007). Teachers and other practitioners should take advantage of such treasure troves of help as Gallaudet's *Shared Reading Project* as resources to help parents become involved in their child's literacy experience. Parents are probably the most underutilized resource in promoting literacy skills in DHH students.

THE ROLE OF WRITING IN LEARNING TO READ

The acquisition of reading skills is based on the premise that students learn the connection between their spoken language and written communication (Nuñes, Burman, Evans, & Bell, 2010). When DHH learners attempt to master reading and writing, this assumption is called into question because children's spoken language may be delayed or, in the case of children who use ASL or hybrid forms of signing, nonexistent altogether. Consequently, it is often the case that children do not develop an awareness of difficult-to-hear word endings (e.g., s, -ed) until they see them in print. This places the language of face-to-face communication and the format of written communication in a unique relationship to one another. We actually know very little about the connections that DHH readers make between the two forms. Some researchers (Geers & Hayes, 2011) have identified a strong correlation between spoken English and writing outcomes. Others feel that DHH students will read better if they are taught a signed form of English (Schick & Moeller, 1992). Still others support that bilingual–bimodal instruction comparing English to ASL is more effective because the brain can handle dual language development (Petitto et al., 2001), and waiting several years for the child to master spoken language may put him or her at risk for linguistic, cognitive, social, or personal development delays (Grosjean, 2008). Wherever students fall along the continuum of languages and modes, DHH students can improve their writing skills with appropriate instruction (Wolbers, 2008). Teachers and other practitioners should observe and assess students frequently and carefully to determine when writing becomes an appropriate tool for teaching reading.

The process of writing is related to reading in that when a child expresses a new concept, the teacher can write it down and provide the child with a visual representation of the new concept and its language-in-print equivalent. For example, if the child has only seen the sign for "invite" and is unable to hear the /t/ sound, her exposure to the printed word may be the first time she realizes that the word contains a /t/ sound. Theoretically, this should enhance her memory of the word meaning and promote sight word recognition of the word. However, this is a critical area needing much research, for we simply do not have sufficient information. The question surrounding the relationship between reading and writing is this: How much language and reading knowledge is learnable and retainable when a printed representation is the source for instruction? Can a child learn and retain a word's meaning by experiencing it in context and then seeing it in print? To what extent can a child learn vocabulary or grammar this way? How many times does a deaf child have to see a word in order to retain it? We simply do not have answers to these questions.

The topic of writing is equally as complex as the topic of reading and, as such, deserves its own book. For this reason, the subject is not covered in-depth here, but we would be remiss in ignoring it altogether. In this section we discuss practices for written language acquisition as they pertain to the acquisition of reading.

SHARED WRITING, GUIDED WRITING, WRITER'S WORKSHOP, AND DIALOGUE AND OTHER JOURNALS AND LOGS

Shared Writing and Interactive Writing

Shared writing is a process of repeated interactions with literacy materials, such as big books or poems, in which the teacher and students navigate vocabulary, concepts, and story elements with embedded mini-lessons focused on language strategies (e.g., conventions of print, sight vocabulary, letter–sound correspondences, etc.; Laurent Clerc National Deaf Education Center, 2010a). Shared writing can involve something as simple as deciding what should go into an invitation to a classroom tea party, or something more grandiose like rewriting a new version of an old classic. Generally, after repeated interactions with and discussions about a particular text, the teacher and students create a product together. Students are encouraged to share their products with their parents or other reading partners. Importantly, mothers' writing mediation, namely shared interactions focused on printed words, during shared reading and writing activities contributed to positive development of alphabetic skills in kindergarten-aged deaf children (Aram, Most, & Mayafit, 2006).

Interactive writing is an extension of shared writing in that the teacher and students share not only ideas but also the role of scribe (Button, Johnson, & Furgerson, 1996). The teacher serves as the facilitator as she and the students create shared written texts while engaging in lessons in the conventions of writing, grammar, spelling, punctuation, and letter formation using chart paper that is visible to all students. The teacher and students negotiate the text, collaborate on construction of the text, engage in multiple re-readings, and display the finished composition in the classroom. Interactive writing can be used to compose a group story, write a letter, create a set of directions, record information from science experiments, etc. Another way of using interactive writing in the classroom is through comic strips (C. Smith, 2000). For example, a teacher might divide students into groups, distribute blank comic strips from the daily newspaper, and have students work together to create captions or stories portrayed by the comics.

One particular format for interactive writing is the *Morning Message.* Morning Message (Englert, Berry, & Dunsmore, 2001; Englert & Dunsmore, 2002; Mariage, 1996, 2001) is a method of interactive writing in which the students and teacher construct meaningful text from student language. In daily 15- to 30-minute sessions, one student generates a topic, the teacher and students ask questions for more details, and they collaboratively add written information to and revise the morning message. The teacher models thinking aloud when needed to demonstrate the conversion process of student language (spoken or signed) to printed text. After each agreed-upon revision, the teacher rereads the message for further discussion. For instruction via sign language, Wolbers (2008) suggested that teachers sign with one hand while pointing to the corresponding text with the other hand to make the direct connection between sign and print. When necessary, the teacher may use fingerspelling to maintain the flow of reading the sentence. Similarly, the teacher can point to the corresponding text for children who use spoken language. Students can also read along with the teacher, reading aloud and/or signing the text as the teacher points. This process continues as the teacher and students move among planning, idea and text generation, revision, and editing. The writing piece is published and shared with an authentic audience, such as within a parent newsletter or school publication.

Wolbers (2008) used a modified setup for DHH students who used total communication (a subset of the category of hybrid signing). The teacher placed student language presented in ASL on one easel and more English-like signing on another. The students and teacher engaged in a translation process to convert ASL to English. For students with limited language for generating a topic, teachers can conduct language experience activities or give parents home journals or semantic maps to collect information on experiences at home and incorporate this information into instruction. After using this interactive writing process, elementary and middle school students improved in their use of appropriate titles, introductory statements, story elements, text coherence, details, and conclusion (Wolbers, 2008). They also increased their accuracy in capitalization, punctuation, spelling, and word identification skills.

At the kindergarten level, students can use individual dry erase boards and markers to capture the sentences generated by the group (Williams, 2011). In a year-long study of interactive writing with six DHH kindergarteners, students made connections between vocabulary from repeated readings of big books and writing activities reinforced by teacher use of thinking aloud and instruction in the conventions of writing, grammar lessons, and student rereading of generated sentences. Comparisons were also made among ASL, printed English, and the sounds of English that were represented by letters. Interactive writing connected the students' face-to-face language with its printed representation and rules for capturing it correctly in text.

Guided Writing

Guided writing is a teacher-scaffolded small-group instructional approach that targets the individual writing needs of students who demonstrate similar needs at particular points in time (Fountas & Pinnell, 2001). Guided writing typically occurs as a 20- to 30-minute portion of Writer's Workshop, after the teacher and class as a whole have generated a writing topic and corresponding background information (Frase, 2008; Gibson, 2008, 2009). Groupings are flexible; all students may not need the same level of guided writing support. Individual student needs are identified through informal observations and assessments. The teacher can quickly review submitted writing pieces to identify common needs among students and tailor guided writing groups accordingly (Frase, 2008). During the small group session, the teacher may demonstrate strategic writing behaviors, provide prompts and feedback to students, assist students in decision making and organization, and provide mini-lessons on writing mechanics, vocabulary, and sentence structure (Gibson). At the end of each guided writing session, students are encouraged to share their writing. Gibson (2008) provided scaffolded guided writing instruction for five typically hearing second-grade students across a three-month time period and reported increases in student use of self-scaffolding, including rereading, self-talk, and use of resources. Teachers can use guided writing instruction with DHH students by identifying their specific writing needs based on classroom performance and observation and addressing them through scaffolded instruction.

Writer's Workshop

Pioneers Calkin (1994) and Routman (1994) envisioned the process of Writer's Workshop as a means for hearing children in general education environments to develop their own ideas, unfold them on the page, and then reformulate them over time through interactive, key processes associated with this approach. These processes are related to the Causal Factors of higher-order thinking skills, communication, explicit instruction, and scaffolding (HOTS and COVES). Writer's Workshop (Fisher, 1995) was re-visioned as a process for DHH students as a daily 50-minute writing process that includes the following components: 10-minute mini-lessons on writing techniques; 30-minute independent writing periods with individual teacher–student conferences; and 10 minutes for students to share their writing with their peers (Laurent Clerc National Deaf Education Center, 2010b). It is appropriate for all DHH children in all communication environments. The format evolves through student selection of a topic, creation of a first draft, and sharing with peers, who ask questions to generate ideas for the student's revision. After editing and engaging in an individual conference with the teacher for specific feedback, the student edits the writing piece and has another conference with the teacher in which they engage in collaborative feedback with a focus on both positive aspects and areas for improvement. Afterward, the student publishes the piece, including a dedication and information about herself, binds it, and shares it with her peers and parents. Student writing pieces are displayed in the classroom upon completion.

Enns, Hall, Isaac, and MacDonald (2007) adapted Writer's Workshop using parallel versions of ASL and English with fourth- and fifth-grade deaf students. First, they used a picture book as a stimulus for writing samples and assessed students' written English skills using the *Kendall* writing levels (French, 1999). Next, they assessed students' ASL abilities through videotaped storytelling using the same picture book. Teachers allowed students the choice of drafting in ASL or English. Students who chose ASL used their videotaped renditions and converted them to written English. Additionally, the teachers used prewriting idea generation to help students select topics and build background knowledge about their topics prior to writing and required an outlined plan of the students' writing prior to beginning the drafting process. Some teachers embedded specific requirements for writing, such as incorporation of dialogue and use of a checklist for grammatical self-evaluation. One mini-lesson focused on the inclusion of dialogue conventions based on the use of role shift in ASL. Increased student ownership, motivation, and mediation between ASL and English resulted from students' participation in this adapted form of Writer's Workshop.

Schleper (2000b) used steps of Writer's Workshop with a newly immigrated deaf student who used English as a third language in addition to limited spoken Mandarin and written Chinese (he was unfamiliar with ASL). After the student generated his story in written Chinese, he shared it through gesture, while the other students in the class generated questions to expand the details of the student's story. These questions were recorded, the student participated in individual mini-lessons with his teacher on the corresponding English vocabulary, and the student published his first shared writing piece.

Research Writing

Research writing is an extension of Writer's Workshop that uses nonfiction topics from content areas, such as dinosaur extinction or the civil rights movement. The students select interesting topics, and the teacher guides activation of background knowledge and research questions using a technique such as a Know, Want to Know, Learned (KWL) chart (Ogle, 1986; Laurent Clerc National Deaf Education Center, 2010c). The students create a project plan, document what they already know, investigate additional sources of information, organize the accumulated information, put it into their own words, and edit, publish, and present their research. Students can work in small groups, pairs, or individually. Mini-lessons might include an overview of plagiarism, how to outline and paraphrase, instruction in technical vocabulary, etc. To meet the varied literacy and language needs of individual students, practitioners might create a specific collection of relevant materials in various reading levels from the library for students to use independently and collaboratively in the classroom.

Content Area Journals or Logs

Journals in math, science, social studies, and language arts classes help students make personal connections to content, connections across content, and connections between content and writing. Consistent opportunities to write in content journals provide students with repeated practice with concepts prior to assessment (Laurent Clerc National Deaf Education Center, 2010d). When using these journals, the focus is on expansion of student knowledge, so teachers might ask students for clarification on their writing and use these journals to monitor students' progress in each content area. Before beginning a new topic, students can record what they already know, as well as questions they may have about the topic, such as "How do caterpillars make cocoons?" or "How is addition similar to multiplication?" Students can use content journals individually or as a group. For example, consider having students make individual contributions to a content journal focused on living organisms or conflicts in U.S. history. Students can read their contributions through an author's chair activity, or the teacher can model fluent reading of student ideas that connect content across classes.

Dialogue Journals

Another practice that the Clerc Center recommends is the use of *dialogue journals* (Bailes, Searls, Slobodzian, & Staton, 1986). Dialogue journals are created with simple composition books to record interactive written conversations over a period of time. Dialogue journals serve as a bridge between natural spoken conversation, with its participants and turns, and the traditional classroom tasks of essay and report writing. They are often used privately between teacher and student but can also be shared among students and their peers. Dialogue journals are generally topic-free, with the student initiating the conversation. The teacher responds, and the conversation continues without requirements or corrective feedback. The teacher provides a model of language every time he or she responds, but dialogue journals do not involve direct instruction in language. There is no age or ability requirement for using dialogue journals. While students may bring limited written language to the journaling process, they can still express themselves in written dialogue prior to mastering all of the rules of writing (Voit, 2009).

How teachers respond to student entries may drive student writing behavior. Peyton and Seyoum (1988) investigated use of dialogue journaling with 12 sixth-grade students who had limited English proficiency and were required to write three sentences a day in their journals. They reported that teacher requests for student responses yielded more student replies but did not elicit an increase in length of student writing. Students did, however, write more freely when the teacher made more personal contributions and when the teacher and student wrote about a topic interesting to both parties. The opportunity to engage in personal dialogue with the teacher may facilitate both a bond with the teacher and accountability in the classroom (Jones, 1991). Anecdotal results from university-level students with limited English proficiency who partici- pated in a 14-week dialogue intervention showed that self-chosen topics were easier to write about and similar to conversations, and writing flu- ency increased as a result of frequent written communication (Holmes & Moulton, 1997).

If time permits, teachers should engage in dialogue journaling on a daily basis with elementary students or two to three times per week with older students across the school year (Staton, 1987). Entries in dialogue journaling are brief, varying from a few sentences to a page in length, and the same topics tend to be discussed and elaborated on for several days. Dialogue journaling is supported by Causal Factor 5, scaf- folding by a more knowledgeable other (Wertsch & Sohmer, 1995), in which the more knowledgeable teacher scaffolds the student's language acquisition through modeling. Teachers should encourage parents to engage in dialogue journaling with their children at home, in English or their native language, to develop language foundations (Schleper, 2000a).

End-of-Class Journal Reflection

Reflection journals are used to help students capture important infor- mation from a lesson in any class, similar to a "ticket out the door." In the last 5 to 10 minutes of class, teachers ask students to write down two important things they learned during the lesson or to generate two ques- tions related to the new information in their reflection journals (Lang & Albertini, 2001). The goals of end-of-class reflections include observa- tion of student ability to construct and prioritize information from a lesson and identification of any student misconceptions or areas of the lesson that may need redirection in subsequent instruction. Additional ideas for reflective writing in the content areas involve creative writing generated from a teacher-given prompt; free writing that includes pre- dictions, observations, and conclusions; and double entries, in which students copy and respond to a relevant portion of text related to the lesson. From a collection of 228 writing samples created by deaf middle and high school science students, Lang and Albertini reported student success with these writing reflections, based on individual abilities, teacher content knowledge, and appropriately leveled prompts and reading materials.

SUMMARY OF RECOMMENDED PRACTICES

In this chapter we focused on literacy practices that have been modified for DHH learners by the Laurent Clerc Center, an organization considered to be an expert entity, placing an evidence base behind these practices. In addition, many other writers in general education, special education, and deaf education have described these practices over time as well. Other well-known expert organizations have websites with useful information, which the teacher and practitioner will want to consult. The practices described are useful for DHH students across the continuum of communication modalities and languages and are directly related to the five Causal Factors highlighted in Chapter 1. Literacy practices that were discussed in this chapter include shared and interactive reading in both the classroom and home environments, as well as guided and independent reading with adequate time and supports in the classroom. We also discussed shared and interactive writing, by which the teacher and students can focus on the connection between reading (decoding) and writing (reproducing) print through the use of shared ideas and language. We highlighted Writer's Workshop and its cyclic process between the teacher and students and writing across content areas, from research writing to content area and dialogue journals. Writing opportunities provide students with access to models and guided mediation during the construction of meaning from printed text within their learning world. Because we know so little about the direct relation and its extent between printed and visual languages, we encourage teachers of DHH students to investigate systematically those strategies that are successful for their students through action research.

RESOURCES

Chiseri-Strater, E., & Sunstein, B. S. (2006). *What works: A practical guide for teacher research.* Portsmouth, NH: Heinemann.

See "Literacy-It All Connects" at http://www.gallaudet.edu/clerc_center/information_and_resources/info_to_go/language_and_literacy/literacy_at_the_clerc_center/literacy-it_all_connects.html.

See books on shared and guided reading at Heinemann Publishing.

See teacher's resources on http://deafed.net (requires registration).

See Spencer, P. E., & Marschark, M. (2010). *Evidence-based practice in educating deaf and hard-of-hearing students.* New York, NY: Oxford University Press.

3 Assessment for Reading Instruction

PURPOSE

As with literacy instruction, the nature of the assessment process has changed considerably over the past decade. Whereas grading the academic performance of children with hearing loss used to be the domain of the teacher of the deaf and assessment the domain of the school psychometrist or educational diagnostician, most assessment and documentation of effectiveness now falls squarely on the shoulders of classroom teachers. Although special education teachers identify a student's present level of academic and functional performance (PLAAF) independent of the general education teacher, they struggle to meet the intention and challenges of high-stakes testing in the general education classroom (unless students are on alternative curriculums). Additionally, DHH children are being served under the model of *Response to Intervention* (RTI), which was originally intended for hearing children with learning disorders (National Center on Response to Intervention [NCRTI], 2010).

Response to intervention integrates assessment and intervention within a multi-level prevention system to maximize student achievement and to reduce behavioral problems. With RTI, schools use data to identify students at risk for poor learning outcomes, monitor student progress, provide evidence-based interventions and adjust the intensity and nature of those interventions depending on a student's responsiveness, and identify students with learning disabilities or other disabilities (NCRTI, p. 2).

RTI is organized into three tiers of support. *Primary-level support* is intended to meet the needs of most students. *Secondary-level support* is intended to provide evidence based interventions for learning and behavior disorders. *Tertiary-level support* involves individualized, intense intervention. When addressing the concept of RTI, many teachers of the deaf (TODs) find themselves trying to fit the proverbial square peg (individualized instruction based on individualized assessment) into the proverbial round hole (RTI), and they struggle with making this model fit the needs of DHH children. In particular, this tiered approach may prevent DHH children from getting the top level of support they need immediately. Recall that the age–achievement gap in DHH children widens rapidly (Kyle & Harris, 2010); postponing access to maximum services contributes to this gap. In this chapter, we provide a look at the literacy assessment options available, the uses for which they were developed, and suggestions for their use. Finally, we review a variety of available assessment tools that may guide teachers in choosing, administering, and interpreting literacy results appropriately, with links to some real classrooms as each child's literacy pattern provides unique challenges.

THE GOALS OF READING ASSESSMENT

Teachers must anticipate end-of-year goals for students and tailor instruction weekly to meet those goals. Frequent assessment and data collection can guide instruction for the individual needs of students, including independent and instructional reading levels. Data collection will also tell the educator if a student needs increased instructional time, if individual goals can be met with less instructional time, or if additional goals should be added. The starting point for reading instruction is to understand what a student does and does not know about the spoken language upon which instruction in reading is based (i.e., English, Spanish, Swahili) (White, 2002). Monthly assessments using running records, for example, allow the teacher to provide immediate feedback for student errors and identify the areas requiring instructional focus. This also allows teachers to identify when a student's goal is mastered and when to establish the next instructional goal. While students with language and reading delays may remain behind their peers with typical language and reading skills, progress can still be demonstrated through effective intervention supported by data collection. Teachers must consider the "needed growth rates for individual students given their delayed starting point and the end-of-year benchmark goal" (Oakes, Mathur, & Lane, 2010, p. 134). Frequent progress monitoring permits documentation of student gain in smaller increments of time across the school year and lets teachers know what is (and isn't) working during reading instruction.

Teachers today spend an incredible amount of time engaged in assessment. Stiggins (1994) estimated that between one-third and one-half of a teacher's class time is spent in one or another type of measurement activity. This is astounding given all that teachers are required to accomplish each day. There are many reasons why we assess; the most common include:

- to determine student eligibility for services under various titles and acts
- to determine appropriate accommodations, modifications, alternative curriculums, and alternative assessments
- to gather large-scale measures (high-stakes tests) of educational outcomes for accountability purposes
- to provide reports to the public on educational outcomes
- to determine if children, teachers, administrators, and schools are meeting standards, achieving goals, and demonstrating performance

- to provide routine monitoring of progress on Individual Education Plan (IEP) goals and objectives and progress in the general education curriculum and to equate performance with grades

However, assessments do not inform educators about what they need to teach the next day. Additionally, this is not always well understood in the case of DHH children because the types of assessments they need are often overlooked in favor of the types of assessment schools require. For example, in order to understand the reading needs of a DHH child, it is very important to assess his or her language skills prior to reading assessment, yet there is rarely sufficient time to do this.

WHAT DO WE ASSESS?

Because the assessment process can be time consuming, schools prefer to use quick assessments such as calculating how many words a child can read in one minute. The problem is that this provides insufficient information with which to plan for instruction. Teachers need to know why the child is reading slowly. A simple assessment of one skill area cannot reveal sufficient information so that teachers can plan instruction. For example, Mrs. Drake, an itinerant teacher in a local school system, who serves a group of early elementary DHH children in a separate (pull-out) group for reading instruction, grapples with a variety of challenges. Besides speech instruction, her students participate in the general education curriculum with interpreters as needed during the remainder of the school day. Case Vignette 3.1 describes how Mrs. Drake addressed Sammy's underlying language problems through assessment. Case Vignette 3.2 describes how she addressed Louisa's reading frustrations. Case Vignette 3.3 introduces the reader to Megan, whose reading problems, we discover, are related to poor vocabulary knowledge. Finally, we meet Thomas (Case Vignette 3.4) whose potential underlying visual impairment has become a noticeable challenge to Mrs. Drake in teaching reading. These cases demonstrate why a closer look at assessment is important.

CASE VIGNETTE 3.1.

Mrs. Drake's Assessment Decisions for Sammy

Sammy is a 7-year-old first-grade student with a moderate-to-severe hearing loss who reads at the pre-primer level. Sammy uses speech accompanied with sign language for communication. Sammy's home language is Spanish. However, Sammy's parents frequently combine some elementary signs with their spoken Spanish when Sammy is home. Sammy's reading difficulties appear to be related to a lack of understanding of the underlying grammar needed for reading. Mrs. Drake decides to assess Sammy's language using the CASLLS Simple Sentence Level form. Because Sammy is new to the school system this year, Mrs. Drake decides to collect this information with the help of his previous teacher, his parents, and his current and former speech language pathologists. She will request only information related to Sammy's grammar use, not the included listening and speech sections of the CASLLS form.

CASE VIGNETTE 3.2.

Mrs. Drake's Assessment Decisions for Louisa

Louisa is a 9-year-old third-grade student with a profound hearing loss who relies on sign language for all communication. During reading instruction in the general education classroom, she is frequently frustrated and engages in behaviors that let her avoid reading tasks. Mrs. Drake has noticed a transfer of these behaviors to the small group reading instruction and thinks Louisa's behavior may be due to the difficulty level of the materials used for reading instruction. Mrs. Drake decides to assess Louisa's reading levels in an effort to reduce Louisa's behavior. Mrs. Drake sits with Louisa one on one and conducts an informal reading inventory using the Johns Basic Reading Inventory. She presents a short reading passage at the pre-primer level for Louisa to read, followed by a few comprehension questions. Mrs. Drake notes the words for which Louisa does not produce a sign but merely glosses over with fingerspelling, even though the words have conceptual signs. After Louisa reads a few passages that become increasingly more difficult for her, Mrs. Drake determines that Louisa's independent reading level is the primer level. No wonder Louisa is frustrated—her instructional reading materials used in the general education classroom are nearly three years above her capabilities!

CASE VIGNETTE 3.3.

Mrs. Drake's Assessment Decisions for Megan

Megan is an 8-year-old second-grade student with a moderate-to-severe hearing loss. Like Sammy, she relies on speech supplemented by sign language for communication. Megan frequently engages in head nodding during conversation, but she seldom offers much information and remains quiet throughout the school day. During reading instruction, she can call out some words verbally or using signs, but she doesn't appear to know very many of the words in the reading materials. Mrs. Drake wonders if Megan has difficulty with the vocabulary. She decides to assess Megan's vocabulary using the Fairview Reading adapted Dolch cards. On one side of each card, a Dolch word is presented in print. On the other side, descriptions of the common signs for the word are provided for the teacher. Because Megan is in the second grade, Mrs. Drake starts with the second-grade Dolch words. However, Megan identifies only two words out of the first 10 that Mrs. Drake displays. Mrs. Drake pulls out the first-grade Dolch word cards, and Megan provides the sign or verbalization of three of the 10 displayed words. Mrs. Drake determines that Megan's vocabulary level is significantly below the vocabulary included in her required reading materials.

CASE VIGNETTE 3.4.

Mrs. Drake's Assessment Decisions for Thomas

Thomas is a 9-year-old student with a moderate hearing loss who primarily uses speech for communication, although he has learned a few signs because he is in the same general education class as Louisa. Mrs. Drake has noticed that Thomas squints and moves reading materials closer to his face when reading. This obstructs his ability to access Mrs. Drake's facial expressions, which are crucial to communication. After confirming that this behavior also occurs in his general education class, Mrs. Drake decides to pursue an assessment of his vision. She contacts Ms. Avery, the vision impairment teacher in her school system. Ms. Avery stops by Mrs. Drake's class one day after school and suggests that Thomas's parents take him to a pediatric ophthalmologist to determine the presence and possible cause of a visual impairment. Ms. Avery also mentions the common use of a functional vision assessment to detect how a vision loss affects academic performance. Ms. Avery explains that this type of assessment measures how well a student uses his or her vision to

(Continued)

(Continued)

perform tasks throughout the day across multiple settings. Ms. Avery agrees to observe Thomas to measure his visual acuity across distances, visual fields, localizing, fixating, tracking, shifting gaze, eye–hand coordination, and color vision. She also suggests observation of Thomas in his different educational settings throughout his school day, including his general education classroom, the resource classroom during reading instruction, PE, and recess. She will also chat with Thomas's parents and his teachers for information on his visual behaviors at home, such as how Thomas moves around his different environments, uses tools within his settings, etc. Mrs. Drake feels relieved to have a plan in place to address possible additional needs Thomas may have.

Below we present the areas that effective teachers include when conducting a comprehensive reading assessment with their DHH students and a sample (not an all-inclusive or exclusive listing) of assessments in each area. Consult the test manuals to determine which tests are age-appropriate for the students in question.

CATEGORIES OF ASSESSMENT

Phonemic Awareness. Phonemic awareness is the awareness that spoken words are composed of sounds called phonemes (Mann, 2003) and that these sounds can be manipulated in syllables and words (Liberman & Shankweiler, 1985). Phonemic awareness underlies the alphabetic principle, or the knowledge that written graphemes, or letters, correspond to the phonemes, or sounds, of spoken words (Scarborough & Brady, 2002). Letter–sound knowledge is one of the most important prereading skills at preschool age and a predictor of variance in both normal reading and reading disability (Anthony & Lonigan, 2004; Lonigan, Burgess, & Anthony, 2000; Wagner, Torgesen, & Rashotte, 1994). Some example tests teachers can give might include:

- the *Early Speech Perception Test* (*ESP*; Moog & Geers, 1990)
- the *Ling Six Sound Test* (Ling, 1989)

Phonological Awareness. Phonological awareness refers to the skills of alliteration, blending, elision, rhyming, and segmentation (Easterbrooks, Lederberg, Miller, Bergeron, & Connor, 2008; Scarborough & Brady, 2002). Teachers assess these skills because they want to know how well children are manipulating their understanding of letter–sound relationships. For example, can the child remove /h/ from "hat" and add /b/ to get the word "bat"? Some example tests teachers can give might include:

- the *Test of Phonological Awareness Skills* (*TOPAS*; Newcomer & Barenbaum, 2003)
- the *Comprehensive Test of Phonological Processing* (*C-TOPP*; Wagner, Torgesen, & Rashotte, 1994)

Decoding. Decoding means the "process of applying one's knowledge of the correspondences between graphemes and phonemes to determine the pronunciation, and hence the identity, of the word represented by a particular letter sequence" (Scarborough & Brady, 2002, p. 324). Teachers assess students' decoding skills because they want to know how well the student can look at a word that is not in his or her sight vocabulary and break it down to unlock its meaning. They also want to know if the student is using phonological strategies or morphological strategies (i.e., structural analysis). If a teacher does not know how the student is attacking an unknown word, then she may not know which skills to teach him or her. Some example tests teachers can give might include:

- the *Decoding Skills Test* (*DST*; Richardson & DiBenedetto, 1985)
- any of a number of decoding tests that curriculums may have as part of their programs

Receptive Vocabulary. Receptive vocabulary refers to that vocabulary the child understands through his or her primary communication mode. If that is the spoken mode, then teachers will present the vocabulary item to the child through speech. If it is the signed mode, then they will present the vocabulary item through sign. Some children use a combined mode and require test items in this manner. Teachers assess receptive vocabulary because they want to know whether or not the child has the underlying concept of the word so that when the child decodes a word, he or she is uncovering the meaning of a known word. Teachers need to be careful, though, that they do not overestimate or underestimate a child's vocabulary knowledge based on complications from the hearing loss. For example, Mrs. Sweet had the following experience with her son:

> "Shortly after our son was diagnosed with a hearing loss (he had just turned 4), we did a language assessment test to see what his level of vocabulary was. They had a picture book and would say a word and ask him where it was. I was surprised when they said 'broom' and he did not point to the picture of the broom, because I would ask him to get me the broom so I could sweep the floor, and he would get the broom for me. I pointed to the picture of the broom and said, 'What is this?' He said, 'a sweep.' The language teacher had me say the phrase a couple of times and told me I put more emphasis on the word 'sweep.' So Stephen had heard 'sweep.' Then we went back through the pictures and asked him what each picture was so we could see what he was calling it. That was a learning moment for me. Then it was not only building his vocabulary but making sure he had the correct words in place."

Some example tests available to the education practitioner include:

- the *Receptive One Word Picture Vocabulary Test* (*ROWPVT*; Brownell, 2000)
- the *Peabody Picture Vocabulary Test,* 3rd Ed. (*PPVT-3*; Dunn & Dunn, 2007)
- the *MacArthur Communicative Development Inventories* (*CDI*; Fenson et al., 1994)
- the *MacArthur Communicative Development Inventory for American Sign Language* (*ASL-CDI*; Anderson & Reilly, 2002)

Expressive Vocabulary. Expressive vocabulary refers to the words that a student says or signs. Teachers assess this because expressive vocabulary is one of the best predictors of later reading success in DHH children (Kyle & Harris, 2006). Some example tests that education practitioners can give might include:

- the *Expressive One Word Picture Vocabulary Test* (Brownell, 2000b)
- the *Comprehensive Receptive and Expressive Vocabulary Test, 2nd Ed.* (*CREVT-2*; Wallace & Hammill, 2001)

Reading Vocabulary. This refers to the vocabulary level at which the child is able to read. Teachers assess this in order to know what level of reading materials to give a child and to determine how large of a gap there is between what the child understands in print and what is expected of him or her reading-wise in the classroom. The student must know the meanings of individual words, or vocabulary knowledge, to understand the complete picture created by a combination of words in text. Educators might assess reading vocabulary via such tests as:

- graded word lists from reading inventories such as the *Basic Reading Inventory* (*BRI*; Johns, 2008)
- *Words Per Minute Correct AVENUE* (http://lt.umn.edu/projects/avenuedhh
- the *Signed Reading Fluency Rubric for Deaf Children* (Easterbrooks & Huston, 2008)

Writing Vocabulary. This refers to the vocabulary knowledge and spelling knowledge that a child can call upon when trying to write. Writing vocabulary knowledge depends on underlying vocabulary concepts and the ability to relate those concepts to print form. This is important because a child may have a perfectly good idea to write down but may not know the printed words to express his or her ideas. Teachers might use some of these tests or practices to assess written vocabulary:

- *Oral and Written Language Scales* (*OWLS*; Carrow-Woolfolk, 1996)
- Analyze fingerspelling. Research on fingerspelling interventions has shown a correlation between fingerspelling and writing in DHH children (Haptonstall-Nykaza & Schick, 2007;

see this article for word lists and a discussion on assessing fingerspelling).

- Analyze written language samples for use of appropriate parts of speech (e.g., nouns, verbs, adjectives, adverbs, conjunctions and connectors, negation, and pronouns).

Receptive Grammar. Grammar refers to syntax (how words are put together within sentences) and morphology (how morphemes, or the smallest units of language, are combined within words). Receptive grammar is the student's ability to understand information presented within phrases and sentences. This is important because vocabulary alone is insufficient to help a child read beyond the fourth-grade level (Kelly, 1996). Grammar is the glue that holds words together and lets them make sense. It is fundamental to text comprehension. For example, a child who does not understand the action/recipient nature of the nouns in the sentence "The car was hit by the debris" may think that the car ran over a pile of junk in the road. Grammar fosters our ability to think beyond the literal. If a child does not understand information presented to him or her in different grammatical forms, whether spoken or signed, then the child will struggle with making sense of information he or she is reading in different grammatical forms. Some tests of receptive grammar include:

- *ACCESS for ELLs* (http://www.wida.us/assessment/ACCESS/TechReports/index.aspx)
- the *Rhode Island Test of Language Structure* (*RITLS*; Engen & Engen, 1983)
- the *Test for Auditory Comprehension of Language*-3 (Carrow-Woolfolk, 1999)

Expressive Language. Expressive language refers to the code that an individual uses to communicate to another person. It can happen through spoken language or sign language. It is the tool that humans use to express ideas to others. (For a comprehensive review of available assessments for examining multiple languages and multiple codes, see Goldstein and Bebko, 2003.) Some examples of available assessment instruments are:

- the *Cottage Acquisition Scales for Listening, Language and Speech* (*CASLLS*; Wilkes, 1999)

- the *Teacher Assessment of Spoken Language* (*TASL*; Moog & Biedenstein, 1998)
- the *Checklist of Emerging ASL Skills* (see Easterbrooks & Baker, 2002)

Conversational Proficiency. Proficiency in conversational language builds a foundation for literate language and thinking about reading. The *Kendall Conversational Proficiency Levels* (*P-Levels*; French, Hallau, & Ewoldt, 1985) assess students' communicative competency using hierarchical checklists and the students' conversational language to identify where students perform on developmental scales. These *P-Levels* also correspond to the *Stages of Literacy Development* (emerging, beginning, developing, maturing; French, 1999), a series of checklists that assess preschool through middle school students' literacy skills in the areas of communicative competency, motivation, background knowledge, and social interactions. For example, P-Levels 3–5 indicate emerging literacy skills.

Text Comprehension Skills. Text comprehension skills are those metacognitive skills that children use to scaffold reading comprehension when they do not understand automatically what they have read. Metacognition refers to a child's ability to think about and be aware of her own thinking, such as identifying when she does not understand presented information. Teachers will want to know which text comprehension strategies a student uses so that they can determine what they need to teach her. Chapter 6 provides a checklist of text comprehension strategies to use to identify which skills students can and cannot use independently.

Reading Comprehension. Of all the skills children must learn, reading comprehension is educators' overarching goal. Educators teach so that students will understand the meaning of the print matter they are struggling with and will be able to learn new information from what they are reading. There are innumerable reading comprehension tests from which to choose, but some of these include:

- the *Gray Silent Reading Test* (*GSRT*; Wiederholt & Blalock, 2000)
- the *Basic Reading Inventory: Pre-Primer through Grade Twelve and Early Literacy Assessments* (*BRI*; Johns, 2008)

- the *Test of Reading Comprehension, 4th Ed* (*TORC 4*; Brown, Wiederholt, & Hammill, 2008)
- the *Woodcock Reading Mastery Test-Revised* (*WRMT-R*; Woodcock, 1987)

Fluency. In reference to children with typical hearing, fluency refers to the ability to read "orally with speed, accuracy, and proper expression" (National Institute of Child Health and Human Development [NICHHD], 2000, pp. 3–5) and is often assessed by counting the number of words a child reads correctly within a one-minute time frame. Teachers need to know how fluently a child reads because the more automatically a child reads, called *automaticity*, the less mental energy he or she has to spend on decoding, and the better a reader he or she will be. Many large-scale assessments such as AIMSweb, a comprehensive K-12 assessment system of the Pearson Corporation contain fluency subtests. We describe fluency assessment in detail in Chapter 6. Some other measures of fluency include:

- the *Test of Silent Contextual Reading Fluency* (*TOSCRF*; Hammill, Wiederholt, & Allen, 2006)
- the *Test of Silent Word Reading Fluency* (*TOSWRF*; Mather, Hammill, Allen, & Roberts, 2004)

Fluency in the signed mode is a different issue altogether. When a child does not use spoken language or when he or she uses it in combination with signs, then reading fluency involves the automatic rendering of print into signed form (Chrosniak, 1993; Easterbrooks & Huston, 2008). Reading fluency in signing deaf children contains three components: accuracy, fluency envelope, and visual grammar (Easterbrooks & Huston, 2008). We will describe this assessment in greater detail in Chapter 7.

Motivation. One of the most important yet least addressed elements of reading is intrinsic motivation, or the internal drive to read. Intrinsic motivation is predictive of reading ability in deaf adults (Parault & Williams, 2010), and the National Reading Panel (2000) identified it as a key component in reading. Motivation results in higher and prolonged levels of reading engagement and self-regulation of reading strategies (Guthrie et al., 1996;

Turner, 1995). Teachers need to consider all possible strategies for encouraging student interest in reading. However, it is rarely assessed or addressed because it is difficult to do so and because there are no commonly used standardized assessments for measuring reading motivation in DHH students. Thus, the teacher must adapt available checklists or create her own classroom-appropriate tools. Possible assessments for hearing students that education practitioners might consider are:

- the *Motivation for Reading Questionnaire* (Wigfield & Guthrie, 1997)
- the *Elementary Reading Attitude Survey* (*ERAS*; McKenna & Kear, 1990)

Pulling It All Together. The various areas of assessment and resulting time expenditures presented in this chapter may seem overwhelming to TODs. However, multiple reading skills can be assessed at one time using available reading inventories that include sight words, fluency, reading comprehension, and a student's current repertoire of reading strategies. When giving this assessment, the teacher begins with the sequential presentation of graded sight-word lists to determine a student's independent and instructional levels for sight words. We suggest beginning with "easier" lists to build a student's confidence. Next, the teacher presents graded passages of running text based on the student's current reading level, one at a time, and conducts a miscue analysis of the student's reading performance. Miscue analysis is the process of uncovering the strategies students use as they read materials on their current level (Chaleff & Ritter, 2001). Using a copy of the reading passage with space in between the lines of text, the teacher notes omissions, substitutions, repetitions, and self-corrections made by the reader while rendering the passage. For students who use some form of sign language or those whose speech may be difficult at times to understand, we recommend videotaping the student's reading performance (with parental permission) for a more accurate scoring of the student's reading ability. In addition to sight words and fluency (described in detail in Chapter 7), a student's reading comprehension can be assessed in two ways: The student can engage in a retelling of the story and answer the comprehension questions that are included with each passage. Again, the reader's independent and instructional levels are determined by the results of the miscue analysis and the comprehension measures. Finally, this comprehensive form of assessment also provides information that allows the teacher to tailor the instruction to the individual needs of students.

READING GAP

Eligibility and placement decisions may appear easy to accomplish on the surface because many states and local school systems now prescribe the specific tests to be given to all students. It is fairly standard for states to expect schools to acquire an audiological, otological, and psychological evaluation on a child whose eligibility for DHH services is under consideration. Please note that all psychological testing must be conducted in the child's preferred mode of communication. Because over half of DHH students spend the majority of their school day in the general education classroom with the general education curriculum, it is a challenge to find the time to address their individual reading needs. Many DHH students need specialized instruction using individualized materials beyond the standard curriculum and data-driven instructional decisions, as opposed to simply using accommodations as replacements for reading instruction (King-Sears & Bowman-Kruhm, 2010).

One important and often overlooked piece of information that teachers will need to gather pertains to the child's current level of reading relative to the demands of daily reading in the classroom. Typically, general education teachers work with children whose reading scores range from below basic to advanced (National Center for Education Statistics, 2009). It requires an inordinate amount of effort to keep a child in the regular classroom if he or she is reading in the basic or below-basic range. This phenomenon frequently occurs for teachers who work with DHH students and means that teachers must scaffold children's learning when their reading is a couple of years behind their grade placement. One way to determine the student achievement/grade-level gap is to give the child a basic reading inventory, such as the BRI (Johns, 2008), to determine his reading grade level, and then see how closely his ability matches that expected in the classroom. If his reading is delayed more than two years compared to his grade placement, then the IEP team should carefully consider placement, modifications, and accommodations. Students whose reading levels are more than two years behind the expectations of the classroom are not maximally placed or served. If teachers find themselves being required to place a student in an instructional environment for social promotion purposes or for administrative expediency, it becomes even more important that they document a student's PLAAF and make this gap clear to the child's parents. Parents are often the best ally in convincing the IEP team to recommend a more appropriate placement.

LARGE-SCALE MEASURES OF EDUCATIONAL OUTCOMES FOR ACCOUNTABILITY PURPOSES

Most states require that DHH students participate in the state's annual assessment programs, similar to the assessments conducted by the National Assessment of Educational Progress (NAEP), and reading is one of the areas that is routinely assessed. In a review of the department of education websites conducted for this book, we found that many states identified a specific assessment for reading, usually conducted from grades 1 through 8 or 3 through 8. Most of these assessments provided a holistic-style rating of outcomes, using language similar to NAEP, such as "does not meet expectations, meets expectations, exceeds expectations" or "not proficient, proficient, advanced proficiency." All students with disabilities, except those who qualify for an alternative curriculum or alternative assessment, must take their state's tests. Teachers may be asked to review their state's reading objectives, framework, or practice tests to prepare their students for the state test. High-stakes assessments are not comprehensive measures of student ability. Student performance can vary based on the sample of questions on the assessment, the student's health on testing day, and many other outside factors (Heubert & Hauser, 1991). Annual standardized assessments do *not* provide information that informs individual student instruction (Cawthon, 2007; Stiggins, 1998);

rather, they provide a comparison of a particular student to her typically hearing same-aged peers on the same testing material. Therefore, teachers working with DHH students need information from a variety of assessments to provide a comprehensive view of student needs and abilities, including auditory, communication, visual, intellectual, attention, social, and memory measures (National Association of State Directors of Special Education [NASDSE], 2006).

ACCOMMODATIONS AND MODIFICATIONS

States usually allow specified accommodations and modifications to assessments based on disability categories, but there tends to be an overlap in their definitions. Hollenbeck, Tindal, and Almond (1999) provided the following definitions for clarification:

> Accommodations do not change the nature of the construct being tested, but differentially affect the student's or group's performance in comparison to a peer group. Also, accommodations provide unique and differential access (to performance) so certain students or groups of students may complete the test and tasks without other confounding influences of test format, administration, or responding. (p. 1)

> Modifications result in a change in the test (how it is given, how it is completed, or what construct is being assessed) and the work across the board for all students with equal effect. Because of the lack of interaction between "group" and "change in test," the modification itself does not qualify as an accommodation. (p. 2)

For example, reading the instructions to a child on how to do a particular task, such as "Read the following examples and circle the correct answer," is an example of an accommodation. If one were to give this same instruction to all children, hearing or deaf, it would not fundamentally change the test item measured and would put all students on an even footing. However, if one were to read a passage to the child about which he had to make some decisions, this would fundamentally change the test from a measure of reading comprehension to a measure of listening/language comprehension and is considered a modification. Table 3.1 identifies categories of accommodations used in the education of DHH children.

Table 3.1. *Commonly Used Accommodations*

Time/Scheduling
- Extended time
- Breaks between subtests
- Frequent breaks within a subtest
- Time of day most beneficial to students

Setting
- Change of location to reduce distractions
- Test in small group
- Test individually
- Environmental modifications: special lighting, noise buffers, carrels

Presentation Format
- Amplification devices (hearing aids, FM systems, cochlear implants)
- Test directions read aloud
- Test directions interpreted
- Test directions repeated
- Test directions simplified
- Test content read aloud
- Test content interpreted
- Use of simplified English

Response Format
- Students sign responses to a scribe
- Computer-administered testing

Other
- Augmentative, assistive, or adaptive technology

Adapted from: Case, 2005; Cawthon & The Online Research Lab, 2007; Tindal, Hollenbeck, Heath, & Almond, 1997.

Phillips (1994) provided five considerations when contemplating accommodations for assessments, including the possibility of a change in the actual skills measured versus the intended skills measured, the meaning of scores under accommodations, any unintended benefit from the accommodations, the ability of the student with a disability to adapt to the standard administration of the assessment, and doubtful validity and reliability in the accommodations. A 2004–2005 survey of 444 educators working with DHH students found that 91 percent completed high-stakes assessments with accommodations (Cawthon & The Online Research Lab, 2007). Educators reported that small group instruction was the most prevalent accommodation (89 percent) during assessment, followed by extra time (82 percent) and interpreting test directions (81 percent). Least frequently used accommodations included simplified English (9 percent) and student signed responses (17 percent). Reading the test items aloud or interpreting the test items was more prevalent in math assessments (26 percent; 24 percent) than reading assessments (6 percent; 4 percent). However, accommodations deemed acceptable for inclusion of a student's score toward adequate yearly progress[1] (AYP) vary across states. Some states accept reading or interpreting test items toward standard administration, while others do not. In addition, some teachers define reading the test content aloud and interpretation of the test content as the same accommodations, while others define these accommodations differently. In the recent past (2005), many states allowed students to be tested at their instructional level rather than their chronological level (e.g., an eighth grader reading on a fifth-grade level would receive fifth-grade instruction and assessment at this level). Today the preference is for all students except those eligible for alternate assessments to be tested at their chronologically equivalent grade level. Accommodations and modifications used in daily instruction typically are the only ones now allowed during statewide assessments.

[1.] Adequate yearly progress, or AYP, is a term found in the No Child Left Behind Act of the U.S. Department of Education. It refers to how school districts score on standardized tests. AYP is determined individually by each state. Schools not achieving AYP receive corrective support and/or more serious consequences.

Best practices for accommodations are "a collection of strategies and principles that help provide satisfactory results in test participation" (Cawthon & The Online Research Lab, 2007, p. 59). The student's mode of communication, academic level (two or more years below grade level in reading), additional disabilities, and test subject are considerations for the accommodations of test read aloud, interpretation of the test, and student-signed response (Cawthon & The Online Research Lab, 2007). However, teachers must remain cautious in the use of accommodations because they can lead to overreliance and circumvention of reading difficulties instead of addressing individual students' reading needs, including their need to develop independent reading comprehension skills (King-Sears & Bowman-Kruhm, 2010). The Test Equity Summit (2008), a group of 12 experts in the field of education, recommended the following to improve test equity for DHH and hearing students: research-based accommodations, advance preparation time for interpreters, instruction in test-taking skills for students, consultations with experts in deaf education during development of assessments, trials of assessments on groups of both hearing and deaf students, and multiple methods of assessments (i.e., portfolios, interviews, etc.) in addition to high-stakes assessments (PEPNet, 2009, Fall).

ALTERNATIVE CURRICULUMS AND ALTERNATIVE ASSESSMENTS

Under NCLB, students with cognitive disabilities who are learning a different set of standards or standards at lesser depth, breadth, and complexity may take an alternate assessment based on the achievement standards identified within their IEP (Cawthon & Wurtz, 2008; NASDSE, 2006). This means that a total of 3 percent of alternate assessments administered may be counted as "proficient" (i.e., if the student's performance was proficient) toward AYP for a school district. It does not mean that only 3 percent of students with disabilities may study different standards or may take an alternate assessment, it just means that their scores may not reflect proficiency in the overall summary of AYP. In a survey of 314 teachers or administrators who worked with DHH students who participated in alternate assessment for the 2004–2005 school year, 32 percent used a checklist, 40 percent used a student portfolio, and 23 percent used out-of-level testing (Cawthon & Wurtz, 2008). In many states, the use of alternative curriculums and assessments means that the student will most likely not be eligible for a high school diploma—only a certificate of attendance. Students receiving instruction from an alternative curriculum and alternative assessment in most cases will need to earn a GED later to continue into postsecondary education.

DIFFERING ROLES OF THE GENERAL EDUCATION TEACHER AND THE TOD

IEP teams have the option of offering a continuum of educational services and settings, yet most DHH students are being placed in the general education classroom, which means that the general education teacher will choose most of the classroom assessments given. These are often tests that do not take hearing loss into account and in some cases (e.g., *DIBELS*, described below) are not recommended by their own publishers for use with DHH students. Assessments may be conducted in the general education classroom or in a resource setting, in a small group or individually. It has been our experience that additional collaboration is needed between the general education teacher and the deaf education teacher to make sure that duplicate testing does not occur. Duplicate administrations of a test invalidate its results and lead to over-testing of the student. When appropriate, assessments should be modified according to the student's IEP. Many times, the TOD is called upon to both modify assessments from content areas (reading, language arts, science, social studies, etc.) and present the modified versions of the assessments to the student. Once any assessment is modified from its original form, validity becomes questionable. Anyone modifying a test needs to ask the following questions:

- With changes, is the assessment still a measure of the intended skill?

- What listening conditions must be in place for the child who uses spoken communication to understand the test sufficiently?
- Does the person administering a test in sign language have the necessary skills? In addition, the TOD or the general education teacher may grade the completed assessment.
- Have the TOD and the general education teacher discussed how the student's grades on modified assessments will be scored and calculated as an overall grade?
- Do the assessments include IEP goals?

Many issues must be considered for a valid assessment of a student's skills. If teachers are using school-selected curricula for reading instruction with modifications, such as benchmarking assessments and basic reading inventories, how are the assessments modified to reflect what a student can actually do? For example, does the teacher provide the meaning of unknown vocabulary words so that comprehension is measured based on putting the words together? Teachers of students with learning challenges above and beyond those that typical children face must take extra measures to evaluate their students' progress in all areas including reading (Perner, 2007). Most grading systems that general educators use are not sufficient to track the growth and change of learning in DHH students, given the slower progress DHH students make across time as compared to their typically hearing peers.

USING ASSESSMENT SYSTEMS DESIGNED FOR HEARING CHILDREN

One test commonly given to children in general education is the DIBELS (Good & Kaminski, 2007). The DIBELS is a collection of measures to assess early literacy skills for students in kindergarten through sixth grade. The measures include initial sound fluency, phonemic segmentation fluency (student production of individual sounds within a word), nonsense fluency, and oral reading fluency within grade-level connected text (https://dibels.uoregon.edu/dibelsinfo.php). Some teachers use sign language when giving this test to meet the communication needs of their students. When teachers conduct assessments using sign language or a supplemental strategy such as Visual Phonics, they must ensure that they are not changing the construct that is measured. For example, if the assessment task is phoneme segmentation, the teacher says, "Tell me the sounds in 'mop,'" and expects a response of "/m/ /o/ /p/" from the student. If an interpreter signs "mop" and the student uses the Visual Phonics hand cues for "mop," the assessment effectively measures the student's knowledge of phoneme segmentation. However, if the target word spoken by the teacher does not have an equivalent in sign language and the interpreter finger-spells the word, such as "of," the student is not segmenting phonemes but rather providing the sounds for given letters. This is not a valid assessment of phoneme segmentation. Further, the DIBELS is a timed test and therefore likely biased against DHH children who need extra processing time. The DIBELS publishers also state that this test is not appropriate for DHH students (https://dibels.uoregon.edu/faq.php#faq_idel4).

USING ASSESSMENTS DEVELOPED FOR DHH STUDENTS

The *Fairview Learning Process* (Fairview Learning Network, 2010) is a reading program developed specifically for deaf students with input from native ASL users and deaf individuals and grew out of a pilot reading project at the Mississippi School for the Deaf. Fairview Learning focuses on basic reading skills by providing direct access to ASL and bridging it to English for reading comprehension. Using the ASL Stories folder, students tell personal stories in ASL to an instructor, who then retells the story while modeling proper ASL. Students use this model to retell their stories on video and link these stories to written English. This folder also contains pages to record and illustrate students' stories, instructional strategies, and assessment forms. Fairview also incorporates Dolch words, or common high-frequency sight words, from pre-primer to third grade levels. In addition, Fairview Learning includes student progress folders with beginning and final assessment forms and daily reading comprehension forms for frequent assessment and data collection. The Fairview Learning Product Checks permit online access to individual record keeping and data analysis, with access to a national comparative database. The assessment focus remains on actual student progress instead of expected student progress. Schimmel, Edwards, and Prickett (1999) reported gains in students' reading levels and teachers' and students' signing skills when using this interactive program with 48 elementary students at a residential school for the deaf.

Other curriculum packages developed for DHH students that contain assessments are *Reading Milestones* and *Reading Bridge.* These were developed with both orally communicating and signing children in mind. Reading Milestones (Quigley, McAnally, King, & Rose, 2001) is a reading curriculum designed for DHH students based on sequential syntactic development, controlled vocabulary, chunking of sentence parts (e.g., separation of subjects, verbs, prepositional phrases), spelling through phonological awareness and sound–spelling correspondences, and placement assessments for students across six levels. The teacher conducts the placement assessments in a small group or with individual students. Reading Milestones was created as supplemental material to help DHH students who are struggling with upper elementary reading materials. Reading Bridge (Quigley, McAnally, Rose, & Payne, 2003) supports the instruction of students from Reading Milestones into fourth- and fifth-grade-level reading materials.

The above authors are developing an online assessment system specifically for DHH students, the *AVENUE* (Miller, Rose, & Hooper, 2011), which will assess various literacy skills. The AVENUE includes several timed online assessments for DHH students: cloze-type reading passages in which students fill in every seventh word from three given choices, a slash test in which students separate connected letters into words, a written response to a given prompt, videotaped retelling of a story presented in ASL, and a picture-naming task to assess vocabulary. For more information about this assessment's progress, go to http://www.cehd.umn.edu/DHH-resources/.

DEVELOPING YOUR OWN ASSESSMENTS

No matter where a student is placed, the teacher or other practitioner is always called upon to document what he or she is teaching, why it is being taught, and how well the student is moving toward mastering the skill or knowledge taught. All educators engage in data collection. Formal, whole-school assessments such as AIMSweb (2010) or *ACCESS for ELLs* (World-Class Instructional Design and Assessment, 2007) can tell us information about a child relative to other children, but they may not provide specific guidance on instruction. For example, Donnie, a 7-year-old child with a moderate to severe hearing loss was given the AIMSweb Maze test and scored 1 out of a target of 5. This tells us that he did not reach the expected target, but it does not tell us what he needs. In addition, Donnie reads *Accelerated Reader* books at the 1.4 grade level and passes the computerized tests at 80 percent. However, his teacher retells the story after he has finished it; discusses the plot, characters, setting, sequence of events, and outcome; and asks him comprehension questions that might be on the test, providing the answer if he misses it. This is not a valid measure of his reading level. Giving him the test without any coaching would be a more valid way of determining what he comprehends when he reads. Instead of these kinds of assessments, teachers need to gather data from a variety of sources. These include checklists, teacher-designed assessments, curriculum-based assessment rubrics, forms with boxes to check as a tabulation of correct and incorrect answers, and portfolios with artifacts.

Checklists

Many authors (French, 1999a, 1999b; Miller, 2001; Rief, 2010) have written teacher handbooks that contain literacy checklists teachers can use to target assessment in specific skill areas. These are very easy to find today online. Simply enter "reading checklists" into a computer browser. For students who cannot yet read, iconic or pictorial checklists work very well. For example, the BRI (Johns, 2008) includes stories that contain only pictures to assess the literacy skills of students whose are at pre-emergent levels.

Teacher-Designed, Curriculum-Based Assessment Rubrics

An *assessment rubric* is a set of general criteria used to evaluate a student's performance in a given outcome area while focusing on the quality of a specific set of performance-based skills.

Rubrics consist of a fixed measurement scale (e.g., a 4- or 5-point scale), a list of criteria that describe the characteristics of products or performances for each score point, and sample resources that illustrate the various score points on the scale. Rubrics can be *holistic* or *analytical*. Holistic rubrics use a scoring procedure that yields a single score based upon the overall impression of a product or performance. The number of points of differentiation used depends on the various degrees of proficiency inherent in the task (e.g., not observed, emerging, developing, or fluent). Analytical rubrics look at specific domains with embedded traits, and each trait receives a separate score. For example, the *Signed Reading Fluency Rubric for Deaf Children* has two domains: fluency envelope and visual grammar (Easterbrooks & Huston, 2008). Typical analytic rubrics have six or seven indicators that are divided into a rating scale of 1 to 4 or 5, with each rating receiving a specific description of the students' expected performance. Each level of proficiency varies from indicator to indicator, so the students must be able to perform specific skills in order to achieve a specific rating. Today's teachers are fortunate in that they can find dozens of premade rubrics on various websites as well as rubric generators from which they can make their own professional-looking rubrics.

There are many reasons why education practitioners might want to use a rubric. First, rubrics narrow the gap between assessment and instruction because they are so integrally related to the instructional task at hand. Next, they help teachers better organize their instructional plans. In addition, students can become engaged in the assessment process because the rubric aids their understanding of what the teacher is expecting and students are able to self-monitor their work, requiring less dependence on the teacher. Teachers can individualize rubrics according to student level and ability during both instruction and assessment to highlight specific desired qualities, set goals with students, and help students become metacognitive thinkers (Schirmer, Bailey, & Fitzgerald, 1999). Finally, rubrics are tangible items that teachers can hand to students or parents to demonstrate growth, development, and change. The key element that makes rubrics so useful is that they create opportunities for teachers to observe student behavior that is related to real-world application of their instruction. They require students to construct responses rather than select responses, and, finally, the scoring method may

Table 3.2. *Steps in Developing an Assessment Rubric*

1. Decide points for your grading system, if applicable.

2. Decide what criteria you are assessing. Use your current curriculum to determine outcomes.

3. Decide which rubric style fits your performance task.

4. Decide who the audience is (i.e., who will be doing the rating).

5. Decide how many degrees of proficiency your rubric will need (across the top of the rubric; e.g., not observed, emerging, developing, fluent).

6. If your task is analytical, decide how many indicators you will evaluate. Four or five is typical.

7. Use descriptive terms to describe differences in degrees of each feature.

reveal patterns in students' learning and thinking that the teacher can use to focus or redirect his or her instruction. Table 3.2 provides a set of procedures for developing assessment rubrics. Various student products can be used within the context of a rubric. Developing an assessment rubric with students helps them understand what the teacher values, sets clear expectations, and gives the teacher a glimpse into what students themselves value. For example, during a story-generation activity, a teacher and student can collaboratively use a writing rubric that includes indicators for the use of nouns, verbs, and adjectives within sentences. The teacher can facilitate self-evaluation by the student while discussing the expected elements from the rubric. Figure 3.1 displays a rubric that a teacher and student used to evaluate the student's writing and direct his revision (Figure 3.2).

Portfolios with Artifacts

One method teachers often use is the portfolio assessment. A portfolio is a collection of work that provides evidence that a student has made progress toward a predetermined set of goals and objectives. Formerly used with many students, this approach is now associated with the documentation a teacher must gather for a student who is receiving an alternative curriculum and alternative assessment (Perner, 2007). Generally, portfolios include artifacts of students' work, that is, permanent products that document effort. These may include such items as student papers,

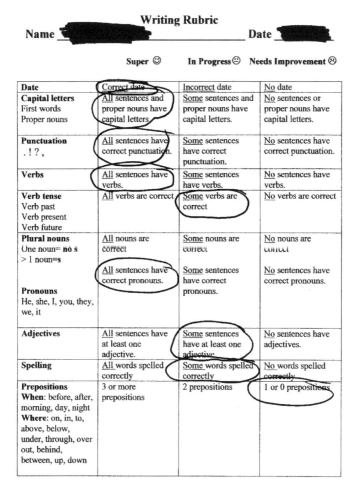

Writing Rubric

Name _____ Date _____

Super ☺   In Progress☺   Needs Improvement ☹

Date	Correct date	Incorrect date	No date
Capital letters First words Proper nouns	All sentences and proper nouns have capital letters	Some sentences and proper nouns have capital letters.	No sentences or proper nouns have capital letters.
Punctuation . ! ? ,	All sentences have correct punctuation.	Some sentences have correct punctuation.	No sentences have correct punctuation.
Verbs	All sentences have verbs.	Some sentences have verbs.	No sentences have verbs.
Verb tense Verb past Verb present Verb future	All verbs are correct	Some verbs are correct	No verbs are correct
Plural nouns One noun= **no s** > 1 noun=**s**	All nouns are correct	Some nouns are correct	No nouns are correct
Pronouns He, she, I, you, they, we, it	All sentences have correct pronouns.	Some sentences have correct pronouns.	No sentences have correct pronouns.
Adjectives	All sentences have at least one adjective.	Some sentences have at least one adjective.	No sentences have adjectives.
Spelling	All words spelled correctly	Some words spelled correctly	No words spelled correctly
Prepositions **When**: before, after, morning, day, night **Where**: on, in, to, above, below, under, through, over out, behind, between, up, down	3 or more prepositions	2 prepositions	1 or 0 prepositions

FIGURE 3.1. Writing Rubric Associated with Figure 3.2

pictures of students participating in activities that demonstrate the task the teacher is documenting, and teacher-made rubrics or observation forms on which the teacher may chart progress. The portfolio must be structured so that it shows clearly where the student began in her understanding or use of a skill, how she progressed, and where she ended at the time of final documentation (Wakeman, Browder, Meirer, & McColl, 2007). The Laurent Clerc National Deaf Education Center provides a product called *Portfolios for Student Growth* (n.d.) that will help teachers develop reading portfolios that will link goal setting with learning.

Monkey is funny. ☺

He eats bananas ~~many 100~~.

Monkey swing *s*   *area* vine green and play *s*.
                  Prep   noun   adj

White tiger play *s* *and*   jump *in* pool *and* splash*es*.
                                  Prep

White tiger eat *s* elk.

White tiger is pretty. ☺

Parrot talk *s* *and* *is* fun.
                  Verb

Parrot eat *s* seeds. ☺

Parrot is ~~color~~ white and cheeks *are* blue.
                                   verb

FIGURE 3.2. Student Revision after Self-Evaluation Using Writing Rubric in Figure 3.1

NEGOTIATION FOR CONTENT MASTERY

Negotiating content for student mastery with the general education teacher is a time-honored strategy used in resource rooms with DHH students to assist with assessment when students' language and literacy levels are below grade level. This involves negotiating a smaller number of vocabulary words, facts, and concepts that the student must master for full academic credit. For example, while typical third-grade students may be required to master 20 spelling words per week, a DHH student may be required to master 10. The process is based on looking at individual students' PLAAF, IEP goals and objectives, and instructional benchmarks.[2] The student is held accountable only for benchmark information and not extraneous words, facts, ideas, and concepts. Content negotiation often takes place in portfolio assessments.

[2.] Benchmarks are expected performances achieved in a specified time that indicate progress toward achievement of an annual goal.

CONSIDERATIONS FOR CLASSROOM TESTING

Teachers routinely test the reading skills of students in their classrooms for ongoing progress monitoring (i.e., for stakeholders) and to assign grades to students' current levels of performance (e.g., report cards). Some of the more commonly used reading assessment formats include short-answer comprehension questions, multiple-choice tests, word banks, and retellings.

Short-answer questions may measure cognitive processes not tapped by multiple-choice formats and are a more accurate reflection of academic and future work settings without the possibility of inflated scores from guessing (Pajares & Miller, 1997; Zheng, Cheng, & Klinger, 2007). When writing a short-answer question, it is helpful to revise the language of multi-clause sentences. For example, the sixth-grade question "What strait, controlled by the United Kingdom, is close to the place where the Mediterranean Sea meets the Atlantic Ocean?" contains a wh-relative clause and a clause with "which is" deleted. With one independent and two dependent clauses, this sentence is actually three sentences in one. To assist the DHH child who may struggle with this level of complexity, teachers can break the question into declarative sentences and add a simple question at the end. For example, a teacher might say, "The United Kingdom controls a strait. The Mediterranean Sea meets the Atlantic Ocean, and the strait is near this place. What is the name of the strait?" As an example from a fifth-grade science test, the question might ask, "Which of the following is a harmful waste material that leaves the blood and travels through the lungs before leaving the body?" In this instance the student is given four multiple-choice answers. The problem the student might face with this question is that it contains an independent clause and two dependent clauses, one of which is a time clause (before), all embedded within a question form. This would be a challenge for a student reading at the basic level. Again, the teacher would put the important information up front, such as: "Look at the names of the harmful waste materials below. Think about the path that each material takes to leave the body." (Give thinking time.) "Which harmful material first leaves the blood, then travels through the lungs, and then leaves your body?" Teachers need to remember to put information into simple sentences at the beginning and then follow this with a simple question. No matter whether teachers use the easier language or the more difficult language, the student will still have to provide the answer, "The Strait of Gibraltar" or "carbon dioxide," and it is more likely that he will answer correctly if he does not first have to figure out a complex question.

The use of a word bank in fill-in-the-blank assessments is a common practice among teachers of students with disabilities, but the evidence base for this practice is limited. We do know that word banks increase accuracy in responses on tests in college students (Glass, Clause, & Kreiner, 2007), but this may or may not be the case with schoolchildren. To use a word bank, teachers list all of the possible answers to a fill-in-the-blank test either at the top or bottom of the test page, and students use the available words to fill in the blanks within the test questions. Although there is no direct evidence that this is effective, we might extrapolate from the evidence on the *maze task*, which is associated with curriculum-based assessment. In a maze task, test designers typically delete every seventh word and replace it with three multiple-choice alternatives (one correct and two incorrect). Students are required to select the correct answers under a time limit. Students' outcomes on maze tests are predictive of their outcomes on standardized reading tests (Shin, Deno, & Espin, 2000). In other words, better readers perform better on maze tests; this might mean that an individual child's reading level influences his or her ability to use word banks to fill in blanks on tests. This practice is used with children who have lower cognitive, language, and literacy skills but is also appropriate for those with better reading skills.

Multiple-choice question formats provide students with the correct answer embedded in a collection of choices. The following is an example reading passage and possible answer choices.

A "Calico" cat must have three colors: black, white, and orange. Variations of these colors include gray, cream, and ginger. Calico cats are usually female. Which is true of a calico cat?

The incorrect choices may include near-misses, such as "A calico cat must have black, white, and ginger." Thematic responses are possible but result from the misconceptions of readers, such as "Calico cats are always female." Unrelated responses are inconsistent with the reading passage given, such as "Calico is a type of car." When given answers are similar in multiple-choice questions, the test taker must engage in higher-order thinking to distinguish the differences in provided answers (Ozuro, Best, Bell, Witherspoon, & McNamara, 2007). Such higher-order skills may include comparing, contrasting, and analyzing. DHH children with limited language abilities may also be limited in the higher-order thinking skills they bring to the multiple-choice task. Students may perform better on multiple choice tests because retrieval cues are provided within given answers, as opposed to short-answer questions. Additionally, they may know the answer but not recognize it within complex language structures. For example, they may know that a calico cat is black, white, and orange, but if the correct answer is "Those cats that do not have orange cannot be called calico," the child may not choose it because of the noun clause and double-negative structures (interpreting the statement instead as "cats do not have orange called calico").

Multiple-choice formats are common for assessments because teachers can score them quickly, conveniently, and objectively (Balch, 2007). Possible negatives of multiple-choice formats include a focus on recall, limited demonstration of deeper knowledge, and the possibility of above-chance performance (Daneman & Hannon, 2001; Zheng, Cheng, & Klinger, 2007). When deciding upon test question format, it is important to consider the purpose of the assessment and how best to measure student ability.

RETELLINGS

When children struggle to express what they have read or when teachers struggle to understand what a child has comprehended, they might consider story retellings as an alternative way to measure comprehension.

In hearing children, the ability to retell stories is an age-sensitive measure of comprehension, narrative quality, semantics, and verbal productivity, but not of morphosyntactic ability, which means that it is a developmentally sensitive measure (Westerveld & Gillon, 2010). When a child retells a story, a teacher has the opportunity to see whether the child understands story structure (e.g., setting, characters, plot, resolution), even though he or she may not be able to write the answer succinctly on a more traditional test. Story retelling is an important evaluation tool for very young deaf children (Robertson, Dow, & Hainzinger, 2006) and for struggling readers, whether hearing or deaf (Gabig, 2008). Materials for gathering story retellings can be found in many traditional assessment products or in materials developed specifically for students who are DHH such as the *Starting with Assessment Toolkit* (French, 1999a). Case Vignette 3.5 provides an example of a teacher's transcription and narrative evaluation of a child's oral story retelling using a picture book.

CASE VIGNETTE 3.5.

Child's Retelling and Teacher's Analysis

In this activity, the teacher read a story she created from the picture book *Carl's Afternoon in the Park*. The story was written to take the students' language levels into consideration. For example, she wrote the story using only simple or expanded sentences without many clauses. The teacher stressed the characters, plot, problem, and resolution over three readings of the story. After reading the story twice and then asking and answering questions about the story, the teacher gave the book to Lily and asked her to tell the story to a friend (Lily used spoken language). The teacher made an audiovisual recording of the process for later reference.

CHILD'S STORY

It going get on that ride there and make noise. Maybe turn page gone be. The baby gonna get on a big, that big dog. The baby wanna hold that puppy. Going in the flower. Carl is digging a hole. Carl is to Carl. But only I going to this! I think. In the pool. Let's see gone pop it. And the baby going go up to the air. Not gonna go sky. Gonna go up in the sky and baby gonna go up. The mommy

---

(Continued)

(*Continued*)

giving the baby the ice cream. That puppy is eating that ice cream. Drips. On the train ride. Look, that on and that one has a new puppy. Going make noise. I going to go at school and ride the Thomas train. I see you. That puppy sitting on that sheep. On the ground right there. That one goes.

TEACHER'S ANALYSIS

Lily is still not using complete sentences in her explanations. She was able to provide characters, setting, and various activities, but she still did not convey the plot that had been stressed to her over two readings and a question-and-answer session. She did not connect that the mother completely missed all the danger that the child had been through and all the struggles Carl had to keep her safe. She was unable to provide a story sequence but instead responded to each picture as if it were a separate story.

SUMMARY OF RECOMMENDED PRACTICES

Assessing a DHH student's reading skills is not an easy task. Expert teachers and practitioners consider many aspects of language as well as reading because a child's receptive and expressive language skills are integrally intertwined with his or her reading skills. Teachers will also face the challenge of assessing reading in both spoken and signed modes. We identified several assessments that have been used with students with hearing loss and presented modifications that teachers might make to tests. Effective teachers will keep themselves familiarized with a variety of topics currently influencing the field, including RTI, high-stakes testing for school accountability, benchmark testing, and progress monitoring. Of course today's teachers must prepare students to read their state's annual reading assessments, but in the classroom, the effective teacher includes inventories of specific skills through checklists, rubrics, and other forms of progress monitoring. Teachers assess not only the language underlying reading but also specific skills in the areas of phonological and morphological decoding, vocabulary, text comprehension, and fluency. Effective teachers and education practitioners will be sure to provide valid and reliable measurements that are implemented with high fidelity and take into account the student's current mode of communication.

RESOURCES

Wren, S., Like, B., Jinkins, D., Paynter, S., Watts, J., & Alanis, I. (2000). *Cognitive foundations of learning to read: A framework.* Austin, TX: Southwestern Educational Development Laboratory.

Search the Intervention Central site for materials and suggestions for assessments: http://www.interventioncentral.org.

Log in to http://www.deafed.net. Go to the section on Instructional Resources. Click on the link to the Virtual Library and then click on "Assessment."

4 Vocabulary: Word Meaning

PURPOSE

Students who are deaf or hard of hearing (DHH) tend to fall behind their typically hearing peers on standardized scores of reading vocabulary. This is because both sources of vocabulary learning (i.e., deliberate instruction and incidental learning; Paul, 1996) can be difficult for them to access. When teaching children to read vocabulary, effective teachers address two parts to the problem: the meaning of the vocabulary the reader is learning and procedures for decoding words. This chapter focuses on the first part of this two-part issue: underlying word meaning (decoding is addressed in Chapter 5). We begin with a discussion of the complexity of the vocabulary learning process and then present the existing knowledge base regarding vocabulary comprehension in DHH readers. We explain key features of good vocabulary instruction, identify evidence-based practices and their associated Causal Factors, and provide case vignettes that demonstrate their application.

VOCABULARY AND HEARING CHILDREN

Multiple researchers have documented that a child's listening vocabulary is related to his or her reading vocabulary (Cunningham & Stanovich, 1997; Penno, Wilkinson, & Moore, 2002; Sénéchal, LeFevre, Thomas, & Daley, 1998). For example, students' receptive vocabulary at the beginning of first grade predicted their reading ability at the end of third (Sénéchal et al., 1998) and eleventh grade (Cunningham & Stanovich, 1997). Once children are on a developmental trajectory for growth in vocabulary, they tend to remain on that trajectory (Farkas & Beron, 2004; Penno et al., 2002). Children who start with smaller lexicons,[1] or vocabularies, add words to those lexicons at slower rates than do students with larger lexicons. As a result, not only must they expand their basic vocabularies more than other children, they must also develop the vocabulary items they have to a greater level of sophistication (Shefelbine, 1990). In other words, if they start out slowly, they continue to develop vocabulary slowly. If they start out rapidly, they continue to develop rapidly. The same holds true for vocabulary trajectories of young DHH children (Connor, Craig, Raudenbush, Heavner, & Zwolan, 2006).

We know a great deal about reading vocabulary and children who can hear. The actual numbers of individual words a hearing child has heard (rather than different words heard) by the time he or she enters kindergarten is quite astounding—somewhere in the following ranges of word tallies: 45,000,000 words (*college-educated families*), 26,000,000 words (*working-class families*), or 13,000,000 words (*lower socioeconomic families*) (Hart & Risley, 1995). Students with typical levels of hearing have learned an average of 6,000 root word meanings by the end of second grade (Biemiller, 2005), and good readers have viewed around 18,600 words in running text, compared to only 10,000 words for poor readers by the end of first grade (Juel, 1988). Good readers know what words mean and can use them. After second grade, the "typical" student acquires an additional 1,000 word meanings a year, which means that by the time the

---

[1.] One's lexicon is composed of the sum total of vocabulary items and all their variations known by the individual.

student is heading into middle school, he or she knows close to 10,000 words, can explain what they mean, and can use them productively in sentences.

Basic vocabulary instruction is essential, but equally important is the time the child spends using the words that he or she knows in "decontextualized" conversations with adults. Decontextualized vocabulary is that vocabulary that emerges naturally during spontaneous conversations about extemporaneous topics, from grocery store advertisements to last night's television show to Sunday's family dinner. Decontextualized vocabulary more accurately predicts reading achievement in hearing children than scores on standardized tests of receptive vocabulary (Tabors, 1996). Teachers and practitioners who want children to learn vocabulary need to talk to them. Conversations contain novel words and figurative phrases and promote higher-level thinking skills in children, such as synthesizing, analyzing, and comparing (Luetke-Stahlman, 1998), all of which are important vocabulary, grammar, and thinking skills that good readers use. For example, one 3-year-old child who heard the word "sharp" in the context of "Your fishing pole is really sharp" engaged in spontaneous analysis as he realized that "sharp" has multiple meanings beyond "the scissors are sharp."

VOCABULARY AND CHILDREN WHO ARE DEAF OR HARD OF HEARING

Typically, DHH students start learning vocabulary later than hearing children, and so the breadth and depth of their vocabularies lag behind. Access to communication imposes a challenge to children's vocabulary acquisition, whether through the spoken or signed mode. Hearing toddlers knew an average of 573 words at 30 months (Fenson et al., 1994). In contrast, DHH children between 1.5 to 4.5 years had only one-fifth the vocabulary of their hearing peers (i.e., a mean of 47 different words for DHH children and 241 for hearing children around four years of age) (Nicholas & Geers, 2003) because limited input leads to limited uptake. Limited exposure to vocabulary receptively leads to limited outcomes expressively (Lederberg & Everhart, 1998; Nicholas & Geers, 2003; Spencer, 1993a). This is especially important to monitor because the productive vocabulary of DHH students is a strong predictor of their reading achievement (Kyle & Harris, 2006).

Uptake leads to vocabulary development, and vocabulary influences reading ability. For example, when the focus of reading turns to vocabulary and information acquisition after fourth grade, reading may decline. Even those DHH students who read on grade level in elementary grades may fall behind. Students with cochlear implants (CIs) who read on grade level when they were 8 to 9 years of age had a reading delay of two years by the time they were 15 to 16 years of age (Geers, 2003; Geers, Tobey, Moog, & Brenner, 2008). Teachers must be aware of this "falling-off" effect when readers start depending more on their ability to learn from text instead of from explicit instruction by a teacher. Although the landscape is changing due to improvements in technology and early intervention, many DHH students are still entering the school years with impoverished vocabularies when compared to children with typical hearing. Such was the case with Megan (see Case Vignette 3.3), who covered up her lack of understanding by making agreeable headshakes that the teacher mistakenly accepted as verification of learning.

Luckner and Cooke (2010) reported that only 10 intervention studies were published in the 40 years prior that were related to vocabulary and elementary DHH students. Vocabulary acquisition varies by degree of hearing loss. Children with mild and moderate hearing losses at 3 years of age had higher expressive vocabulary scores and quicker vocabulary acquisition than those with severe and profound losses, and this significant gap in expressive vocabulary increased with age (Kiese-Himmel & Reeh, 2006). Such was the case with Louisa (Case Vignette 3.2), who did not have early support for vocabulary, resulting in a large gap between her age and her ability as measured on the *Basic Reading Inventory*. In addition, DHH children use more directives and requests, because these can be done through nonverbal communication, and fewer statements or questions that require the exchange of information through the production and understanding of language (Lederberg & Beal-Alvarez, 2011; Nicholas, 2000). While DHH children continue to use nonlinguistic communication throughout preschool (i.e., simple words and gestures), hearing children transition to linguistic communication (i.e., expanded grammar) with faster increases in communication skills than DHH children (Lederberg & Everhart, 1998; Nicholas, 2000).

What is involved in helping DHH children develop their vocabularies? We know that DHH children need intensive, daily instruction and discussion of vocabulary in rich and varied contexts, including sentence construction supplemented with picture representations and multiple exposures to the spoken, signed, and printed forms of the target words (de Villiers & Pomerantz, 1992; Paatsch, Blamey, Sarant, & Bow, 2006; Robbins & Hatcher, 1981). Vocabulary uptake involves a child's active recognition, interaction, and response to communication (Harris, 1992) and may include self-correction of language errors by students (Heift, 2004). Corrective feedback is also provided to children by others through the use of recasts, although some recasts are more productive than others (Sheen, 2006).

Parent's interactions with their children also have an effect on vocabulary acquisition. With reference to children who are learning sign language, the signing ability of their parents varies widely, with most mothers signing only a small proportion of what they actually say (Lederberg & Everhart, 1998). There is a direct relation between the number of words a mother signs and the number of words a child signs (Nicholas & Geers, 2003; Spencer, 1993a). When parents do sign, DHH children typically miss between 20 and 30 percent of their parents' visual communication (Lederberg & Everhart, 1998) because parents do not wait for the child's visual attention before communicating or because the child has not learned to look at his or her parents for information. Parents may forgo the needed repetitions of signs (five to eight times) for child acquisition of the meaning connected to signs. Sign language vocabulary was highly correlated with reading vocabulary in those children who used sign language (Hermans, Knoors, Ormel, & Verhoeven, 2008b). With reference to children who are learning spoken language, access to good amplification, reliance on spoken communication, and structured teaching by their parents resulted in better spoken language (Musselman & Kircaali-Iftar, 1996). Participation in intervention, degree of hearing loss, and cognitive ability significantly predicted language outcomes in preschoolers who used spoken language and together accounted for almost 60 percent of the variance in vocabulary (Sarant, Holt, Dowell, Rickards, & Blamey, 2009). In addition, for children who received CIs and were learning spoken communication, age at implantation affected word learning (Hayes, Geers, Treiman, & Moog, 2009), and there was a clear value added for early implantation (Connor et al., 2006). Finally, whether DHH children used spoken language or sign language, it was important for them to have experiences with the decontextualized language use that resulted in better vocabulary outcomes. It is also important in light of Causal Factor 2, which emphasizes that children whose teachers (or parents or other communicating partners) are better communicators have better communication outcomes than children who interact with poor communicators.

Exposure to early storybook reading has an influence on vocabulary acquisition in DHH children no matter whether they use spoken language or sign language. Storybook reading is a very important event in early childhood, although many hearing parents of DHH children tend not to read to them sufficiently often. When hearing mothers of children with CIs used more complex techniques to facilitate language during storybook reading, such as recasts, open-ended questions, parallel talk, and expansion, their children scored higher on language assessments than children whose mothers used lower-level techniques such as labeling, imitation, directives, and closed-ended questions (DesJardin, Ambrose, & Eisenberg, 2008). Recasts present the same information in a different structure (Nelson, 1998). For example, the child may say, "Mmm. Vanilla. That my best ice cream," and the teacher may respond, "Mmm. You like vanilla ice cream. It's your favorite flavor." Open-ended questions are used when the adult asks the child a question that he or she can answer using multiple words, such as "What is happening here?" These kinds of questions would have shown Megan's teacher (Case Vignette 3.3) that Megan did not really understand her. When the adult provides commentary for a picture at which the child is looking, this is referred to as parallel talk. Expansion is the addition of information to a child's utterance. Mothers' mean length of utterance (MLU[2]) and word types (i.e., nouns, verbs, adjectives, adverbs, prepositions) positively related to their children's receptive and expressive spoken language skills, and their use of recasts was positively associated with children's receptive abilities, MLUs, and number of word types (DesJardin & Eisenberg, 2007). In addition, mothers' increased use of open-ended questions and decreased use of labeling and directives positively related to children's expressive language skills (DesJardin & Eisenberg, 2007).

A vicious cycle exists between vocabulary and reading: Students with impoverished vocabularies are limited in their reading abilities, reciprocally affecting their ability to learn new vocabulary from text and their desire to read (DeVilliers & Pomerantz, 1992; Juel, 1988). Good readers in fourth grade frequently read on their own about four nights per week, while poor readers may read on their own only once per week (Juel, 1988). Many children with hearing loss do not have access to a rich vocabulary until a) they get their first hearing aids or cochlear implants, b) they receive intervention (early or otherwise), or c) someone starts communicating effectively with them in the language or mode most appropriate for that individual child. When provided with consistent use of amplification, early intervention support, parental education, and early integration with hearing peers, DHH kindergarteners with profound hearing loss who used spoken language showed no significant differences from their hearing peers in terms of initiating and maintaining conversations, although the DHH students provided less information during these conversations (Duncan, 1999). These findings support the need for teachers to provide and expand student vocabulary during informal conversations to facilitate conversational competence of DHH students.

[2.] An MLU is a common measure of linguistic productivity in young children traditionally calculated by dividing the number of morphemes in a sample of 100 utterances by the number of words in the sample.

WORDS REPRESENT IDEAS

Figure 4.1 demonstrates the complexity of the relationship between ideas and vocabulary, which accounts for many of the challenges DHH children face when learning vocabulary, whether through the spoken mode, signed mode, or some combination thereof.

A fundamental aspect of learning vocabulary is that objects and ideas can be represented by words. The largest circle in Figure 4.1 represents all of the possible ideas that are in the world. The next smaller circle represents the words and grammar that we can use to represent these ideas. We learn vocabulary our whole lives because the source of ideas in this world is endless. The next smaller circle represents the vocabulary and grammar we are able to produce, which ties vocabulary together in meaningful ways. Just being able to say or sign a word does not necessarily mean one understands it. For example, someone might be able to

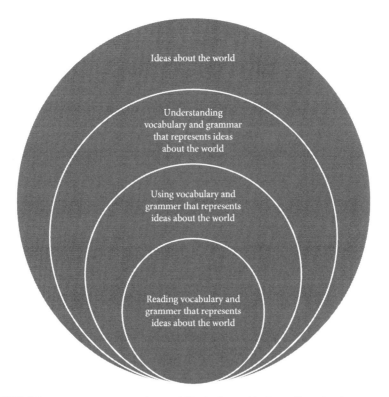

FIGURE 4.1. Relationships among Ideas and Words. Created by Susan Easterbrooks

pronounce the word, "ethyldichloroarsine" or fingerspell it, but without the knowledge that it is a chemical agent that causes blisters, the spoken or fingerspelled rendition would be meaningless. Think about what this means for the deaf child who is reading along with his classmates and comes to a word he does not know. Typically, to the best of his ability, he may fingerspell or pronounce the word and then move on. If he does not know the underlying meaning that the word represents, then that word is hollow.

Vocabulary items may be categorized as either lexical or functional. Lexical items have specific meaning and form the basic building blocks of sentences (i.e., nouns, verbs, adjectives, adverbs, and prepositions). Lexical items are limitless: New words are invented every day (e.g., Skype®, blog, carmageddon). Functional items, such as "of" or "the," make no sense in and of themselves (Chomsky, 1995) and have meaning only when paired with a lexical item (e.g., *The caboose is at the rear "of the train"*). While functional words are still vocabulary items, they are important because they are related to the grammar that holds phrases and sentences together in meaningful ways. Many aspects of grammar must be taught to children. Consider this sentence: "What is, is; what was, was; what will be will be." Just knowing the words (what, is, was, will, be) does not assure understanding unless we realize that the word "what" is used as a pronoun and not a question: It is easier to read a language if one understands both the lexical and functional vocabulary items of which it is comprised. This was the challenge that Sammy (Case Vignette 3.1) faced in trying to learn to read. His teacher measured his grammatical skills on the *CASLLS* and found significant gaps in his knowledge of functional and lexical vocabulary.

THE PROBLEM WITH SIGHT-WORD LISTS

Many schools use sight-word lists, such as the Dolch word lists (Dolch, 1948), in their instruction of reading vocabulary. Sight-word lists typically contain those words that are the most commonly found in children's texts and literature, and a surprising number of these fall into the functional category rather than the lexical category. The assumption is that if a child can learn to read a key set of sight words, then he or she should be able to figure out the rest of a passage. There are several problems with this assumption. First, it overlooks the fact that most sight words violate the decoding strategies young children learn. For example, the word "know" violates several conventions of letter–sound correspondence. Next, because many sight words are in the functional category (i.e., meaningless in and of themselves) (e.g., *a, too, if,* and *so*), they must be taught within a phrase or sentence. Also, words on these lists are common because they have multiple meanings. For example, the word "on" has at least 14 primary meanings (e.g., location, recipient of an action, around, in close proximity to, continuance, about, and manner of conveyance) and dozens of figurative uses (Easterbrooks, 1985). It is difficult to teach the underlying meaning of many words from sight-word lists because they are grammatically complex; however, many children still need to learn a basic set of words by sight (see Figure 4.2). Figure 4.2 represents a common display of sight words within a classroom.

FIGURE 4.2. Classroom Display of Sight Words on a Word Wall

CHALLENGING VOCABULARY COMPONENTS

Helping DHH children learn basic vocabulary at a rate commensurate with hearing children is certainly an important challenge because vocabulary knowledge is one of the key factors associated with good reading comprehension. Yet facility with reading vocabulary is far more complex than just mastery of basic vocabulary. Most languages, and therefore their print versions, are composed of abstract applications of words and phrases, including multiple meanings of words (both concrete and abstract) and sophisticated figurative language expressions. Additionally, a special lexicon surrounds the process of testing and assessment (e.g., *Decide which choice best completes the statement or answers the question*). These abstract and multiple meanings embedded within phrases pose special challenges to effective instruction.

Multiple Meanings

Because DHH students are exposed to language in context less often than their hearing peers, they miss not only basic vocabulary but also the multiple meanings of words. Compared to their hearing peers, DHH students performed much lower when selecting multiple meanings for high-frequency words. They selected the primary meaning (instead of the secondary meaning) most often, and their scores did not improve with age (Paul & Gustafson, 1991). All languages use individual words to represent a number of concepts. For example, the word "cut" might refer to an action (to cut), a condition (to have a cut), a portion of (cut of the profits), one's status (a cut above), removal from (cut from the roster), and a myriad of other meanings. It may be combined with a preposition to form a verb idiom (e.g., cut off). DHH children learning spoken language may hear only a limited number of meanings for a given word. DHH children learning through a hybrid sign system may not understand a word in context. Finally, DHH children learning ASL may see multiple concepts expressed through different signed expressions and not realize that one English word can represent multiple concepts.

Figurative Language

While DHH children, whether using spoken language, a hybrid sign system, or ASL, can understand idioms and figures of speech in English, they tend to be at least 3–4 years delayed relative to their hearing peers (Easterbrooks, 1983). The amount of figurative language in print material is overwhelming, yet we know very little about how figurative language influences DHH children's reading comprehension (Rittenhouse & Stearns, 1990). Marschark, West, Nall, and Everhart (1986) noted that deaf children produced just as many instances of figurative language in sign language as their age-matched hearing peers produced in English. Consequently, while deaf children *can* learn figurative language in English and in ASL, we simply do not have the evidence base to explain the most effective means of teaching figurative language, especially as it applies to improvements in reading comprehension. Further research is needed on this topic.

The Language of Testing

In order to take most tests, students must understand the vocabulary used in the test questions. For example, in the question *"Which statement below best shows the relationship between the two main characters?"* we might expect a student with poor vocabulary to struggle with the concepts of "statement" and "best shows." Most likely the teacher would have explained the terms "relationship" and "main characters" but may expect that the student already understands more common vocabulary and recognizes it in print. DHH students have a tendency to recall concrete terms better than abstract terms (Lang & Pagliaro, 2007); a literal interpretation might distract the student from the true meaning of the question. Vocabulary such as *characterize, reasonably conclude,* and even *circle the most likely answer* can cause confusion during test taking. In many instances, it is the vocabulary in the question that may cause the student to answer incorrectly rather than a lack of knowledge of the answer. Effective teachers will take the time necessary to examine the vocabulary within printed questions and will include instruction in these within the student's curriculum.

EFFECTIVE INSTRUCTION OF READING VOCABULARY

The remainder of this chapter presents effective practices that lead to positive growth in meaningful reading vocabulary comprehension and specific strategies that have an evidence base. When a practice does not have direct research to support its use, effective teachers can consider whether the practice is based on factors known to cause positive learning outcomes. Recall that Causal Factors are those cognitive, psychological, or social practices known to cause positive learning outcomes but are not necessarily methods, strategies, materials, or practices, per se. Good teaching practices that cause positive learning outcomes are 1) promotion of higher-order language and critical thinking skills (HOTS); 2) a good match between teacher/child communication (Co); 3) visual representation of ideas, concepts, and processes (V); 4) explicit instruction (E); and 5) scaffolding and mediation by a more knowledgeable person (S). First we present general practices related to Causal Factors that lead to positive learning outcomes. While these practices may not necessarily have direct evidence of their treatment efficacy (i.e., effectiveness and efficiency), they are founded in sound instructional principles. Next we describe strategies that have a known evidence base.

General Practices

Focus Instruction on Acquiring Meaning. According to Paul's (1996) semantically based knowledge model, vocabulary activities must fit into a student's semantic repertoire rather than into a particular context. In other words, effective teachers will relate new vocabulary to constructs in the individual child's lexicon rather than to an external construct. For example, when teaching the word "severe," the student may learn it better when it is related to a personal experience (e.g., a severe injury) than to an expository story about weather. This is consistent with Causal Factor 5 (scaffolding). The knowledge model argues that when a child learns a word within the context of a sentence, he is unlikely to transfer his knowledge of that word to different contexts. The semantic-based knowledge model includes the following components: integration of words into multiple contexts; repetition; and meaningful use in natural, contextual situations. Students should learn vocabulary in depth and as it relates to their whole world instead of mastering a word's meaning in an upcoming passage. This helps establish a mutual relationship between syntax and semantics (Kelly, 1996) because syntax influences word meaning. Further, poor DHH readers do not glean as much from context as good readers and may tend to invent meanings of unknown words in a passage (DeVilliers & Pomerantz, 1992).

Employ Explicit Instruction. Deaf children learn vocabulary better through direct instruction than through context. Effective teachers use explicit instruction (Causal Factor 4) in all aspects of teaching vocabulary meaning, including multiple meanings of words, synonyms and antonyms, examples and non-examples, semantic elaborations, and connections among words and related concepts (Paul, 1996). Deaf students who are better readers are able to provide synonyms, antonyms, and analogies for words and phrases they see in text (Luetke-Stahlman & Nielsen, 2003), and students' ability to define words, identify similarities and differences among words, and provide multiple attributes for nouns positively affected reading comprehension scores across nine years (Nielsen & Luetke-Stahlman, 2002a). Case Vignette 4.1 provides a teaching example describing explicit instruction.

CASE VIGNETTE 4.1.

Vocabulary Instruction by Examples and Non-examples

Mrs. Drake is explicitly teaching animal vocabulary to Shawn, a preschool student who uses speech to communicate. Mrs. Drake shows Shawn a photo of a dog. She tells Shawn, "This is a dog," while modeling the spoken production for dog and tracing the dog in the picture. "This dog has four legs, a snout, and fur," Mrs. Drake says, as she points to each feature and emphasizes the pronunciation of each word. Mrs. Drake shows Shawn a photo of a German shepherd and repeats, "This is a dog." She continues with photos of a poodle, a Pomeranian, and a St. Bernard, labeling each photo as a dog. Next, Mrs.

(Continued)

(Continued)

Drake shows Shawn a photo of an alligator. "This is not a dog," she says, as she emphasizes the word "not" by extending its duration. She shows him a photo of a flamingo and repeats, "This is not a dog." Mrs. Drake has explicitly shown Shawn multiple examples of a dog, reinforced this concept with the spoken word "dog" each time, and shown Shawn two non-examples of a dog. Mrs. Drake can check for comprehension by displaying the photos of the German shepherd and alligator on the table for Shawn and prompting, "Show me the dog." She can repeat this with the photo of the St. Bernard and the flamingo. If Shawn correctly points to the dog each time, Mrs. Drake knows he understands the concept for "dog."

Teach Both Breadth and Depth of Vocabulary

Breadth includes words that students will encounter across a variety of settings, and depth includes an expanded knowledge of the various ways in which a single word may be used in text and conversation, including multiple meanings, antonyms, synonyms, and figurative uses. The more information students know surrounding one word, the better they forge patterns of information throughout the brain. Beck, McKeown, and Kucan (2002) suggested breaking words into three tiers. Tier 1 words are words students are likely to know (e.g., sad, funny). Tier 2 words appear frequently in many contexts (e.g., regardless, compromise), such as across reading, social studies, and science classes. Tier 3 words appear rarely in text or are content-specific (e.g., irascible, biogenetics). Instruction focused on Tier 2 targets words students are likely both to need and to learn well throughout repeated opportunities in multiple settings. In place of traditional fill-in-the-blank sentences, vocabulary instruction should include learning words in semantically rich environments, with multiple examples and explicit relationships highlighted among words. For example, the word "book" should be explored as a collection of items (book of matches), an activity (book a room, book a suspect), with various morphemes (bookish, bookings), and as figurative expressions (throw the book at). This practice addresses higher-order thinking skills (Causal Factor

1), better communication with the teacher (Causal Factor 2), explicit instruction (Causal Factor 4), and scaffolding of new information onto old (Causal Factor 5).

Engage in Repetition. In addition to breadth and depth, students need frequent and repeated opportunities to master vocabulary words. This includes instruction across multiple activities and settings to increase word knowledge, fluently retrieve word meanings in different contexts, and apply word meanings for reading comprehension (McKeown, Beck, Omanson, & Pople, 1985). For example, in a story a character might *throw* her hands *up* in frustration, in health one might *throw up* when sick with the flu, in math one *throws* a ball *up* to measure the speed of gravitational pull, and in science an owl *throws up* a pellet of mouse fur and bones. Up to 12 exposures may be necessary to develop deep understanding of a new word, and students who struggle with reading may need additional opportunities (Roberts, Torgesen, Boradman, & Scammacca, 2009). Repetition is a component of explicit instruction (Causal Factor 4).

Teach All Processing Levels

There are three levels at which we process vocabulary knowledge: association processing, comprehension processing, and generation processing (Stahl, 1986). This means that vocabulary instruction needs to go beyond simple traditional rote memorization to multiple levels of processing and understanding vocabulary (Causal Factor 5). In association processing, the student connects a new word to a synonym or a specific context by associating new words to old words. She accesses her prior knowledge and associates the new to the old. For example, if the student comes across the word *wheelbarrow* in a story, the teacher might say, "You told me about a blue dirt cart. You said that Grandpa pushes a blue dirt cart in the garden. 'Wheelbarrow' is the same thing as a dirt cart." In comprehension processing, the student uses associative knowledge of the word, such as using the word to complete a sentence or categorizing the word with other words based on certain criteria. Teachers help students incorporate new words into existing ideas or categories, such as explaining, "A hyena is like a dog, but it is not a pet." Finally, in generation processing, the student creates a new category for the word using known information. For example, the teacher might explain, "Yes, you are on the right track. Even though a salamander is similar to a reptile, it is an amphibian." This practice engages students in higher-order thinking skills (Causal Factor 1) and improved vocabulary interaction with the teacher (Causal Factor 2).

Use Visual Organizers

Vocabulary instruction should be interactive and supplemented with visual support (Causal Factor 3). Visual (or graphic) organizers provide visual representation of the connections and relationships among words. They can highlight specific vocabulary, hierarchical relationships, categorizations, and word patterns; build anticipation; and link new information to students' previous knowledge. Teachers provide the visual structure, and students provide the information. Types of visual organizers include Venn diagrams for comparisons and differences among topics, hierarchical organizers to point out main ideas and supporting details, sequential organizers to identify a sequence of steps, KWL (Know, Want to Know, Learned) charts, and diagrams to illustrate key topics. Visual organizers also include graphs, maps, word webs, and flowcharts (Egan, 1999; Smith, 2002). Teachers can develop visual organizers with students prior to a reading activity to activate prior knowledge and highlight vocabulary, during the activity to document new vocabulary and concepts, or after the activity as a formative assessment to recall newly learned information. Teachers can also provide copies of visual organizers to students for independent review. Semantic/structural feature analysis is another strategy using visual support. In this procedure, a teacher and students connect related concepts from a reading passage via a web. The arms of the web show the syntactic relationships between words and connect the topic idea to different concepts. For example, a teacher might demonstrate new vocabulary through visual metaphors from a story about animals by connecting boxes with pictures or labels of animals (e.g., dogs, birds, and fish) connected by the phrase "are covered with" to boxes containing labels about their coverings (e.g., fur, feathers, and scales). Middle school students identified with learning disabilities

(LD) learned more vocabulary through structural feature analysis and semantic mapping than students who received direct instruction (Bos & Anders, 1990). When students with and without LD used organizers across content areas, they had higher performance than those who did not (Horton, Lovitt, & Bergerund, 1990). Stoner and Easterbrooks (2006) found that visual organizers supported increased use of adjectives in DHH students' written stories. While definition instruction leads only to surface learning in a context-free manner, interactive vocabulary instruction with visual support activates students' prior knowledge, incorporates their personal connections, and provides language for students to use to make predictions, all while making relationships among printed words explicit. Detailed information on how to use visual organizers is available on many websites.

Relate to Prior Knowledge

Vocabulary develops best within conversations and social contexts; effective teachers engage children in conversation to expand their thinking (Causal Factor 1) and communication skills (Causal Factor 2). Some very young DHH children are able to use their prior knowledge of known words to identify novel words (Lederberg, Presbindowski, & Spencer, 2000) (Causal Factor 5). Teachers should start with what the students know about a vocabulary term so they have something they can relate it to. For example, when discussing the Civil War, the teacher might ask students what they know about the word "war," then relate this term to times they were mad at their friends, how they reacted to the situation, and the resulting outcome. Then the discussion can expand to the larger problem of how Americans felt about taxation with no representation and how this led to a war because both sides could not agree.

EVIDENCE-BASED STRATEGIES TO TEACH VOCABULARY MEANING

Vocabulary knowledge provides labels for ideas students already have within their minds (Paul, 1996). In the remainder of this chapter, we describe a list of strategies for which an evidence base exists. Some are strategies for the teacher, while others focus on strategies students can use themselves.

In-depth Discussion

This strategy includes relating vocabulary words to students' previous experiences and providing multiple exposures to the word and its multiple meanings through in-depth discussions (Paul, 1996; Paul & Gustafson, 1991). It also is based on Vygotsky's (1978) concept of the *more knowledgeable other* (Causal Factors 2 & 5). We learn by our conversations with others who know something more about a topic than we do (Easterbrooks & Baker, 2002). We pick up vocabulary incidentally through socially based conversational interactions, both spoken and signed, surrounding a topic of mutual interest (Saffran, Newport, Aslin, Tunick, & Barrueco, 1997). One promising practice that has recently appeared in the literature is the concept of *elaborative reminiscing* (Reese & Newcombe, 2007). In elaborative reminiscing, parents provide children with elaborated accounts of experiences they have had together, much in the same manner as teachers use storybooks or dialogic reading strategies to encourage children's connection to the language in books. This is consistent with Causal Factors 1, 2, and 5.

Pre-teaching Vocabulary

One time-honored approach to teaching vocabulary has been to pre-teach it prior to its use in actual instruction. This is related to Causal Factors 1 and 5. Evidence exists that pre-teaching is an important component of instruction to make that instruction most effective and efficient (Cannon, Easterbrooks, & Fredrick, 2010). While seemingly obvious, this strategy requires careful consideration in the light of newer models of lexical acquisition. Pre-teaching finds its support in the concept of lexical priming in relation to word learning (Neely, 1991). Lexical priming research tells us that children learn words better if they have a semantic (SHOE-SOCK) or phonological/graphemic (BEE-SEE) schema for the word already in their lexicon. This relates to the *knowledge model* in that teachers should employ instructional strategies that prime the student's readiness to acquire words by accessing categorical associations. This would suggest that when pre-teaching vocabulary, categories of words should be taught together, or new words should be taught in relation to categories of words already known. For example, when teaching the word "pomegranate," ask the child to name some fruits he or she knows, and then explain that a pomegranate is a fruit. However, we must apply this strategy mindfully because hearing children with reading disabilities have disruptions in their ability to benefit from different priming strategies (Miles & Stelmack, 1994). Teachers of DHH students should not assume that all of their students would benefit from this strategy and should consider using progress monitoring strategies or action research in the classroom to assess the effectiveness of this strategy when suspicious that a DHH student might have an additional reading disorder.

Pre-teaching involves the following steps:

1. Collaborate with the general education teacher to negotiate words on which the student will be tested.
2. Assess the student's vocabulary to determine which words he or she already understands and which ones he or she needs to learn.
3. Teach the meaning of each new vocabulary word as it pertains to the context in which it will be used in the general education classroom and later work on expanding multiple meanings and multiple concepts for the word.
4. Check comprehension of the new words, language, and concepts after the student has attended the class through a quick assessment, such as the "ticket-out-the-door" strategy, and then re-teach any information not mastered.

Using Semantic Equivalents to Teach Multiple and Figurative Word Meanings

Hermans et al. (2008) used the term "fossilized" to describe the nature of many DHH students' vocabularies. By this, they meant that whatever meaning a student attaches to new words, that meaning takes primacy (i.e., supersedes other meanings) in her lexicon, and she has difficulty incorporating additional meanings into her vocabulary. Precisely because DHH students tend to fossilize word meanings, it is important to use a *semantic equivalence* perspective when teaching figurative word meanings. We find support for this in Causal Factor 4 (explicit teaching). Entertaining the child with art projects to highlight the literal meaning of a phrase (e.g., drawing someone pulling your leg) engages the primacy function of lexical knowledge, and DHH students may tend to retain the silly meaning rather than the actual meaning. Teaching the semantic equivalent (e.g., "You're pulling my leg" means "You're teasing me") may provide immediately accurate information that will take on the prime role in the lexicon. The student will not have to learn two meanings, the correct and the incorrect, only to be faced with having to ignore the wrong but often more tantalizing meaning.

Visual Materials

The use of pictures and photographs provides scaffolding for students who lack the needed language to represent concepts, such as descriptions of home, families, communities, etc. (Tarulli, 1998). For vocabulary for which students have no concept, such as an *impala* or a *pyramid*, simple online searches can quickly produce multiple photographs of a concept or object. Teachers can use the Picture-to-Picture strategy from *Visualizing and Verbalizing* (Bell, 2007) to develop students' productive vocabulary (Causal Factors 1, 2, 3, and 4). In this strategy, the students hold and describe a picture, which is unseen by the teacher, using expressive vocabulary. The teacher asks contrasting questions to prompt students, such as "Is the clown's hair yellow or orange?" thereby modeling productive vocabulary and giving students a choice with which to respond. The teacher can also provide gestures or signs for vocabulary words that are unknown to students, further modeling language. After students have described 12 various elements (what, size, color, number, shape, where, movement, mood, background, perspective, when, and sound), the teacher describes the mental picture formed by the students' words. After her description, the teacher finally sees the picture and discusses if her mental image matched the picture based on the students' given description. Specific vocabulary words from this activity can be linked to print, multiple meanings, and signs and used in additional contexts to increase students' productive vocabulary in reading, writing, and conversation.

Word Walls

Because DHH students benefit from visual environments, effective teachers often create print-rich classrooms. Print-rich classroom environments contain planned arrangements and student interactions with a collection of literacy materials (Wolfersberger, Reutzel, Sudweeks, & Fawson, 2004). Walking into a print-rich environment, one might see an independent reading corner, a guided reading center, a multitude of printed labels around the classroom, "centers" with literacy materials, literacy programs on computers, procedures for classroom routines displayed in text, a daily letter to the class on chart paper, big books, etc. An effective teacher calls the students' attention to these literacy materials, models how to use them, engages the students in discussions and activities using these materials, and provides opportunities for independent student use of the materials. Exposure to and interaction with print-rich environments may increase student reading achievement. From a sample of over 4,000 preschoolers who attended day care, more than 10 percent were deemed "early precocious readers," as defined by their abilities to read more than five words on pre-primer word lists (Johns, 2004) and lines of text from *The Runaway Bunny* (Neuman, 2004). These early reading abilities were attributed to print-rich environments found in day cares (i.e., print materials, signs, props, reading spaces, read-alouds, meal-time conversations, small group activities, etc.) and community environments (i.e., available books, signs, reading spaces, etc.) (Neuman & Celano, 2001). Word walls are part of a visible (Causal Factor 3) and accessible print-rich environment. Word walls contain collections of specifically chosen words displayed on a designated wall within a classroom for the purpose of word study and exploration through teacher and student interaction (Brabham & Villaume, 2001; Harmon, Wood, Hedrick, Vintinner, & Willeford, 2009). See Table 4.1 for ways to organize and use word walls.

Table 4.1. *Organizing and Using Word Walls*

Visual Organization

Themed word walls (example: characteristics of Harry Potter)

High-frequency word walls (Dolch words, etc.)

Outline shape of words using different colors of paper as background or outline words in black marker

Words that lack predictable spelling patterns

Ways to Use Word Walls

Word analysis

Word families (king, ring, fling, etc.)

Root words (hop, fight, see, etc.)

Prefixes and suffixes (un-, dis-, -ly, etc.)

Count, chant, and/or clap letters in words

Clap word parts (en-chant-ment)

Compare word lengths

Sign word, fingerspell in motion of sign (example: "can" with c-a-n in downward motion of sign for "can")

Match beginning sounds (bite, black, bank, etc.)

Rimes (-ight, -ound, etc.)

ABC word wall of student names

Decoding by analogy ("If 'f-i-g-h-t' is 'fight,' then 'n-i-g-h-t' is _____.")

Using key anchor words to relate new words when spelling ("Bunch" is spelled like "lunch.")

Irregular past-tense verbs (fought, saw, caught, etc.)

Mathematical words to explain math symbols

Homophones (blew, blue; allowed, aloud; etc.)

Contractions

Multiple spellings for vowel phonemes

Content words

Theme words from units of study (Civil War, Confederate, Union, etc.)

Content vocabulary

Categorize and connect words (verbs, nouns, adjectives, adverbs, etc.)

Student self-selection of words

Students can select the words for the word wall based on their interests

(Continued)

Table 4.1. *(Continued)*

Physical activities

During spelling of words, students squat for each short letter (e.g., a, o, e, n), stand straight for each tall letter (e.g., b, d, f, h), and hang their arms toward the floor for hanging letters (e.g., g, j, p, q)

I spy ("I spy a word that starts with 'f' and has 6 letters and 1 syllable.")

Students draw the word wall word on personal dry erase boards and outline it to practice the positions of short, tall, and hanging letters to "establish a visual image of the word."

Flashcard games with word wall words

Students use sound boxes to separate the individual sounds of the word wall words, placing letters that create one sound into one box (digraphs, vowel combinations).

Words are color-coded to a definition on a card, and students identify 3 ways to define the word (definitions, examples, synonyms, antonyms).

Students give a real-world example of word wall words.

Sentence completions: Students receive a card with a missing word and select a word from the word wall to accurately complete the sentence.

Adapted from: Bourne, 2006–2007; Brabham & Villaume, 2001; Harmon, Wood, Hedrick, Vintinner, & Willeford, 2009; Williams Phillips-Birdsong, Hufnagel, Hungler, & Lundstrom, 2009.

Word walls typically display three categories of words: theme-related words, high-frequency words, and words related to spelling patterns. Word walls can be portable to meet students' individual needs. For example, students can carry personalized word lists in their binders that include words divided by nouns, verbs, and adjectives to assist with writing, or their word lists can provide spellings for high-frequency or difficult-to-spell words, or they can include separate lists of content words, such as terms from social studies and science classes. Word walls can be cumulative or dynamic, depending on the teacher's intended purpose and the students' needs. For instance, struggling readers may benefit from systematic and explicit instruction that is personalized (Brabham & Villaume, 2001).

A teacher may also create separate word walls based on distinct purposes. A teacher who is focusing on acquisition of signs may create a word wall divided into words represented by categories of handshapes (e.g., onion, apple, key under an illustration of the corresponding common handshape). A teacher whose students are developing spoken language might build a word wall around sounds that the students have mastered in their productive speech or words than have the same initial sound. To maximize the effectiveness of word walls, teachers must model and interactively use them frequently and intentionally as an integrated instructional strategy to enhance student vocabulary learning (Harmon et al., 2009). Students vary in their independent use of word walls across grade levels and academic abilities (Williams, Phillips-Birdsong, Hufnagel, Hungler, & Lundstrom, 2009). Teacher strategies while using word walls should include associations between words and images (Sadoski & Paivio, 2004), connections to students' previous experiences and background knowledge through conversational scaffolds (Brabham & Villaume, 2001; Harmon et al., 2009), and in-depth word study through higher-order thinking skills (analyzing, comparing, evaluating, etc.).

Storybook Reading and Repeated Readings

Storybook reading provides multiple opportunities to both model vocabulary and give feedback. Storytelling provides vocabulary in context, and the addition of role-playing the story with student-made crafts (masks, setting, etc.) increases opportunities for repetition of target vocabulary through active participation with the language in context (Tavil & Soylemez, 2008). Dialogic reading, an interactive reading process involving questions and dialogue based on storybook reading between an adult and child, significantly increased receptive vocabulary scores of DHH children using spoken language (Fung, Chow, & McBride-Chang, 2005). Dialogic reading provides opportunities for teachers to model language and "thinking aloud," ask open-ended questions, provide vocabulary, expand on children's language, and give appropriate language feedback (Arnold, Lonigan, Whitehurst, & Epstein, 1994). This process also increases students' opportunities to interact with storybooks through repeated readings, reinforcing language via multiple opportunities. Repeated readings, combined with asking children to provide the definition for a target word, resulted in a 22 percent gain in children's vocabulary, while repeated readings combined with explicit instruction of target words resulted in a 41 percent increase in vocabulary (Biemiller & Boote, 2006). Therefore, utilizing dialogic reading as an instructional strategy can increase students' vocabulary in an engaging activity.

Incremental Rehearsal

Incremental rehearsal (IR; Tucker, 1989) is an instructional strategy for teaching new words by interspersing them with known words in a 10-percent-unknown to 90-percent-known format. A teacher should first pre-assess a student to identify known and unknown words. Next, the teacher presents all of the words in print, one by one, with a 2-second wait time for each word, allowing the student to produce the sign or verbalization for each known word. If the student does not know a word, the teacher provides the verbalization or sign for the word and has the student repeat the word. Next, the teacher uses it in a sentence that the student repeats. The teacher can help the student rehearse the new word across opportunities until it becomes a known word. The teacher sets the criteria for both wait time and the number of correct productions required based on the individual processing and language skills of each student. Incremental rehearsal provides increased opportunities for students to respond and has resulted in increased reading fluency and comprehension for students with learning disabilities (Burns, 2002; Burns, Dean, & Foley, 2004). To address the individual needs of students, teachers can provide repeated exposure to vocabulary words using incremental rehearsal.

SUMMARY OF RECOMMENDED PRACTICES

Students who possess a broad receptive vocabulary and the ability to use these words expressively are better readers. Once a child starts on a vocabulary learning trajectory, he or she tends to follow it across time. Therefore, effective teachers attempt to influence a student's trajectory with practices that have an evidence base or are supported by Causal

Factors. Effective teachers address vocabulary instruction as a multilayered process: They ensure that their students understand a concept and the related spoken or signed phrase that represents the concept, followed by the relation between the spoken or signed concept and its representation in print. DHH students, regardless of their communication mode, need repeated opportunities to interact with known and novel vocabulary across contexts and environments. Decontextualized conversations and storybook reading with more knowledgeable language models provide opportunities for students to apply and expand their current lexicon with new words and concepts. Effective teachers pair explicit vocabulary instruction with visual strategies and cement novel words to students' prior knowledge and experiences.

RESOURCES

Georgia Pathway to Language and Literacy: http://www.georgialiteracy.org
Log in to http://deafed.net. Click on "Knowledge Base and Calendar." Click on "Resources for Use in Support of General Education Teachers," scroll down, and click on "Ten Things You Should Know about Reading Vocabulary and Students with Hearing Loss."
Cornerstones: http://pbskids.org/lions/cornerstones/introduction.html
Center for Accessible Technology in Sign (CATS): http://www.cats.gatech.edu/

5 Vocabulary: From Phonological Decoding to Word Work

PURPOSE

Teaching vocabulary requires a two-pronged approach: helping readers understand the underlying meaning of words and helping them to unlock the meaning of printed words that they do not know. In Chapter 4 we described ways to teach underlying word meanings, and we stressed that expressive vocabulary is the strongest predictor of later reading achievement in DHH students with severe to profound hearing loss (Kyle & Harris, 2010). This chapter presents a discussion of ways that students must learn to take apart and put back together those printed words that they do not understand by sight. Students need to learn decoding strategies and engage in higher-level word work, such as syllabification and examination of root words, to read unknown words in print. Effective teachers and practitioners establish a balanced approach to vocabulary acquisition that has both top-down and bottom-up features and that supports the development of basic vocabulary comprehension. There are many things teachers can do to help a child decode a word he or she does not know. They can use phonological, morphological, structural, intonational, and contextual strategies, which we present within the next two chapters. However, before we continue we want to stress once more that if a student is decoding words (saying, signing, or fingerspelling) without knowing their meaning, then the student is merely learning how to be a word caller.

In this chapter we describe some of the various categories of decoding, explore the research, and present evidence-based practices. We relate these practices to their intrinsic Causal Factors (i.e., HOTS and CoVES). Further, we describe promising instructional practices that may not yet have a sufficient evidence base in the hopes that teachers will try them and document their effectiveness in their classrooms using action research (after scrutiny for inherent Causal Factors). Finally, we provide case vignettes to demonstrate the use of different instructional practices and strategies that are most useful with students in a variety of educational environments.

PROBLEMS WITH DECODING

Struggling readers can learn to decode words, but unless they understand the word's meaning within the context of the phrase in which it is located, they tend to read one word at a time. This is referred to as "word calling" and is a chronic problem among most struggling readers, whether typically hearing or deaf. Unfortunately, it is often accepted as evidence that the child can read. But the traditional skills associated with reading printed passages do not necessarily assist all readers. There are many types of word callers among hearing children, and most likely these patterns exist among DHH children. The facility with which a child reads a word out loud is determined by a combination of comprehension, fluency, and decoding ability (Rupley & Slough, 2010; Valencia & Buly, 2004). *Automatic word callers* have good decoding and fluency skills but poor comprehension, such as Megan, whose story you read in Chapter 3. *Struggling word callers* have poor decoding, fluency, and comprehension, such as Makouika (Chapter 7). *Word stumblers* have poor decoding and fluency but good comprehension, such as Max (this chapter) *Slow comprehenders* have good decoding and comprehension skills but poor fluency, such as Shawn (Chapter 4). Some students are *slow word callers* with good decoding but poor fluency and comprehension, like Gregory (Chapter 7). Finally, some readers, like Thomas, introduced in Chapter 3, are considered *disabled readers* because they lack skills in all three areas. Many DHH students struggle with the same mix of decoding, fluency, and comprehension difficulties as do hearing children.

In order to decode most words, readers must mix together base words (e.g., *touch*), word parts or affixes (touch-*ing*, touch-*able*, *re*-touch), verb idioms (*touch up*), and patterns of inflection (e.g., when the word *content* is accented on the first syllable, it means "the elements that comprise something," but accented on the second syllable, it means "to be happy with") to figure out a whole word. Combinations of these elements allow speakers to derive the meanings of a large variety of words. Vocabulary meaning can be concrete (e.g., a fish) or abstract (e.g., to fish for some information). Likewise, phrases can be concrete or abstract. For example, the English phrase "He's a real prince" when spoken one way can mean "He is actually a prince." Spoken with another inflection it can mean "He's a very wonderful person," and spoken with yet another inflection it can mean "He is a worthless person."

Finally, strong readers are able to learn new words through context, but struggling readers (i.e., those with patterns of poor comprehension, fluency, and decoding as well as weak vocabularies) do not learn well through context and require more explicit instruction (Cain, Oakhill, & Lemmon, 2004). Effective teachers know the strengths and weaknesses of their students across all areas necessary for good reading, including vocabulary comprehension, decoding, and fluency, and design instruction that facilitates improvement in areas of weakness while capitalizing on areas of strength.

DEFINITIONS USED IN DESCRIBING DECODING

In order to decode words, a reader must master several systems associated with the printed word. The phonemic system is composed of phonemes (e.g., /s/ or /v/), which are the individual sounds within words. The morphemic system comprises morphemes (e.g., base words and affixes), which form the parts of words. The orthographic system is composed of visual forms (e.g., letters, digraphs) that represent a sound in a word. Several structural systems (e.g., syllabication, Latin and Greek word roots) can also be used to unlock an unknown word. Sometimes readers will use the surrounding context to provide support when decoding a word. While these types of decoding work together, they are also independent of each other. One type of decoding alone is not sufficient for mastery of reading, and children use different types of decoding at different ages. As typical readers become older, the use of phonological decoding decreases and morphological analysis increases (Deacon & Kirby, 2004; Singson, Mahoney, & Mann, 2000), most likely because after children master phonology, they rely on the orthographic features of words they are decoding. For instance, when presented with the word *windshield*, a first grader may use a phonological approach to decode the individual sounds that form the words *wind* and *shield*, but a fourth grader may use a morphological approach to decode the meaning-carrying morphemes *wind* and *shield*. Researchers are still unclear as to whether orthographic knowledge increases *as* DHH children learn to read or *because* they learn to read. That is, while some DHH children may learn that the morpheme "-s" makes a singular word into a plural word before they learn to read, others may learn that "-s" on the end of the word makes it plural because they now see it in print. Further research is needed in this area (Harris & Moreno, 2004).

Children use multiple routes to decoding to become fluent readers. In the following paragraphs, we provide definitions for each type of decoding and strategies for working with DHH students.

PHONOLOGICAL DECODING DEFINITIONS

When most people think of decoding and phonological awareness, they think of phonics. Phonics refers to the skill of associating graphemes (printed letters and letter groups) with phonemes (speech sounds). For example, the English phoneme /f/ can be represented by the graphemes f (*fish*), lf (ha*lf*), ph (*ph*one), or gh (cou*gh*). Similarly, a grapheme can represent more than one sound. The grapheme "c" can be pronounced /s/, as in "city," or /k/, as in "cut." The 26 letters of the English alphabet represent 45 sounds with 398 different possible spellings (Morrison, Trezek, & Paul, 2008). For this reason, English orthography is referred to as an opaque orthography; there is not a one-to-one correspondence between letters and sounds. Many other languages, such as Farsi, are much more transparent and have a clearer, one-to-one relationship between graphemes and phonemes, making it easier for students to decode words phonetically. Letter sounds, letter names, and letter forms (lowercase and uppercase) are among the alphabetic principles that children must learn in order to read. *Phonological awareness* is the broader term for a collection of decoding skills that are based on the relationship between graphemes and phonemes.

Phonemic Awareness. Phonemic awareness is the awareness that spoken words are composed of sounds called phonemes (Mann, 2003) and that these sounds can be manipulated in syllables and words (Liberman & Shankweiler, 1985). Phonemic awareness is the ability to notice, think about, and work with the individual sounds in spoken words. This involves the detection, discrimination, and identification of individual sounds. Phonemic awareness activities are all done through listening alone. They do not involve recognition of letters or names of letters. Sometimes teachers will use the printed letter as a visual tool to help students see what they are demonstrating, but alphabetic knowledge is not the intention.

Letter–Sound Correspondence and the Alphabetic Principle. The reason we learn phonemic awareness is to support the alphabetic principle, or the knowledge that written graphemes, or letters, correspond to the phonemes, or sounds, of spoken words (Scarborough & Brady, 2002). Letter (grapheme)–sound (phoneme) knowledge is one of the most important prereading skills at preschool age and a predictor of typical variance in both normal reading and reading disability (Anthony & Lonigan, 2004; Lonigan, Burgess, & Anthony, 2000; Wagner, Torgesen, & Rashotte, 1994). Below we describe aspects of phonemic awareness.

Initial Letter Identification and Alliteration. Alliteration refers to the skill of identifying words that begin with certain sounds (e.g., Teacher says, "B-oat. Boat. What is the first sound you hear in b-oat, boat?").

Elision. Elision refers to the skill of dropping a sound or part of a word and producing the new word (e.g., Teacher says, "If I take /b/ away from boat, what word do I have? Yes, *oat*.").

Segmenting. Segmentation is the skill of identifying how many phonemes are in a word (e.g., Teacher says, "B-oa-t. How many sounds do you hear in b-oa-t? Yes, three sounds."). Segmentation also includes identification of the number of syllables in a word (e.g., Teacher says, "Bas-ket-ball. How many word parts do you hear in bas-ket-ball? Yes, three word parts").

Blending. Blending is the skill of taking parts of a word and putting them together (e.g., Teacher says, "B-oa-t. What word do you get when you put b-oa-t together? Yes, *boat!*").

Rhymes, Rhyming Words, and Rime. Two words rhyme when they share a stressed vowel and all the sounds that come after it (e.g., right/ flight; neck/speck). The beginning parts of each word are different and are referred to as the "onset" (e.g., r/fl; n/sp), and the part of the word that begins with the vowel and carries the rhyming sound is called a "rime" (e.g., ight; eck) (Scarborough & Brady, 2002).

While phonological awareness is not the only factor required for skillful reading for hearing or DHH children (Bryant, Nunes, & Bindman, 1997), it plays an integral part in the reading process. The development of phonological awareness skills as a foundation for later literacy learning in DHH students is undoubtedly one of the more controversial areas of literacy acquisition. Proponents of its instruction insist that DHH learners cannot master literacy skills without it, and opponents of its instruction insist that it is of minimal consequence. In a study of 31 teachers across 16 OPTION schools[1] (www.oraldeafed.org), 56 percent indicated that they taught rhyming activities, and 56 percent indicated that they included work on word families in their phonemic awareness

---

[1.] An OPTION school is a school where children with hearing loss learn spoken communication through auditory/oral instruction.

and phonics instructional practices, but only 22 percent of the teachers indicated that they engaged in instruction for blending and segmenting. Perhaps this is because blending and segmenting have not been taught in the past and remain controversial topics (Easterbrooks, Stephenson, & Mertens, 2006).

Some researchers state that the reading process for DHH readers is "qualitatively similar but quantitatively delayed" when compared to their hearing peers (Paul, 1998; Trezek, Wang, & Paul, 2010). Because children learn to read a written system that is based on spoken language, they access elements of that spoken language to various degrees and in various ways (Perfetti & Sandak, 2000). We do not know exactly when, how, and to what extent DHH readers may use phonology. Some DHH children access phonology, or the sound system of language, via speechreading (Kyle & Harris, 2006, 2010) and residual hearing, while others may not. Those who do access phonology may use it after they learn to read, as opposed to hearing children who use phonology as a prerequisite to reading (Kyle & Harris, 2010). Some DHH students used phonological awareness to a certain degree for rhyme judgment (Campbell & Wright, 1988; Waters & Doehring, 1990), when reading pseudowords (nonsense words) aloud (Leybaert, 1993), and during spelling (Campbell, Burden, & Wright, 1992; Hanson, Shankweiler, & Fischer, 1983; Leybaert & Alegría, 1995). DHH readers who use phonology may depend on their access to sound and their own speech intelligibility (Kyle & Harris, 2006, 2010; Perfetti & Sandak, 2000). Regardless of when and how DHH readers use phonology and speechreading, these two skills alone are not enough to crack the reading code (Paul, Wang, Trezek, & Luckner, 2009).

Phonological Working Memory

Another component of phonological decoding involves remembering words by their collection of sounds. This is done through the use of the phonological loop, a mechanism for temporarily storing new combinations of sounds until they move to the long-term memory (Baddeley, Gathercole, & Papagno, 1998). Children with phonological memory store the sound structure of a word phonologically, creating a direct auditory path to the new word in addition to a visual pathway created from the printed version of the word (Gathercole, Hitch, Service, & Martin, 1997). The ability to remember information in two ways, both visually and auditorily, strengthens a reader's ability to recall a piece of information (Paivio, 1991). Children with poor phonological short-term memory may have difficulty retaining words phonologically, reducing the pathways for recall of the word (Cain et al., 2004). By storing words in their spoken forms, children can "analyze and reflect upon them" and engage in higher-level thinking about how words are formed (Berninger, Abbott, Nagy, & Carlisle, 2010, p. 154). Phonological coding may be enhanced through the addition of a visual tool for access to phonemes, such as Visual Phonics or Cued Speech (see "Instructional Strategies" below).

PHONOLOGICAL DECODING STRATEGIES

DHH children learn to decode in multiple ways. Effective teachers examine each student's strengths and weaknesses and choose the most appropriate way, or combination of ways, to teach him or her to decode. They determine the type (auditory, visual, hands-on) and level (mediation and scaffolding) of support the student needs and then try to fade out that support as they see that the child is mastering traditional phonics. Effective teachers use tools such as the *Early Speech Perception* (ESP) test (Moog & Geers, 1990) to differentiate between children who have usable access to sound for learning to read and those who need instruction via additional modalities (Easterbrooks, Lederberg, Miller, Bergeron, & Connor, 2008).

Auditory Representation of the Grapheme-Phoneme Relationship

One way children represent a grapheme is by saying the corresponding phoneme (e.g., the student says /b/ when she sees the letter "b"). They represent the printed letter by saying the sound of the letter. They use phonological skills "in the air," that is, through residual hearing without visual support. Some students with cochlear implants and those who receive great benefit from their hearing aids may be able to manipulate some phonemes without any form of visual support, such as speechreading support.

Visual Representations of the Grapheme-Phoneme Relationship

Visual strategies for representing phoneme–grapheme correspondence are based on Causal Factor 3. Most of the available research in this category has focused on very young children rather than those in the early, middle, and upper grades. Phonological awareness "does not have to be auditory in nature" (Akamatsu, Mayer, & Hardy-Braz, 2008, p. 149). Older deaf students or those with less-than-sufficient access to sound may be able to comprehend the Grapheme-Phoneme relationship through lipreading (Kyle & Harris, 2006), fingerspelling, kinesthetic feedback from speech, and orthography (Leybaert, 1993). Some visual forms of representation that have been used successfully are *Cued Speech* (LaSasso & Metzger, 1998), *Visual Phonics* (Trezek & Wang, 2006), and lexicalized fingerspelling (Haptonstall-Nykaza & Schick, 2007). Effective teachers familiarize themselves with the research on these strategies and incorporate them into their teaching repertoires. Below we provide a description of these visual strategies. When using Visual Phonics or Cued Speech, it is necessary to take the appropriate training courses or workshops to develop the critical level of proficiency.

Visual Phonics. The strategy receiving the most attention at present is Visual Phonics (International Communication Learning Institute, 2008) because there is a growing evidence base that this strategy is effective with DHH students across the continuum of hearing loss and communication modes. Combining Visual Phonics with traditional phonics activities provides additional support for manipulating the building blocks of a spoken language to which DHH students may not have full access. Visual Phonics is a multisensory instructional tool that includes 45 handshapes and movements that provide clues to the tactile production of each spoken sound in English (Waddy-Smith & Wilson, 2003). Explicit instruction in the alphabetic principle supplemented by Visual Phonics increased young DHH students' access to grapheme–phoneme correspondences (Beal-Alvarez, Lederberg, & Easterbrooks, 2011; Trezek & Wang, 2006; Smith & Wang, 2010), pseudoword decoding (Trezek & Wang), and phonological awareness skills (i.e., segmentation, deletion, onsets, and rimes; Trezek, Gampp, Wang, Paul, & Woods, 2007) and middle schoolers' acquisition and generalization of phonemic awareness and decoding of pseudowords (Trezek & Malmgren, 2005). For example, a student who knows the corresponding Visual Phonics hand cues for the sounds /b/, /ō/, /t/ can distinguish the difference between the final sounds in the words *boat* and *bow*, even though he or she might not be able to hear the final /t/ sound in *boat*. Visual Phonics is a strategy appropriate for a student like Justin, featured in Case Vignette 5.1.

CASE VIGNETTE 5.1.

Ms. Rose's Use of Visual Phonics

Justin is a kindergarten student who received a cochlear implant at age 3 This means he has been "listening" auditorily for about two years, but his oral vocabulary is limited, and he frequently uses some signs to express his wants and needs. Ms. Rose and Justin's kindergarten class are working on letter–sound relationships. Because she wants to provide full access for Justin, Ms. Rose attended a workshop and became certified in Visual Phonics. When she introduces the new sound for the week, she uses the Visual Phonics hand cue along with the phoneme, and all of the students in her class have adopted the use of these visual cues. When she works with Justin individually on his decoding skills, she provides visual support for phonemes when needed. For example, Justin is tracing the letters "c-a-t" while saying the sounds. When he is stuck on the sound for /t/, Ms. Rose cues him with the Visual Phonics hand-shape. Justin produces the /t/ sound, repeats blending "c-a-t," and says "cat!" aloud, pointing to the printed word. Visual Phonics serves as a bridge between his limited vocabulary and the new skill of letter–sound relationships.

Lexicalized Fingerspelling. Some DHH students use fingerspelling as a coding system to remember new words (Bonvillian, 1983; Chamberlain & Mayberry, 2000; Hirsh-Pasek, 1987). Receptive fingerspelling ability is directly related to reading vocabulary (Sedey, 1995). Neutral fingerspelling refers simply to spelling a word letter-by-letter. In contrast, lexicalized fingerspelling refers to words whose spellings have become sign-like in movement, such as the "loan signs" #BANK or #STYLE in ASL (Haptonstall-Nykaza & Schick, 2007). While certain letters may appear omitted in lexicalized fingerspelling, the addition of movement represents a level of phonology that DHH students may use for coding. When we compare the links between word learning accompanied by sign versus fingerspelling, we find higher word learning for lexicalized fingerspelling, showing that fingerspelling may solidify cognitive connections between print and signs (Haptonstall-Nykaza, 2004; Haptonstall-Nykaza & Schick, 2007). Fingerspelling also has a high correlation with later English print vocabulary (Haptonstall-Nykaza & Schick, 2007; Mayberry & Waters, 1991; Padden & Ramsey, 1998, 2000; Sedey, 1995). Further, some deaf children have demonstrated the ability to master the phoneme–grapheme code through fingerspelling (B. S. Schick, personal communication, July 20, 2011). Case Vignette 5.2 describes how Mrs. Miller uses lexicalized fingerspelling with her students.

CASE VIGNETTE 5.2.
Mrs. Miller's Use of Lexicalized Fingerspelling

Mrs. Miller is working on word families with her second-grade students at a day school for the deaf. All of her students use sign language to some extent during instruction. Mrs. Miller is using fluent fingerspelling to teach word families. This week the class is focusing on words that end in -tion, such as "motion," "lotion," and "potion." Mrs. Miller has these words grouped together on her word wall under a "-tion" heading. To demonstrate that each word has the same ending, Mrs. Miller repeatedly demonstrates the phonological unit of "-tion" in a fluent manner, which provides the basis for lexicalized fingerspelling. This means that instead of fingerspelling each individual letter in a stilted manner, she blends the four letters of the manual alphabet into a fluid motion, beginning with the "t,' popping the pinky up for the "i," and fluidly moving into the "o" and "n." Mrs. Miller shows her students that the beginning of each word is different by highlighting the initial letter, followed by her fluent version of the rime, or word ending. Her students imitate this fluid manner, and in the process they create a phonological unit from these four letters. This phonological unit then becomes the foundation for which lexicalized fingerspelling is used to represent signs. Now Mrs. Miller's students can use the fluent fingerspelled word "lotion" instead of the sign string SQUEEZE-BOTTLE (ABOVE-HAND) + RUBBING HANDS TOGETHER.

Cued Speech. Cued Speech is a manual system for coding spoken English and over 40 other languages that helps students differentiate phonemes and syllables that look similar on the mouth (Hage & Leybaert, 2006). It was created by Cornett (1967) as a tool to help DHH students become efficient readers by increasing speech reception skills. During spoken conversation, the person providing the cues holds one hand near the mouth in specific handshapes (eight for English) to represent consonants and specific locations (four for English) to represent vowels; this helps the student distinguish the components of speech. The handshapes and locations must be combined with speech movements in order to carry meaning (Leybaert & Charlier, 1996). DHH students who received early and intensive exposure to Cued Speech demonstrated improved rhyming skills (Charlier & Leybaert, 2000; LaSasso, Crain, & Leybaert, 2003), spelling skills (Leybaert, 2000; Leybaert & Lechat, 2001), and speech reception skills (Alegría, Leybaert, Charlier, & Hage, 1992; Nicholls & Ling, 1982). However, most Cued Speech research has been conducted with children who use French (Spencer & Marschark, 2006), a language with a more transparent orthography (i.e., fewer inconsistencies between graphemes and phonemes) than the more opaque orthography of English (i.e., multiple phonemes are represented by multiple graphemes and vice versa) (Trezek et al., 2011). More classroom intervention studies are needed for DHH students who learn spoken English (Spencer & Marschark, 2006; Trezek et al., 2011). Cued Speech is typically used with DHH children whose parents have chosen this approach, and training is required to master the Cued Speech system. Case Vignette 5.3 provides an example of how one mother used Cued Speech to read stories to her child.

CASE VIGNETTE 5.3.

Darla's Use of Cued Speech

In using Cued Speech with her son Kellen, Darla began with cueing every phrase or sentence with him because she learned through research and the help of parent advisors and other resource professionals that we learn language and how to read by hearing (seeing in Kellen's case) language spoken

(Continued)

(Continued)

in a natural, conversational manner. It was in that way, then, that her son was ready to receive the lyrical language that picture books can provide for all children. Because Cued Speech is based on phonemes of spoken language, she could cue sound-for-sound on her hands and lips what the book said, and Kellen would receive word-for-word what was written on the page. She also read nonsensical types of books, such as Dr. Seuss, and Kellen could appreciate the rhyming that picture books often contain. In the very beginning of reading with Kellen, Darla did what all parents do. She sat him on her lap, facing her. As he got older, he sat beside of or in front of her. Then, together, they looked at the illustrations. Darla would point to the book and then direct Kellen's attention to her face, which was where the expression and information would first be introduced to him. Darla would show excitement and say some exclamation about what was happening, such as: "Wow! A dog! Look—he has a car!" (Go, Dog, Go! was one of his early favorites). When Kellen was very young, they didn't go over each word. Instead, Darla and Kellen talked about what was happening in the pictures as though THAT was the story. They made their own story to accompany the pictures in the book. Sometimes Darla would point out words to him, especially as he started to recognize sight words. Cued Speech made this story-time experience as enjoyable and natural as it felt when Darla read to her hearing child. The only difference was the importance of Kellen looking at her face and hands for the information presented. Cued Speech helped to make all the drama and fun of a story come alive. Because of their shared reading experiences at home, Kellen entered kindergarten already a good reader. Cued Speech worked so well with phonics that sounding out the words on the page ended up being a natural progression for Kellen, from their early cued story times all the way to reading on his own.

Semantic Representations of the Grapheme-Phoneme Relationship

Another way to show the grapheme-phoneme relationship is to relate a sound to a meaningful semantic concept, such as a picture, and then transfer that picture/sound relationship to the printed letter (Bergeron, Lederberg, Easterbrooks, Miller, & Connor, 2009). This is called the semantic association strategy and allows teachers to represent the letter–sound relationship via a meaningful picture. To use the semantic association strategy, effective teachers follow these steps. First, teachers engage students in an activity that practices repetition of a sound meaningfully

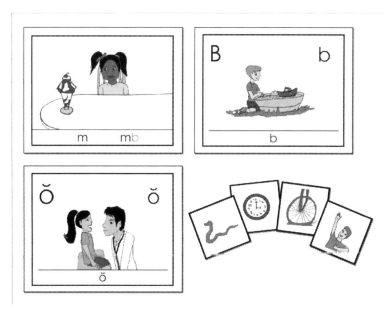

FIGURE 5.1. Concept Cards for Various Sounds. Figures Courtesy of Elissa and Elizabeth Miller. SOURCE: *Foundations for Literacy* (Lederberg, Miller, Easterbrooks, & Connor, 2011)

(e.g., let children go down a slide and encourage them to yell "eeee"). Next, teachers show them a picture of a child going down a slide. Each time they see the picture, they must say, "eeee." Such a picture is referred to as a *concept card*. Concept cards can be used for phonological awareness activities, such as blending the sounds in words or separating words into individual sounds. Figure 5.1 provides several examples of concept cards. Case Vignette 5.4 gives an example of how concept cards are incorporated into phonological awareness activities.

CASE VIGNETTE 5.4.

Ms. Li's Use of the Semantic Association Strategy

Omar is a preschool student with a severe hearing loss who wears hearing aids. He attends a small preschool class with DHH peers. He has a deaf mother and a hearing father, so Omar negotiates between sign language and speech very well, although his access to speech sounds is affected by his hearing loss. Omar and his teacher, Ms. Li, are working on early literacy skills.

(Continued)

(Continued)

Omar has learned phonemes through the semantic association strategy. When he sees a picture of a boat, he knows it represents /b/ after his class played with boats in a tub of water and took turns saying "/bbb/." A few days ago, Ms. Li taught him the new sound /e/ by having the kids take turns sliding down the playground slide and saying "/eee/." Ms. Li places the boat and slide pictures next to each other. "What sound is this?" she asks Omar as she points to each concept card. He points to the boat picture, says /b/, and then points to the slide picture and says /e/. Ms. Li points to each picture and says the corresponding phonemes, at a slightly faster speed than Omar. He repeats. "Do you hear a word?" Ms. Li asks. Omar blends the sounds one more time and says "bee!"

PHONOLOGICALLY BASED DECODING CURRICULA (PHONICS)

Foundations for Literacy is an emergent literacy curriculum that was developed specifically for DHH preschoolers (Lederberg, Miller, Easterbrooks, & Connor, 2011). Foundations focuses on letter–sound relationships, phonological skills, vocabulary, fluency, and shared reading experiences through a semantic-association strategy as described above (Bergeron et al., 2009). For example, the letter "b" is associated with the phoneme /b/ through a story in which a character places a boat in a tub and says /bbb/ as the boat circles around the tub. A picture of a boat semantically connects the phoneme and grapheme (see Figure 5.1). Students also engage in language experiences directly related to the semantic experience, such as placing their own packages of popcorn in the microwave and practicing /p/. Students experience multiple opportunities to practice isolated phonemes in engaging contexts. Instruction with Foundations provides multisensory support through a combination of sign language, voice, and visual support (Bergeron et al., 2009; Morrison et al., 2008) and follows guidelines for systematic and explicit instruction (Carnine, Silbert, Kame'enui, & Tarver, 2004; Trezek et al., 2010). Foundations initially introduces the most common sound for a letter (such as the long sound for a vowel), separates instruction for letters that sound or look the same (such as /b/ and /p/), and introduces the most useful letters first. For those students who require additional visual support, Foundations can be paired with Visual Phonics to make the articulatory features of phonemes more explicit (Beal-Alvarez, Lederberg, & Easterbrooks, 2011).

Other Visual Strategies for Phonological Skills. Teachers can model the segmentation of words in a hierarchical visual manner. While holding a picture of a target word, such as "basketball," beneath one's mouth, a teacher can say the word slowly and nod her head to each syllable as she says it. Students can count the parts of the word on their fingers as the teacher says the word. Teachers can also show students the number of parts in "basketball" by holding up three fingers: Pointing to the first finger, the teacher says the first syllable of the word ("bas") while cueing the students to her mouth; the teacher points to the second finger and says the second syllable ("ket") and repeats on the third finger for the third syllable ("ball"). The students and teacher can also clap the syllables or tap the syllables on the tabletop or with their feet. These strategies can also be used with segmentation of phonemes with a word. The teacher can say, "'Time.' I hear three sounds in 'time.' What are the sounds?" while pointing to three fingers as she slowly says the word. For additional visual support, the teacher can refer to the corresponding grapheme or semantic cue for each sound as she directs students' attention to each of her fingers, either by pointing to the cues displayed next to her or by actually sticking the cues on each finger.

Many of these skills can be reversed for the blending of words. The teacher can point to three fingers, one at a time, while saying a particular phoneme: "/m/ . . . /ē/ . . . /t/. What word do you hear?" The teacher can also use the semantic association strategy during blending for visual support. See Case Vignette 5.4. Finally, the teacher can present pictures of two or three known words, label each one, and give the student a target word to blend. "This is 'bee' (point to bee). This is 'me' (point to me). Listen to this word: /m/ . . . /ē/. Which word do you hear?" Students can point to the correct word or repeat the word, based on individual student ability. Students can also blend the word themselves by referring to picture card cues or using graphemes for known phonemes.

Instruction in initial sound can also include visual strategies. Teachers may use the Visual Phonics hand cue for the initial sound in a word. They can begin with a closed, or limited, set of phonemes for the initial sound with picture cues. For example, the teacher may set up a bowl for /m/ words and another for /ē/ words, labeled with picture cues. Holding a picture of an eagle, the teacher can say "'Eagle.' What is the first sound in 'eagle'?" and point to each bowl. The student can simply point, place the picture card in the labeled bowl, repeat the phoneme, etc., based on student ability. As children begin to master initial sound, the teacher can gradually remove picture supports and/or offer more choices to increase discrimination skills.

MORPHOLOGICAL DECODING DEFINITIONS

English word forms are the product of a highly developed morphemic system (Gaustad & Kelly, 2004; Gaustad, Kelly, Payne, & Lylak, 2002). Through morphological analysis, students learn word meanings by dividing the parts of words into units of meaning (morphemes), analyzing the meanings of the individual morphemes, and then putting the pieces back together to analyze the combination of morphemes as a whole. DHH college students who scored better on a test of morphological decoding skills exhibited higher scores on a test of English skills (Clark, Gilbert, & Anderson, 2011). Children's awareness of the relationship between root words and their affixed forms increases with grade level, is age dependent, and contributes to both reading comprehension and vocabulary growth (Freyd & Baron, 1982; Singson, Mahony, & Mann, 2000; Tyler & Nagy, 1990). Morphological skill predicts vocabulary knowledge for hearing students (McBride-Chang, Wagner, Muse, Chow, & Shu, 2005; Nagy, Berninger, Abbott, Vaughan, & Vermeulen, 2003) and assists in the reading and spelling of words that are low frequency (e.g., the words *hesitate* and *ignore* may appear in a second-grade story but not as frequently as most words associated with that grade) (Berninger et al., 2010). Morphological skill is also related to reading ability from third grade through college (Singson et al., 2000; Tyler & Nagy, 1989) and contributes to reading ability beyond the effects of phonological awareness, vocabulary, and verbal short-term memory. The rate at which students add affixes to known root words is astounding. Skills in analyzing an unknown word by its morphological elements will assist children in meaningful decoding.

We expand, modify, and change words almost without thought when we affix single and multiple morphemes to the front or end of a root word. Think of all the pieces that make up the word "antidisestablishmentarianism." Each morpheme carries meaning. Morphemes can be root words (i.e., "friend") or can be bound to the root via a system of affixes. Affixes include prefixes (e.g., un-, re-, dis-) and suffixes (e.g., -ly, -ment, -s, -ness). The word "unfriendly" contains three morphemes: the prefix "un-," the root word "friend," and the suffix "-ly." For a student to understand the semantic features of this word, he or she must know the meanings of all three morphemes. Figure 5.2 demonstrates the material one teacher used when helping his students learn about root words and affixes.

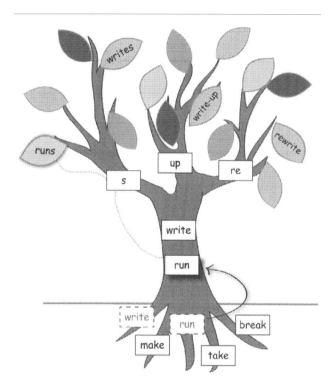

Trees have roots, and so do words!
1. Make cards with a variety of root words on them. Place them at the tips of the roots on a bulletin board or smart board.
2. Identify affixes and attach them to each branch.
3. Each day, take one word from the roots and place it on the trunk of the tree.
4. Help the students create new words to be the "leaves" of the tree.

FIGURE 5.2. Visual for Explaining the Relationship between Root Words and Affixes

Morphological decoding is an important skill for a number of reasons. More than 82 percent of the words contained in the Academic Word List, a tool that identifies 570 of the most frequently used words across academic contexts, are of Greek or Latin origin (Coxhead, 2000). Decoding of prefixes, root words, and suffixes can unlock words and ultimately lead to their meaning. Through third grade, students typically learn an inclusive bank of root words and their meanings. When students reach fourth grade, two changes occur: They encounter an increased number of words with prefixes (Nagy & Anderson, 1984; T. White, Power, & White, 1989), and they begin to read to accumulate new information, so they depend on root words and the individual meanings of affixes (i.e., prefixes and suffixes) to assist in decoding for meaning. Words with Latin roots increase in seventh grade and throughout college, so mastery of morphological decoding is vital for reading success (Nagy & Scott, 1990). Table 5.1 identifies the averages of root words, inflected words, and derived words that children know by fourth grade.

We create new words through the addition of two types of morphemes: inflectional and derivational. An inflectional morpheme is a morpheme that is attached to a noun or verb (e.g., tree/trees or grow/grow*ing*) and relates to number and tense within noun–verb agreement. A derivational morpheme takes one part of speech and changes it to another, such as

Table 5.1. *Averages of Root Words, Inflected Words, and Derived Words by Grade*

Grade	Root words	Inflected words	Derived words
1	3,000	2,700	1,800
2	3,700–5,200	3,200	3,200
3	4,500	4,100	5,600
5	6,700–8,400	5,200–5,600	12,200–16,000
8	8,800	6,500	24,800
11	10,500	7,300	30,200
Total new words added to vocabulary per day		3–7	
Total new words added to vocabulary per year		540–1,260	

Adapted from: Anglin, 1993; Biemiller & Slonim, 2001; Sullivan, 2006.

from a noun to an adjective ("spot" to "spot*ed*") or from an adjective to a verb ("familiar" to "familiar*ize*"). Inflectional morphemes are usually mastered in spoken language before kindergarten and in a fixed manner for children with typical hearing (Berko, 1958; Brown, 1973). Children who are 5 and 6 years of age use inflectional morphology to some extent for spelling (Treiman & Cassar, 1996). Student knowledge of inflection is related to academic progress in first and second grades (Carlisle, 1995; Carlisle & Nomanbhoy, 1993; Vogel, 1977). Significantly, inflectional morphological awareness measured in second grade predicted reading comprehension in fifth grade for hearing students (Deacon & Kirby, 2004).

Mastery of derivational morphemes seems to involve a longer, more open-ended course than that of inflectional morphemes (Nagy, Diakidoy, & Anderson, 1993; Tyler & Nagy, 1989). The hearing child's awareness of roots and affixes begins to appear somewhere in second or third grade; production of derived forms is related to reading ability in first grade through high school (Carlisle, 1995; Carlisle & Nomanbhoy, 1993; Fowler & Liberman, 1995). The use of derivational morphology skyrockets around third grade (primarily because of the increased presence of Latin and Greek word roots in higher grades [e.g., *herbivore* and *carnivore* both refer to a kind of diet; *herb* makes it a vegetarian diet, and *carni* makes it a meat diet]), when it plays a role in spelling (Henderson, 1985). Student performance measures of morphological awareness predicted reading ability as accurately as student performance on either phonological or vocabulary measures (Singson et al., 2000).

Another way morphemes are combined is in compound words (e.g., doghouse), which are made up of two free morphemes (i.e., morphemes that have meaning alone, such as "dog" and "house"). However, when put together to form one word, the meanings of the individual morphemes change to form a word with a new definition. Some researchers report that hearing readers process compound words by separating them into individual morphemes and tend to focus on the first morpheme in a compound word for decoding, even though the meaning of the compound word is frequently held within the second morpheme (Andrews, Miller, & Rayner, 2004). Awareness of compound words is a predictor of reading comprehension, even across languages (Cheng, 2008). While we know that hearing children begin to use compound words within their language before kindergarten, we do not know how they use them within reading and at what age.

Because text is based on spoken language, DHH students without full auditory access to a spoken language, regardless of their mode of communication, may not know the combinations of letters (i.e., morphemes) that create units of meaning. Therefore, they may not know how to accurately break words apart into root words and affixes (Gaustad & Kelly, 2004). For example, DHH college students performed similarly to hearing middle school students on their abilities to use inflectional and derivational morphological decoding (Gaustad et al., 2002), which affects their reading across content areas such as science and math (Kelly & Gaustad, 2007). However, DHH students may benefit from morphological training, as demonstrated by elementary-aged DHH students who received nine weeks of morphological instruction (Bow, Blamey, Paatsch, & Sarant, 2004).

MORPHOLOGICAL DECODING STRATEGIES

Effective teachers are familiar with the sequence of acquisition of morphemes in spoken language and use this to guide instruction in morphological decoding (see Table 5.2). For example, hearing children may add the suffix "-ing" as early as two years of age (Akhtar & Tomasello, 1997) and plural inflections (e.g., -s, -es) as early as 21 months of age (Tomasello, Akhtar, Dodson, & Rekau, 1997). Acquisition of morphology is a gradual process, and consistent use of a particular morpheme may take up to a year for hearing students to master (deVilliers & deVilliers, 1973). As students' productive language increases, students add morphemes to words. Hearing students of elementary and middle school ages who received instruction in the meanings of specific affixes generalized this knowledge to novel words (Baumann, Edwards, Boland, Olejnik, & Kame'enui, 2003). However, keep in mind that DHH students frequently arrive at school significantly behind their hearing peers in language development.

Table 5.2. *Sequence of Morphological Development in Spoken Language*

1. Present progressive verb + ing; as early as 2; 1

2. The preposition "on"

3. The preposition "in"

4. Plural inflections (e.g., -s, -es); as early as 1; 9

5. Past inflections on irregular verbs

6. Possessive inflections (e.g., the dog's ball)

7. Uncontractible copula ("is," "am," "are")

8. Articles ("the," "a," "an")

9. Past inflections on regular verbs (e.g., -ed); -ed as early as 2; 9

10. Regular third-person forms (e.g., s as in "He writes well")

11. Irregular third-person forms (e.g., "they have")

12. Uncontractible auxiliary forms (e.g., "does")

13. Contractible copula (e.g., -'s and -'re)

14. Contractible auxiliary forms (e.g., -'d)

* Morphemes 1, 4, 6, and 9 are acquired by 4 years of age for typical language development. Adapted from Akhtar & Tomasello, 1997; J. G. deVilliers & deVilliers, 1973; Brown, 1973.

Because of this, they may likely be behind in their acquisition of morphological skills and may need extra time to acquire and master each morpheme.

Whether a student is learning morphological decoding through spoken language, by including signed morphemes (e.g., *Signing Exact English*), or through a signed explanation of the printed morpheme, effective instruction for morphological decoding must be explicit and early (Causal Factor 4), not only for root words, prefixes, and affixes but also for irregular spellings, complex word structures, and low-frequency words (Gaustad & Kelly, 2004; White et al., 1989). One way to do this is to use contrast to highlight the difference in meanings between similar root words with different morphemes, such as "happy" and "unhappy" or "joke" and "joker." All DHH children, no matter their language or communication mode, will require instruction in the morphosyntax of print. Children who sign may also benefit from a discussion of the morphemic features of signs (Paul, 1998). For example, teachers can show children the movement pattern for fingerspelling *er* and then have them add this pattern to various root words (e.g., dancer, reader). Teachers can explicitly teach the link between a printed morpheme (e.g., -ing) and signed forms of morphemes. For instance, teachers may distinguish the difference between "run" and "running" when signing by pointing out that the repeated movement in "running" relates to the suffix of -ing on the root word "run." Teachers can follow this discussion with the signs "run, finish" for the printed word "ran," highlighting the same root word of "run" but with a change in spelling to denote past tense, as shown by the sign "finish."

While there is a longstanding controversy in the field of deaf education regarding whether or not one should use the signs for morphemes available in systems such as Signing Exact English (SEE; Schick & Moeller, 1992), teachers can use the signs for morphemes as a tool to help them demonstrate the concept of decoding words morphologically. For example, Luetke-Stahlman and Nielsen (2003) reported that students who received five or more years of exposure to SEE read at significantly higher levels than their peers who had less exposure and posited that this was due to increased exposure to the morphology of the spoken language. While teachers' abilities when using SEE vary (Luetke-Stahlman, 1989; Mayer & Lowenbraun, 1990), some signers improved their accuracy of SEE when provided with feedback and direct instruction (Luetke-Stahlman & Moeller, 1990; Mayer & Lowenbraun, 1990). The use of SEE during morphological instruction is one tool teachers may find effective with some of their DHH students.

Morphological decoding of English print may be effective with DHH students in all communication modes because the patterns of letters are visually available. Morpheme–grapheme correspondence is more stable than phoneme–grapheme correspondence in English and therefore may be more reliable as a decoding tool for some readers. Skilled readers who are deaf pay attention to the form features of English text more so than poor readers, and the ability to apply morphemic knowledge to decoding of text is highly correlated with skilled readers' reading comprehension performance (Kelly, 1996). Finally, spellings derived from morpho-graphemic analysis are more stable than spellings from phonic analysis. For example, the root word "bio" has a stable morpheme–grapheme relationship and always refers to science, but the long /a/ sound can be represented through *a* (crazy), *ai* (pail), *a_e* (cane), *ay* (day), or *eigh* (sleigh) and can form thousands of words with different meanings. Given what we know about morphological development in hearing readers, the limited research available for morphological instruction with DHH readers, and their common delays in language, we must consider this as another avenue to decoding in multiple contexts, including conversation, reading activities, and direct instruction, using the students' primary mode of communication. Further research is needed in this area, but implementing this approach should not wait.

INTONATION-BASED DECODING

Another way in which we decode words and phrases is by their intonational patterns. The way in which a child breaks sentences down into phrase chunks (e.g., *This is the dog* that chased the cat *that ate the cheese...*) influences both interpretation of meaning and fluent spoken and signed production of the phrase. Because the information this provides a child is closely related to concepts surrounding the discussion of fluency, we address this form of decoding under the discussion of fluency in Chapter 7. Brevity in this location does not imply lack of importance.

CONTEXTUAL DECODING

Contextually based decoding refers to using the known words surrounding an unknown word within a sentence to figure out its meaning. Written language is lexically richer than spoken conversation, and we can likely surmise that it is richer than the forms of sign language that many DHH students experience in home and at school. In order to use context cues, students must know the concepts and their related printed representations that surround the target word. Typically hearing college students who learned English as a second language needed to know 98 percent of the surrounding words in text before they could use contextual decoding for an unknown word (Hu & Nation, 2000). These cues may be structural (containing features of both morphological and syllabic analysis) in that they are found within the unknown word (e.g., "-tion"). This means that in order for young children to learn to use context cues, effective teachers must make sure their students understand the vocabulary contained within the contextual print. For example, in the sentence "The king and queen rode to the palace in their chariot," a student needs to know the printed words and concepts behind *king, queen, palace,* and *rode* to use these words as contextual cues for the unknown target word *chariot.* Useful cues can be found near the unknown word within the same sentence or reading passage and can be addressed by focusing on semantic and grammatical knowledge.

Syntactic and semantic cues also assist in contextual decoding. Syntactic cues refer to those based on the knowledge of the structure of sentences, usually from knowledge of oral language (Farrington, 2007). For example, if a child substitutes "poked" for "parked" when reading the following sentence, we know that he is aware that a verb must go in the sentence: "The limo driver parked his car by the fire hydrant." Semantic cues refer to the meaning of text. When the student substitutes "poked" in the preceding sentence, he will need to reread the sentence to see if it makes sense; reflect that another verb, such as "parked," makes more sense; and replace his guess with a more semantically appropriate word. For hearing children, the majority of reading errors are semantic (Farrington, 2007). Contextual analysis also requires the activation of prior knowledge. Consider the following sentence: "New York City has many vehicles in the streets: taxis, buses, cars, vans, and trucks." If a student doesn't know the word "vehicle" but is familiar with taxis, cars, vans, and trucks from his prior knowledge, he can likely deduce the meaning of the word "vehicle" using a combination of semantic cues (the word is related to types of cars) and syntactic cues (the word appears to be a noun).

Students who spend an average of 25 minutes of reading daily on their own may encounter 20,000 unfamiliar words per year (Nagy, 1988). However, even the best vocabulary instruction can address only a small portion of these words across a school year, with estimates around several hundred (Nagy, 1988). Students learn words from a single exposure in context only 5–10 percent of the time (Nagy, Anderson, & Herman, 1987; Shu, Anderson, & Zhang, 1995), and students who struggle to read need repeated exposures to words before mastery. Contextual decoding is one strategy that students can add to their toolbox to assist with unlocking unknown words while reading.

The amount of assistance that context provides can vary by reading materials. Some material may provide little information in regard to semantic relationships within the text and unknown word. Other contexts may provide synonyms or more explicit information. Consider these two examples:

Allison and her family stayed in a *yurt* on their vacation. She couldn't wait to tell her friends all about it.

Allison and her family stayed in a *yurt* on their vacation. She liked it better than a tent because the roof had a hole for stargazing.

The first sentence provides very little information in context for decoding *yurt*. A *yurt* seems novel in that Allison stayed in it on vacation and wants to tell her friends, but no additional information about the unknown word is given. In the second example, contextual cues are provided: A *yurt* is related to a tent but has a hole in the top. A student's ability to use contextual cues depends on the amount of detail provided within the context. It also depends on the student's knowledge of the other words within the reading passage and his or her prior knowledge and ability to apply this knowledge to the present reading task. Readers who are younger and those who have not mastered phonological decoding may rely more heavily on context for decoding (Nicholson, 1991; Stanovich, 1980). Unfortunately, rich, detailed context is not typical in reading materials (Gough, 1984), and enough information may not be provided for the student to decipher any meaning.

Because DHH students typically begin with smaller lexicons (Mayne, Yoshinaga-Itano, Sedey, & Carey, 2000) and slower vocabulary trajectories than their hearing peers, they have fewer known words to which they can refer when faced with unfamiliar context cues. Based on their receptive vocabulary scores using the *Peabody Picture Vocabulary Test* (*PPVT*), DHH students seem to have significantly reduced learning rates of vocabulary. Of a sample of 311 DHH students between the ages of 4 and 18 years, Boothroyd, Geers, and Moog (1991) reported that profoundly deaf hearing aid users had a learning rate of 0.43 to 0.60 times that of their hearing peers, while DHH students who received cochlear implants at an early age had a rate of 0.63 and later implantees a rate of 0.45 (Connor, Hieber, Arts, & Zwolan, 2000). Based on these learning rates, the average 18-year-old profoundly deaf student has a vocabulary of about 12,000 to 18,000 words (Marschark, Spencer, & Nathan, 2011), while his or her average hearing peer has an average vocabulary of more than 330,000 words (Nagy & Herman, 1987). Because of these smaller lexicons, DHH students require explicit instruction in both the meaning behind vocabulary and how to use their known vocabulary as contextual cues within text. DHH students require highly detailed ("rich") or explicit context cues to derive partial meanings of unknown words, and the ability to use context cues is strongly related to levels of reading comprehension (deVilliers & Pomerantz, 1992). Poor readers had difficulty even with explicit contextual cues. Students need to read to improve their vocabulary skills, but they need vocabulary skills to become good readers.

Effective teachers provide explicit instruction in contextual decoding. The teacher can "think aloud" while modeling the use of contextual cues and ask students to explain how she arrived at her answer. While practice and feedback, such as "Yes, you were right!" or "No, that word means… " leads to learning of target vocabulary words using contextual cues, practice that includes student explanations for how they derived their answers leads to greater gains (Brandão & Oakhill, 2005; Siegler, 1995). The teacher can ask students, "How did you know that?" When students generate explanations for their thinking (i.e., metacognitive analysis), they may become more aware of what the text actually says. Hearing children learn to use context even better when they are asked to explain how they figured out a word's meaning (Cain, 2007), and it is likely that DHH children would benefit from this type of instruction as well, although we have no research yet to document this. Finally, simple rule explanation (e.g., Teacher says, "Use all the words in the sentence to help you figure out the meaning of the word you don't know") may be sufficient for hearing children (Fukkink & de Glopper, 1998), but it may not be sufficient for DHH children.

For students who need explicit instruction, the teacher can even use a marker to highlight the words in the text that led to her decoding of the unknown words, demonstrating that these words may come before or after the unknown word. Hearing readers were less likely to use those cues that followed the unknown word than those that preceded the unknown word (Cain et al., 2004; Chern, 1993), so explicit instruction may direct students to multiple ways of accessing words through context. Case Vignette 5 5 presents an example of instruction using context cues.

CASE VIGNETTE 5.5.
Ms. Gillian's Use of Context Cues

Max is a fourth-grade student with a profound hearing loss who uses sign language to communicate. Ms. Gillian and Max are working on decoding skills for unknown words using context cues from a brief reading passage in the fourth-grade reading curriculum used by his general education teacher. Max reads: "The pigeons live in many urban roosts," fingerspelling "pigeons," "urban," and "roosts." Max looks back at the word "pigeons," looks at Ms. Gillian, and says, "We learned that word in science! It is a kind of bird!" Max finishes reading the sentence and again pauses after "urban roosts," looking at the phrase in puzzlement. "What do you think 'urban roosts' means?" Ms. Gillian asks. She watches Max silently reread the sentence. He points to "lives" and says, "I think it means something like 'lives.'" "Okay," Ms. Gillian says, "Where do pigeons, or birds, live?" Max knows that birds live in nests. "What do you think 'urban' means?" Ms. Gillian prompts. Max is unfamiliar with this word and doesn't recognize any word parts within the word. "So far you know that the birds, called pigeons, live in nests. 'Urban' means in the city. What does this sentence mean?" Ms. Gillian watches Max's face light up as he says, "It means pigeons live in nests in the city! I wonder where they make nests." Ms. Gillian says, "Right! How did you know that?" Max looks at the text, then explains, "I knew pigeons are birds, birds live in nests, and 'urban' means city. I think 'roosts' means nests."

Contextual decoding occurs deliberately (i.e., the student reads a given passage and derives the meaning of target words) and incidentally (i.e., in a natural setting for reading where the student acquires meanings of unknown words on his or her own) (Paul, 1996). Students can use a "guess and check" strategy by substituting a word they think may work based on context cues and rereading the sentence to check for meaning (Farrington, 2007). Contextual decoding for DHH students may be most effective when combined with discussions about word meanings and their related concepts (Paul, 1996). Effective teachers help students to mediate the definition of a word based on the child's personal experiences. Using examples of target words in context and providing definitions are two avenues for accessing the breadth and depth of a vocabulary concept (Stahl & Fairbanks, 1986).

STRUCTURAL DECODING THROUGH SYLLABIFICATION

There are two types of structurally based decoding. The first is based on the rules for syllabification, and the second pertains to advanced work on Latin and Greek word roots. The relationship between syllabification (i.e., breaking words into their syllables) and reading is unclear when it comes to DHH children, as most of the literature on the subject pertains to the development of speech, not reading. For example, when we break words into their syllable units, as in dis/en/tan/gle/ment, this artificial breakdown of the word may make meaning obscure. In particular, the word "tan" has nothing to do with the meaning of the word "disentanglement"; "tangle" is the more appropriate breakdown for helping with meaning. Generally, we learn to break words into syllables for pronunciation purposes; this is different from morphemic structural analysis.

Latin and Greek word roots have a clear relationship to the literacy process in students with learning disabilities (Ebbers & Denton, 2008). Paul (1998) identified procedures for instructing DHH students to understand and use morpho-graphemic correspondence, beginning with basic knowledge of root words, suffixes, and prefixes and moving toward understanding of Latin and Greek word derivatives. Effective teachers teach root words, then compounds, and then expanded word meanings, in that order, followed by highlighting affixes (e.g., -s, -ed, -ing, -er, -able, -ly, -ness, and -y) through morphological analysis. Students break words into their smaller, meaningful parts to identify the complete definition of the words in a meaning-based way. For example, one might break the word "unlawfully" into four parts (un-, law, ful, -ly) and discuss the meaning of each part, putting the word back together to demonstrate the word's complete meaning. Teachers can address morphological analysis, structural analysis, and complex Latin and Greek root words in the following sequence and under the following conditions (adapted from Paul, 1998):

1. Always teach decoding and comprehension separately.
2. Teach students to decode unknown vocabulary in the context of known grammar and vocabulary. Give them as many context cues as possible.
3. Teach morphographs by visually highlighting the changes they make to base or root words or to other morphographs (e.g., "happy" versus "unhappy").
4. Teach basic verb inflections (-ing, -er, -s, etc.).
5. Teach prefixes and suffixes.
6. Teach Latin roots for numbers, as they are the most easy to demonstrate visually. They also are among the Latin prefixes/roots associated with the largest number of derived words.
7. Teach base word meanings such as *turb* and *script*. To teach Latin and Greek affixes and roots, focus on recognition of their meaning.
8. Teach within the context of created sentence groups. For example, when teaching the meaning of "unicycle" (assuming that the child knows that *uni* means "one"), tell a story where the root "cycle" clearly appears elsewhere in the passage. ("When I was little, I had a tricycle. My parents bought me a bicycle when I was six years old. One day, when I am brave enough, I want to learn to ride a *unicycle*. What does *unicycle* mean?")
9. Teach all possible derived forms of a word to show the possible ways an affix can change the meaning and grammatical

category, helping students to examine all of the different words that can be derived from one base. This is a teacher-directed activity. Next, have students brainstorm as many words as possible with a given affix or root (e.g., cycle, bicycle, unicycle, cyclical). This is a student-directed activity. The teacher might give students passages in books that have the targeted root word.

SUMMARY OF RECOMMENDED PRACTICES

To effectively decode printed words in reading materials, students must know how to unlock the printed code of words, and they must know the underlying meaning of the words they decode. That is, they need to have a large repertoire of tools they can use to take apart and meaningfully put back together the printed words that they have not mastered by sight. These tools may include phonological decoding (i.e., grapheme–phoneme relations) and morphological decoding (i.e., grapheme-morpheme relations). These strategies create the foundation for engagement in the higher-order word work involved in structural analysis (e.g., syllabification, root words, and suffixes) and contextual analysis (i.e., figuring out the meaning of a word or phrase from the language that surrounds it). Finally, teachers can use intonational decoding, mentioned in the chapter on fluency. Within the DHH population, varying levels of access to sound may affect how students unlock print. An effective teacher uses current assessment data to select the most appropriate decoding strategies within different contexts for individual students, from visual approaches to phonological decoding to helping students create multiple pathways for memory storage and retrieval of decoded words. Effective teachers model "thinking aloud" to demonstrate how they make decisions regarding unknown information in text and ask students how they figure out unknown information to provide needed levels of scaffolding during decoding.

RESOURCES

What Works Clearinghouse: The WWC has examined the evidence base of numerous literacy programs that focus on decoding and provides a statement about the level of effectiveness of these programs: http://www.whatworks.ed.gov.

Laureate Learning: http://www.laureatelearning.com

Cannon et al. (2010) reported that when used with teacher mediation, Laureate Learning's *Language Links* program improved DHH students' morphosyntactic skills.

6 Grammar and Text Comprehension

PURPOSE

Text comprehension refers to the ability to understand meaning conveyed by print. It is not merely a reason for teaching reading; it is the primary objective. We begin this chapter with a discussion of grammar because it is a fundamental component of text comprehension. Grammar imparts a large share of meaning (above and beyond vocabulary) to a phrase, sentence, paragraph, or extended narrative during and after the early years of literacy learning. The chapter proceeds with discussions of theories that explain text comprehension, research on how hearing and DHH learners acquire the ability to comprehend or understand text, and evidence-based instructional practices associated with text comprehension skills. We describe a variety of comprehension strategies that have a developing evidence base (e.g., language experience approach, story maps, narrative story grammar), all of which may be used whether the child is using spoken language, a hybrid sign system, or a natural sign language. We focus on those text comprehension strategies known to be effective (e.g., activating prior knowledge, predicting and summarizing, among others) with hearing and deaf children (no matter their language or mode). As with the previous chapters, these strategies are grounded in case vignettes. We identify the Causal Factors associated with the practices discussed. Causal Factors are good teaching practices that result in positive literacy outcomes and may provide guidance for a practitioner when other evidence is minimal. Cognitive, psychological, and social factors that cause positive learning outcomes are 1) promotion of higher-order language and critical thinking; 2) a good match between teacher and child communication; 3) visual representation of ideas, concepts, and processes; 4) explicit instruction; and 5) scaffolding and mediation by a more knowledgeable person.

GRAMMAR KNOWLEDGE AND ITS RELATION TO TEXT COMPREHENSION

When we read, we read a language; we do not simply move from squiggles on the page to formal thought. When working with DHH students, two languages require consideration. First, teachers and other practitioners must consider the spoken language of the culture in which they teach (e.g., English, Chinese, Farsi, Hindi), including both the spoken and signed renditions of that language in addition to the printed versions. Second, teachers and other practitioners must consider the indigenous sign system of the culture (e.g., American Sign Language, Icelandic Sign Language, Slovakian Sign Language). Text comprehension issues differ depending on whether the student is moving from 1) the spoken language to its print form, 2) a signed version of the spoken language to its print form, or 3) a natural sign language to a printed language. First we address the grammar of language (i.e., morphology and syntax) and how it relates to text comprehension, and then we address practices. Although the majority of teachers in the United States (52 percent) use speech only, and an additional 35 percent use a combination of signs and speech, any discussion of grammar must also respect the 11 percent of teachers who use the indigenous sign language of the United States, American Sign Language (ASL; the remaining 2 percent use Cued Speech or 'other'; Gallaudet Research Institute, 2008).

When Readers Use Their Country's Spoken Language

Deaf and hard-of-hearing students' weak grammar knowledge is a primary contributing factor to their struggles with text comprehension. In many countries (M. Nikolaraizi, personal communication, March 14, 2008), students who are DHH have difficulty moving past the fourth-grade reading level. One contributing reason is that many have never mastered the grammar of the spoken language of their country, and print employs the same grammatical structures. Table 6.1 lists grammatical structures that are especially difficult for deaf students (see Easterbrooks & Baker, 2002; Easterbrooks & Estes, 2007, for extensive reviews of grammar acquisition in DHH children).

In order to understand the meaning of a spoken or written sentence, students must be able to carve out the underlying syntactic relationships within a sentence. This is called *parsing*; we parse sentences to make meaning (Clifton & Duffy, 2001) by pulling meaning out of chunks of words within a sentence. Table 6.2 summarizes some of the strategies by which we parse the sentences of spoken or written English. When teaching a child to read for understanding, the teacher will want to know whether he is capable of parsing the grammar used to create printed sentences in the manner needed. Look at the examples of syntactic parsing in Table 6.2. In order to parse the example sentences, the child would have to know that *down* "belonged" with *the road* in Sentence 2 and with *drove* in Sentence 3. He would parse meaning differently by how he related the word "down" to the other words in the sentence. Although we have evidence regarding parsing in children who hear (Clifton & Duffy), little is known about how to teach deaf children to parse sentences meaningfully, and more research is needed in this area as it relates to parsing printed sentences. Teachers might try parsing a passage by picking several sentences from instructional-level reading material that might be parsed in different ways to see how a student attacks confusing sentences. Teachers themselves

Table 6.1. *Grammatical Structures Posing Challenges for DHH Students*

Structure	Examples
Negation in the correct form and location in a sentence	I have no money. He is not tall. Aren't you coming? She never finishes her homework.
Question forms that must be answered by an adverb, an adverbial phrase or clause, a relative pronoun, or by a complement form	How often do you jog? Frequently. Where is the light switch? Behind the door. Why did she leave? Because… What did she say? That she is going to be late.
Advanced verb tense, especially using do-support	Doesn't that surprise you? He might have been late. Next month they will have been living here for 10 years.
Adverbial phrases and clauses	While driving down the road, he noticed a strange noise in his engine.
Pronominalization, especially intrasententially (within a sentence) and intersententially (between sentences)	Although she is a well-known singer, Amanda was not chosen to be in the play. She was not happy about this.
Passive voice	The cookies were eaten by the dog. The car was struck by the bus.
Relative clauses	John, whose wife is a teacher, rides his bicycle to work every day.
Complementation	For her to leave her desk was unusual. That the dog was so old came as a surprise to the girl.

Sources: Easterbrooks & Baker, 2002; Quigley & King, 1980; Quigley, Montanelli, & Wilbur, 1976; Quigley, Power, & Steinkamp, 1977; Quigley, Smith, & Wilbur, 1974; Quigley, Wilbur, & Montanelli, 1976.

need to understand how to chunk, or group, parts of the sentence in order to help their students understand the meaning held within the grammar.

Historically in the English-speaking world, several programs were developed based on syntactic parsing (e.g., *the Fitzgerald Key* [Fitzgerald, 1929], *the Apple Tree Curriculum* [Anderson, Noren, Kilgore, Howard, & Krohn, 1999], and *Teaching Competence in Written Language: A Systematic*

Table 6.2. *Examples of Sentence Parsing Strategies*

Strategy	Explanation	Example
Syntactic Strategy	We process chunks or phrases and modify meaning as we go along. In Sentence 1, "The garden gate" sets up a picture in your head that you modify when you read the next part. In this case, the relative clause structure (which was used as a stretcher) holds the key to changing the meaning. Although Sentences 2 and 3 look identical in form on the surface, syntactically the word "down" is a preposition in S2 but is part of a verb idiom in S3. If a reader were to interpret "down" in S3 as a preposition, the sentence would make no sense.	S1. The garden gate, which was used as a stretcher, carried many of the wounded to makeshift hospitals. S2. He drove *down the road.* S3. He *drove down* the prices.
Lexical Strategy	We use the meaning of parts of sentences to help us understand the meaning of other parts. In Sentences 4 and 5, the information in the prepositional phrase (by the trick horse) helps us back up and reinterpret what "was thrown" means. We know after reading the last part of the sentence that the verb in S5 refers to a physical action, whereas it refers to a mental action in S4.	S4. He was thrown by the trick horse. S5. He was thrown by the trick question.
Prosodic Strategy	We change the meaning of a sentence by the prosodic contour (intonation, accenting, stress) with which we read it. Sentence 6 could mean that the customer had a mean look on his face or that the salesman gave the customer a mean look. Meaning is made when we apply the appropriate prosodic features.	S6. The car salesman angered the customer with a mean look.

(Continued)

Table 6.2. *(Continued)*

Strategy	Explanation	Example
Semantic Strategy	Although two sentences may have almost identical structure, one word can change the entire context. In Sentence 7, the word "easy" means that someone else understood Ray, but in Sentence 8, Ray is doing the understanding.	S7. Ray was easy to understand. S8. Ray was eager to understand.
Context Strategy	We parse sentences and parts of sentences by the broader context in which we find them. The sentence "I'm studying" is identical in both sequences, but the first context (Sentence 10) refers to an experience in the present, and the second context (Sentence 11) refers to an experience in the future.	S10. What are you doing? I'm studying. S11. What are you doing Saturday? I'm studying.

Source: Clifton & Duffy, 2001; Snedeker & Yuan, 2007; Speer, Kjelgaard, & Dobroth, 1996.

Program for Developing Writing Skills—Second Edition [Phelps-Teresaki, & Phelps-Gunn, 2000]). However, there is an insufficient evidence base regarding syntactic development in DHH students. Specifically, what elements of grammar cause the most problems? Is the developmental sequence of grammatical acquisition in young DHH children different than that of typically hearing children or just delayed? The most comprehensive information to date is the work done in the 1970s by Quigley and others (Quigley, Power, & Steinkamp, 1977) that was conducted with adolescents. More research is needed that addresses syntactic parsing at the emergent and developing grammar stages.

When Readers Use Their Country's Signed Language

When children use the signed language of their country for communication purposes (e.g., British Sign Language or isiZulu Sign Language) but must learn to read the spoken language of their country (i.e., English or Zulu), a bilingual–bicultural philosophy is often considered. This philosophy encourages the development of knowledge, context, and academic skills through ASL (Strong, 1988) or the country's formal sign language. Because there is no written version of most of the world's indigenous sign languages (i.e., natural sign languages such as ASL, Al-Sayyid Bedouin Sign Language, etc.), we cannot use the printed form of that language (L1) to teach the printed form of the second, spoken language (L2). For example, if an English reader were trying to learn Italian as a second language, he or she could compare the two printed words (e.g., hello = ciao) or phrases (e.g., I do not understand = No capisce) side by side. However, sign languages do not have a printed form, so we must make direct comparisons between the signed form of the first language and the print form of the second language. This notion of learning L2 from comparison to L1 is based on Cummins' Linguistic Interdependence Hypothesis (Cummins, 1984, 2000). According to Cummins, L1 and L2 share a common foundation, referred to as a common underlying proficiency (CUP), or interdependence of cognitive and linguistic skills that leads to cognitive and linguistic transfer between languages. For example, if a student knows the concept of "cat" in her first language, she needs only the label for the concept in her second language (i.e., "gato" in Spanish). Linguistic transfer refers to transfer of knowledge related to language, such as the Systematic Rules Principle (Easterbrooks & Baker, 2000), which states that all languages are governed by rules. If a student understands this, then learning another language is less complex (Wilbur, 2000). However, students need adequate exposure and interactions in both L1 and L2 through spoken and written forms to permit transfer between languages and to expand one's CUP (Cummins, 2000). Therefore, with linguistic interactions, students can expand both their cognitive and linguistic skills through a common underlying proficiency to acquire a second language.

Critics of the application of this hypothesis to deaf learners cite the double-discontinuity hypothesis (Mayer & Akamatsu, 2000; Mayer & Wells, 1996). ASL has different structure and syntax compared to English, and ASL does not have a written form. In addition, most deaf people lack full access to spoken English. Therefore, they must learn a second language that occurs in a different mode (oral) with a written system based on a spoken mode. While Mayer and colleagues agree that cognitive transfer is possible, they contend that the grammatical differences between ASL and English are too great for ASL to serve as a basis for reading English. This may not be the case when children use signed forms of English. Again, the knowledge base in this area is growing.

Although this may change in the near future, at the time of this writing only one school for the deaf in the English-speaking world (C. Zinszer, personal communication, November 11, 2010) had a published ASL curriculum. This curriculum was founded on the premise of ASL literacy, a concept that reflects how deaf learners of ASL interpret texts based on their membership in the deaf community and its related social settings (Snoddon, 2010). ASL literacy occurs on two levels: functional ASL literacy (decoding and production of ASL) and cultural ASL literacy (understanding and appreciating the cultural significance of ASL literacy). This ASL curriculum includes four strands: ASL linguistic structure; ASL literature; ASL text; and ASL media arts and technology, such as the creation and editing of ASL stories via video recordings (Snoddon, 2010). Using this strategy, two deaf adult storytellers were video recorded while sharing ASL renditions of their life stories with 16 deaf students. During reviews of these stories, students and their teachers discussed aspects of ASL literacy, such as the ASL concept of name signs, ASL discourse, and ASL identity, and created and edited their own life stories. However, information regarding the specific time line for teaching ASL linguistic structures has not yet been identified. Table 6.3 identifies some of the practices that have been used in ASL/English bilingual programs.

THEORIES OF TEXT COMPREHENSION

In addition to debates surrounding top-down and bottom-up practices described in Chapter 1, another classic debate pertains to whether visual strategies (e.g., sight words, brainstorming maps) or verbal strategies (e.g., phonological awareness, decoding) are more important in the reading process. As we write this, the field of reading is focused on acquisition of phonological awareness and decoding skills as a means for improving reading

Table 6.3. *Strategies Used in ASL Bilingual Classrooms*

Discuss all instructional issues using ASL or the sign language native to a particular country.

Develop student understanding or comprehension in ASL as the foundation for comprehension of written English.

Use ASL to discuss features of the spoken language and access spoken language primarily through print.

Use direct comparison of equivalent structures (e.g., "upset" in English has an equivalent sign in ASL) and nonequivalent structures (e.g., it is acceptable to repeat the sign "car" to indicate plurality in ASL but not acceptable to say it repeatedly in English).

Use space and directionality (i.e., the direction in which one produces a sign) to convey grammatical structure (e.g., to show the recipient of an action in the passive voice sentence "The boy was bitten by the duck," the teacher would establish the location of the boy then demonstrate the duck's action). The developers of the proprietary sign system, Signing Exact English (Gustason & Zawolkow, 2006; Gustason, Zawolkow, & Lopez, 1993) recommended that teachers incorporate natural gestures and spatial features associated with ASL into English-oriented sign systems to clarify meaning.

Compare the languages beginning with the easiest comparisons and progressing to the hardest comparisons.

Show the language learner forms that exist in both the signed and the spoken languages (e.g., pluralization either through reduplications in ASL or the -s morpheme in English).

Show the language learner forms that do not exist either in ASL or English (e.g., "much dogs" does not occur in either ASL or spoken English).

Show the student the mismatches between ASL and written English and instruct students in compensating for this mismatch, such as the presence of classifiers in ASL but not in English.

Have students demonstrate in some manner (e.g., using manipulatives, role-playing, ASL) that they understand the meaning of the English printed word before trying to write.

Use code-switching, a process of switching between languages, for clarification. "Code switching between ASL and English is extremely common in classrooms where the teacher is fluent in both languages" (Nover, Christensen, & Cheng, 1998, p. 68).

(Continued)

Table 6.3. *(Continued)*

Use bridging materials from the Fairview Reading Program (Schimmel, Edwards, & Prickett, 1999) to parse verb idioms as semantic equivalents. Students learn the different signs, for example, for various versions of "take off," such as "remove" (take off your shoes) or "leave" (take off work early), or specifically to describe an airplane rising from the runway.

Sources: Gustason & Zawolkow, 2006; Gustason, Zawolkow, & Lopez, 1993; Luetke-Stahlman, 1998; Nover, Christensen & Cheng, 1998; Paul & Quigley, 1994; Schimmel & Edwards, 2003; Schimmel, Edwards, & Prickett, 1999; Schimmel & Rushton, 2010; Strong, 1988.

outcomes. However, as described in Chapter 5, there are many children who have good decoding skills yet cannot comprehend decoded reading material (Johnson-Glenburg, 2000; O'Connor & Klein, 2004); this reminds us that phonological awareness and decoding are not the only skills children need in order to read. Further, we must keep in mind that some children use spoken language and others use various hybrid sign systems or ASL, and the needs of each group may vary. We are still gathering research evidence to establish how and when these skills may benefit DHH readers.

One theory that might help us understand the relationship between visual and verbal strategies in reading is the *dual-coding theory* (Paivio, 1986, 1989; Sadoski & Paivio, 2004). This theory speculates that there are two separate and distinct systems that children use to represent and process information. One of these systems is the verbal system, which pertains to spoken or signed language. This system responds to linguistic information and specializes in sequential processing. For example, this system cares whether we say, "My have Daddy car" or "My Daddy has a car." The other system is the visual system. This system deals with image-based information (also called *imagery*) and specializes in spatial processing of picture-like information. Associative links between the verbal and visual systems allow these systems to link their codes and share their references. For example, if one were to say, "Big, hairy, ugly dog" in spoken English, many listeners would process the words sequentially in their linguistic system. They would not immediately be comfortable if they heard "dog, ugly, big, hairy." Simultaneously, one's visual imagery system puts a picture of this creature in one's mind. If we think about it long enough, we will remember the picture and the description. Later, the description will evoke the picture, and the picture will evoke the description (shared references). Thus, any programs, materials, or practices that support visual representation of information as a way to help students parse meaning into useful chunks, figure out inferences, and see the relationships among printed words is likely to be of benefit to DHH children. Although we have a limited evidence base to support this assumption, it is consistent with Causal Factor 2, a good match between teacher/child communication levels, and Causal Factor 3, visual representation of ideas, concepts, and processes.

RESEARCH ON TEXT COMPREHENSION IN HEARING AND DHH LEARNERS

What is it that children who comprehend well actually do? If we knew this information, it might help guide our decisions about instructional choices and future research. Luckner and Handley (2008) reviewed the work of well-known researchers in the field of literacy acquisition (e.g., Gersten, Fuchs, Williams, & Baker, 2001; Vaughn & Linan-Thompson, 2004) and identified the following elements to be characteristic of good comprehenders.

Good comprehenders:

1. *Set goals for reading.* Many of the text comprehension strategies described below can be written as personal goals for students to use while they are reading.
2. *Apply their knowledge and experiences to the text.* Reading becomes a fluid process for a student between checking personal experiences against the information in the text and then revising the meaning based on the student's own font of knowledge.
3. *Read words and phrases fluently.* We discuss reading fluency in detail in the next chapter because it is a multifaceted issue for DHH children.

4. *Use strategies and skills to construct meaning before, during, and after reading.* We provide numerous examples and a listing of these strategies and skills in Table 6.5.

5. *Adapt strategies that match the text and their goals.* This means that they understand different purposes of print (e.g., narrative, expository, persuasive, etc.), different forms of print (e.g., newspapers, chapter books, how-to guides), and different genres (e.g., mystery, science fiction, historical novels).

6. *Maintain task persistence.* Students who can ask structured questions about a passage read for longer periods of time and understand more than poor comprehenders (Gunn, 2008; Hirvonen, Georgiou, & Lerkkanen, 2010).

7. *Recognize the author's purpose.* This involves knowledge of purposes, forms, and genres of print mentioned in point 5.

8. *Can learn to distinguish between facts and opinions* (Dixon & Rossi, 1995).

9. *Draw logical conclusions.* This is made possible when the reader combines all of the previously mentioned skills during the reading process.

In their review of 52 data-based articles written on the topic of deafness and reading comprehension, Luckner and Handley (2008) also found a tentative and developing evidence base for five comprehension strategies:

1. explicit comprehension strategy instruction (consistent with Causal Factor 4)

2. teaching students story grammar[1] (consistent with Causal Factor 5)

[1.] The term "story grammar" may be confusing because it does not refer to the morphology or syntax foundational to a story but to the elements of title, author, setting, main characters, conflict and resolution, events, and conclusion. Some additional elements known as "events" are the initiating event, internal response, attempt, consequence, and reaction. Narrative story grammar is explained later in this chapter.

3. modified Directed Reading Thinking Activity-DRTA (Stauffer, 1969)[2] (consistent with Causal Factor 5)
4. activating background knowledge (consistent with Causal Factor 1)
5. use of well-written, high-interest texts (consistent with Causal Factor 2)

Easterbrooks and Stephenson (2008) also examined the evidence base for literacy instruction in deaf education. They identified 10 literacy strategies most commonly cited in the literature and then examined their evidence extensively. They concurred that we have very little actual evidence about what works and what does not work with DHH children. They found developing evidence for the following general categories of instruction for comprehension:

1. use of technology (consistent with Causal Factor 3)
2. metacognitive reading strategies (consistent with Causal Factors 1 and 5)
3. use of content area reading materials (consistent with Causal Factor 1)

Additionally, Shandilya (2010) found that 74 percent of teachers in oral OPTION[3] schools reported using story retellings to teach comprehension, 65 percent engaged children in answering comprehension questions, 42 percent had students act out the stories, and 39 percent incorporated sequencing activities into instruction.

We caution here that exclusion from the lists above does not mean that an instructional practice is ineffective; it simply means that we have no research in support of the practice specific to outcomes for DHH children. More research is needed in this field before we will have a clear picture of the best way to help children comprehend text.

---

[2] DRTA is a process whereby readers apply an explicit strategy containing the following sequence: introduction/what we know, prediction, prove or modify prediction, and reflect. The modified version is explained below.
[3] "OPTION schools" refers to an international network of over 50 private, oral programs for DHH children.

EVIDENCE-BASED INSTRUCTIONAL PRACTICES

We have organized the discussion of evidence-based practices here into three categories. The first is a set of general programs, practices, and approaches that have an evidence base. These are unrelated in that they do not have a unifying basis save that they are teacher-directed (Causal Factors 2 and 5). The second set of practices is associated by their focus on the visual representation of information to support children in learning to unlock the meaning of print (Causal Factor 3). The final set is composed of text comprehension strategies that children use before, during, and after reading to help them unlock the meaning inherent in the text (Causal Factor 5). Although initially taught by the teacher, the expectation is that children will incorporate these strategies independently into their repertoire for routine use before, during, and after reading.

Teacher-Directed Practices

Explicit Instruction

Explicit instruction is a systematic instructional approach that accounts for both design components and delivery components and is appropriate for use in all languages and communication modalities. There is growing evidence that explicit instruction of literacy skills provides far better outcomes than holistic approaches (e.g., whole language; Luckner & Handley, 2008). This has been reported with DHH children in the areas of phonological awareness (Beal-Alvarez, Lederberg, & Easterbrooks, 2011; Bergeron, Lederberg, Easterbrooks, Miller, & Connor, 2009; Colin, Magnan, Ecalle, & Leybaert, 2007), vocabulary instruction (Cannon, Fredrick, & Easterbrooks, 2010; Loeterman, Paul, & Donahue, 2002; Paatsch, Blamey, Sarant, & Bow, 2006), fluency (Bergeron et al., 2009; Krammer, 2007), and text comprehension (Kraemer, Kramer, Koch, Madigan, & Steely, 2001).

The Directed Reading Thinking Activity (DRTA)

DRTA (Stauffer, 1969) was developed 40 years ago as a group problem-solving approach during which children read segments of text, made predictions, and then followed a group process in challenging one another's assumptions using questioning and conversation to think critically about the reading passage (Causal Factors 1 and 5). It is useful across languages and modalities. DRTA was one of the precursors to direct, explicit instruction (see above) and the reading strategies movement (see below) popular through the 1980s and into the 1990s. One limitation of the original research (Satchwell, 1993) is that DRTA has always been examined in a "modified" context that included several other classroom practices; this problem remains in more recent reports as well. Taken from a historical perspective, we see this research as contributing to the body of work that went into the development of the concept of reading strategies; however, DRTA has not been studied separately nor investigated adequately with DHH students, and so we cannot conclude that it has a sufficient research base. It does have a strong history of successful use, support from expert opinion, and a growing evidence base across communication modalities, and it is consistent with Causal Factor 5. Additionally, the field has moved past a strict adherence to DRTA as a separate approach to its incorporation in more inclusive approaches to reading strategy instruction. Even though there is not strong research in support of DRTA with DHH students, it is a strategy that deserves further research because it encourages interaction between the text and the student's thoughts about the text in an environment of shared communication.

The Language Experience Approach

The most commonly used approach for teaching new grammar within the context of print is the *language experience approach* (LEA). Extensive information on this topic is available at http://www.gallaudet.edu/Clerc_Center/Information_and_Resources/Info_to_Go/Language_and_Literacy/Literacy_at_the_Clerc_Center/Literacy-It_All_Connects/Leading_from_Behind_Language_Experience_in_Action.html. LaSasso and Mobley (1997) found that 81 percent of the school programs they investigated identified themselves as LEA users. Shandilya (2010) reported that 65 percent of teachers in oral OPTION schools reported using experience stories in their programs. It may come as a surprise to many that there is no high-quality research supporting the effectiveness of this ubiquitous approach to language and literacy. LEAs have enjoyed such popularity that no one bothered to develop an evidence base. Much has been written about how to apply the practice (e.g., Moog, Stein, Biedenstein, & Gustus, 2003; Schleper, 2002), but as previously reported, a comprehensive examination of six university library search engines uncovered not one data-based article to provide support for this practice. Teachers and other practitioners can find newer iterations of this time-honored practice that do have an evidence base with DHH students (e.g., *Morning Message*; Wolbers, 2008). Remember, also, that lack of an evidence base does not mean something is an ineffective practice; just that it has no evidence in either direction. In fact, as we suspect with LEAs, it may be an effective practice, has the support of expert opinion, and is consistent with all five Causal Factors. Additional research-based documentation on its effectiveness is needed.

Language Experience Stories. Language experience stories are the heart of the LEA approach and typically begin with a shared experience between the teacher and students that serves as a catalyst for language and writing activities. It is appropriate across languages and modalities. These stories use natural, student-centered language, creating both "text-to-life" and "life-to-text" connections (Laurent Clerc National Deaf Education Center, n.d.). For example, a trip to the zoo or a hands-on learning activity during the school day may result in a guided lesson of recall and vocabulary development. Rangel (2000) depicted how smelling pizza in the classroom next door served as a topic for a language experience that extended from writing a letter and formulating questions to math concepts such as fractions, graphing, and how credit cards work. After a shared experience, children recount the events and the teacher records these on chart paper or a dry erase board or helps the children put their dictation onto a piece of paper. These charts or individual papers are usually accompanied by pictures. A series of experiences can be combined into a book, and students can practice the language by rereading the story to themselves or to someone at home.

Foundations for Literacy, a research-based emergent literacy curriculum developed for DHH preschoolers (Beal-Alvarez et al., 2011; Lederberg, Miller, Easterbrooks, & Connor, 2011; Bergeron et al., 2009; Easterbrooks,

Lederberg, Miller, Bergeron, & Connor, 2008), includes a weekly LEA to which daily instruction is tied. For example, while learning the sound for /ee/, students engage in a "plan, do, and recall" experience that involves planning for sliding down a slide, engaging in the actual experience, and recalling the experience following the activity as the teacher documents and expands the students' language into a language experience story. The /ee/ sound is used because it represents the squealing sound a child makes when sliding down a slide. Helms and Schleper (2000) reported on how adolescent DHH students used a cooking activity as a plan, do, and recall language experience and the various ways students used writing on their own throughout the activity, including letters, lists, and creating a story about the process.

Read-Alouds

According to the National Academy of Education's Commission on Reading (1985), "[t]he single most important activity for building the knowledge required for eventual success in reading is reading aloud to children" (p. 23). While generally thought of in the context of young children (Akamatsu & Andrews, 1993), the *read-aloud* process is also an important contributor to literacy in middle school and high school students. After the early elementary years, most students increase their vocabularies and funds of knowledge by reading. For the older student who is language delayed or reading below grade level, development of vocabulary and world knowledge become stunted. To compensate, teachers must read persistently and consistently to DHH students of all ages. Read-alouds are especially beneficial in content areas, as they allow teachers to:

- introduce students to new topics
- present those topics in an authentic context (e.g., reading passages from *A Rumor of War* to the students in preparation for a lesson on the Vietnam War)
- expose students to new vocabulary and to known vocabulary in new contexts
- present science and social studies concepts in accessible and enjoyable language (e.g., reading *The Magic School Bus Inside a Hurricane* to students in preparation for a lesson on weather)

- ask and answer questions
- clarify misunderstandings
- go beyond the information given in the book
- reinforce new vocabulary and grammar skills
- prepare students to participate in *guided free writing* activities in which they summarize what they have learned at periodic points in time through a lesson (Lang & Lewis, undated)

In addition to an available evidence base, instruction generated through read-alouds relates to most of the Causal Factors.

Narrative Story Grammar

Another organizing strategy that deserves mention is the use of story structure, also called narrative story grammar. Narrative story grammar refers to elements such as the main character, setting, problem, attempt at resolution, and resolution, all of which help in the anticipation and prediction of future story events, defined in Table 6.4. Narrative ability is an important predictor of reading comprehension ability in deaf children (Crosson & Geers, 2001), whether they use spoken or signed language. Available studies reporting results of narrative research with deaf students find it a useful tool in evaluating narrative discourse competence (Akamatsu, 1988; Griffith & Ripich, 1988; Griffith, Ripich, & Dastoli, 1990; Stoner, Easterbrooks, & Laughton, 2005; Yoshinaga-Itano, Snyder, & Mayberry, 1996). For example, DHH students who used sign language increased their recall of narrative events and their use of ASL classifiers when given the opportunity for repeated retellings (Beal-Alvarez & Easterbrooks, 2012; Morgan, 2006). Narrative skills in 8- and 9-year-old DHH students correlated significantly with speech perception, language syntax, and reading test scores (Crosson & Geers, 2001). DHH students tend to go through the same phases of narrative development, from simple sequences through focused chains to true narratives, as do students with typical levels of hearing, albeit at a slower rate (Klecan-Aker & Blondeau, 1990). Narrative instruction is based on Causal Factors 1, 4, and 5 and involves discussions of stories with teachers and peers. Although we have no research evidence for its use with DHH children, many teachers anecdotally report that they enjoy using Braidy, the Story Braid® and the

Table 6.4. *Story Grammar Elements Used in Rating Students' Narrative Productions*

Element	Description
Main Character	A minimum of three statements attributed to the protagonist. He/she must do, think, act, or feel something.
Initiating Event or Problem	The main character or second character must initiate some action sequence.
Internal Response	The main character must have a reaction (i.e., thought, idea, or feeling about the situation or event; this generally utilizes some word of emotion) *or* internal plan (i.e., a statement revealing how the main character may solve the problem). Some authors separate these two responses.
Attempt	This is some action taken by the main character to solve the problem; there may be more than one attempt before any consequence occurs.
Consequence/Outcome	This is the event that follows the attempt; there may be more than one consequence for each attempt.
Resolution/Reaction	The main character must have some resolution, feeling, or thought about the consequence.
The Overall Story Grammar Score is the total number of elements in the story out of 6 possible elements.	

Sources: Dimino, Taylor, & Gersten, 1995; Klecan-Aker & Blondeau, 1990.

Story Grammar Marker® (http://mindwingconcepts.com) programs to teach the structure of narratives. Research is needed on currently popular tools.

Making Learning a Visual Process

DHH students require visual support to help them organize what they are learning (Causal Factor 4). Visual strategies are a way to compensate for the transient nature of the auditory signal in children who struggle to hear a complete message and the visual signal in signing deaf learners who must grasp the visual content before it is gone (Luckner, Bowen, & Carter, 2001). Visual organizers promote comprehension, retention, and recall of information (Luckner et al., 2001; Stoner & Easterbrooks, 2006) and are one way to assist students in developing and capturing visual imagery surrounding a story (Schirmer, 1993). Visual organizers can be effective tools in helping DHH students increase their use of adjectives in descriptive writing (Stoner & Easterbrooks, 2006). Luckner and Handley (2008) included such organizers as webbing (semantic and concept), thematic organizers, and anticipation guides in their review of reading comprehension strategies. Additional visual means of representing information include the use of three-dimensional objects, simulations, demonstrations, pictures (Gentry, Chinn, & Moulton, 2004), and videos. The research base in this area is still sparse but is developing, and the trend is toward positive research support in favor of visual tools. Thinking maps (Hyerle, 2009) are a subtype of visual organizer that promotes higher-order, critical thinking about a topic (Causal Factor 1). Knowledge of story grammar structure (described below under text comprehension) is another form of visual organizer.

Visualization. The ability to look at words on a page and create a mental image or picture of what is transpiring is an important visual strategy for reading comprehension (Causal Factor 4). For example, if one reads the sentence "The clown drove a tiny car," the reader likely envisions a clown and car with specific features, even though these features may vary across readers. Students who struggle to read often have problems visualizing what words mean (Hibbing & Rankin-Erikson, 2003). Printed English is a sequential stimulus; deaf children can remember complex visual schemas and figures, but this skill erodes as parts are presented and remembered sequentially (Todman & Seedhouse, 1994). Paivio (2008) demonstrated that imagery is one of two types of cognitive code (i.e., visual and verbal codes). Because children must alternate between sequential and simultaneous codes as they work back and forth between word and image in developing a mental representation of text, opportunities for erosion of both codes exist. Even for the visually oriented DHH students, the ability to visualize text is a learned skill (Causal Factor 1). One program teachers may find useful is the *Visualizing and Verbalizing for Language Comprehension and Thinking* Program (Bell, 1991), as it may provide teachers with guidance in helping DHH students to develop visual imagery as a means of enhancing text comprehension.

Story Maps. Another way that teachers may scaffold text comprehension is through the use of story maps that represent thematic patterns. A story map allows the teacher to demonstrate what can be expected in a story (e.g., characters, setting, problem, resolution) and to demonstrate language patterns that are incorporated repetitively in a story (e.g., *Is Your Mama a Llama?*; Guarino, 1989). Once a child becomes familiar with a story map and its associated grammatical structures, he or she can use this knowledge as a scaffold to understand a new story with a similar theme (H. Litterst, personal communication, September 16, 2009). Starting in kindergarten, teachers might want to build a reading program around themes. In a study of teachers in oral OPTION programs (Shandilya, 2010), 71 percent reported using theme units with their young students. Instructors should teach one theme approximately every nine weeks and follow these steps:

1. Read several stories that follow a particular theme (e.g., prey/predator stories, quest stories, etc.).
2. Present a story map that goes along with the theme and demonstrate how to map a known story onto the visual organizer.
3. Read a story as a group, developing the visual organizer with the students as you go along.
4. Have students read a story independently and map the story.
5. Provide additional opportunities for students to read other stories of the same theme independently.

Each theme will have an associated visual map; students use this map as a tool for understanding the sequence of the story, developing predictions, and as a memory device.

Technology Innovations. The Institute of Education Sciences recently released a randomized, controlled trials study (considered to be the highest level of evidence available) of the effectiveness of 16 reading and math software programs (Dynarski et al., 2007). Thirty-three districts, 132 schools, and 439 teachers participated in the study. The authors found that test scores in reading and math were not significantly higher in classrooms that used software than in control classrooms. This news is both good and bad. The good news is that we have evidence that software does not take the place of a good teacher. Software is a tool for teachers to use during instruction; it is not instruction itself. The bad news is that this may cause administrators to question the cost of software. The primary benefit of software is that it saves teachers hours and hours of creating materials by hand. The evidence base demonstrating that it does much else is limited. For this reason, we must investigate whether the technology applications we use are efficient and effective; we must also understand the level of teacher support required to get the highest value added to instruction.

Locally Produced DVDs. In an effort to develop reading materials that take the needs of signing DHH students into consideration, many schools for the deaf have developed signed versions of books (Causal Factors 2, 3, and 5). These include, but are not limited to, the *Novel Signs* project at the Horace Mann School for the Deaf; *Visual Storyreading in American Sign Language* from the Kansas School for the Deaf; a series of short stories and mysteries by the Texas School for the Deaf; and the signed DVD series by the Atlanta Area School for the Deaf (AASD). The AASD materials are based on short stories at the emergent and beginning reading levels from AlphaKids (Sundance Publications: http://www.sundancepub.com) and Newbridge Publications (http://www.newbridgeonline.com). Staff and students at the school interpreted approximately 400 titles into ASL and contact sign versions (i.e., hybrid signs). Math titles used in a single subject study of vocabulary acquisition were found to be effective in helping students master math vocabulary (Cannon, Easterbrooks, & Fredrick, 2010), and repeated viewings and retelling opportunities of a subset of these stories resulted in increased classifier production for students who used ASL (Beal-Alvarez & Easterbrooks, under review). These DVDs are available from the school at no cost when providing evidence of purchase of the storybooks.

Text Comprehension Strategies

The concept of "text comprehension strategies" refers to a clearly deter-mined, top-down process of teaching readers to take responsibility for their own reading through the use of strategies that assist them in unlock-ing the meaning of phrases, sentences, and written passages.

Instructional scaffolding of text comprehension strategies permits learners to master these strategies and advance their comprehension independently (Vygotsky, 1978). Teachers help students through four phases of instructional scaffolding pertinent to text comprehension. In the first phase, the teacher engages in *modeling* while mediating through a verbal commentary. In the second phase, the student attempts to *imitate* the skill he or she saw the teacher perform, and both the teacher and stu-dent engage in commentary. During this phase, the instructor must con-stantly assess student understandings and offer frequent assistance and feedback. In the third phase, the teacher begins to *remove the scaffolding*. He offers progressively less assistance and feedback to his students as they begin to master new content and/or skills. Students are in the fourth stage when they have achieved *mastery* and can perform the new skill or strat-egy without any help from their teacher (Byrnes, 2001).

Scaffolding techniques fall along two primary continuums. The first continuum is the level of the teacher's involvement, and the second is the place in the reading process in which the teacher or child uses the scaf-fold. Along the continuum of high to low teacher involvement are model-ing of desired behaviors, explaining information, providing a tool (such as an organizer) for the child to use in order to participate, verifying and clarifying student understandings, reminding students of the scaffold and how to use it, and providing hints and cues. The teacher's goal in using scaffolding techniques is to offer just enough assistance to guide the stu-dents toward independence and self-regulation. The second continuum involves whether the teacher and child use the technique before reading, during reading, or after reading.

Teaching Reading Comprehension Strategies. The ability to comprehend text is a complex process that involves intentionally thinking about what one is reading (i.e., metacognition). Text comprehension strategies require students to think critically about what they are reading (Causal Factor 1) and to scaffold their own knowledge (Causal Factor 5). Literally dozens of strategies exist that students may apply to the process of unfolding meaning (Stebick & Dain, 2007). A growing research base points to the effectiveness of teaching text comprehension strategies to school-aged deaf children (Brown & Brewer, 1996; Ewoldt, Israelite, & Dodds, 1992), making text comprehension one of the few literacy practices with an available evidence base. Luckner and Handley (2008) reviewed the literature on comprehension strategies with DHH students and found compelling evidence for the support of the following comprehension strategies, for which we provide several examples from practicing classroom teachers:

- prediction: the use of prior knowledge to connect what the child has read to inferences about what he or she might find upon further reading (see Case Vignette 6.1)
- questioning: the use of self-questioning to make sense of unfamiliar language, implicit information, and the less tangible elements of literacy such as mood and emotions
- imagery: the activation of sensory images to create a mental "movie" of the sights, sounds, smells, tastes, and feelings conveyed by a story (see Case Vignette 6.2)
- connecting: the use of personal experiences before, during, and after reading to help the reader make a personal connection to the story that will enhance its meaning
- summarizing: the process of distilling the main ideas for the purpose of writing or retelling essential elements of a story (see Case Vignette 6.3)

Many other strategies to promote text comprehension are available. We define several of these in Table 6.5. Teachers can incorporate them into instruction one at a time until students are skilled with each practice. Teachers should monitor students' progress to document the benefits that the strategies provide to the students. Table 6.6 provides a sequence of the process of teaching reading strategies.

CASE VIGNETTE 6.1.

Ms. Helen's Prediction Activity

Ms. Helen teaches a group of preschoolers at a day school for the deaf. She is working on prediction during shared reading time using *Is Your Mama a Llama?* by Deborah Guarino. This book has a repeated pattern in which a young llama asks his animal friends if their mamas are llamas, which leads the llama to find his own mother. After reading the first few pages that present two repetitions, Ms. Helen asks her students: "Who do you think is her mama? She has flippers and eats fish." The students volunteer shark and dolphin. Ms. Helen adds, "You remember 'shark' and 'dolphin' from our aquarium trip! What other animals did we see?" The students think about their visit and shout out "snake!" and "whale!" Ms. Helen reminds the students that "We saw the man with the pail feed fish to this animal." The students enthusiastically shout "seal!" Ms. Helen replies, "You guys are right! You thought seal, and look... here is the mama seal!" as she turns the page.

CASE VIGNETTE 6.2.

Mrs. Crawford's Imagery Activity

Mrs. Crawford is an itinerant teacher who works with a group of three middle schoolers in a separate classroom for an hour a day. They are currently reading *Sarah Plain and Tall* by Patricia MacLachlan and discussing the scene when Caleb sees the buggy in the distance. "He sees dust from the wagon and a yellow bonnet. What do you think that looks like?" she asks Chanda, who replies by describing the wagon in the far distance with a huge cloud of dirt around it and a tiny bit of yellow. Mrs. Crawford asks Jeremy to expand on Chanda's image. Jeremy replies that he sees two people sitting in the front of the wagon, one with a tall black hat and the other with a yellow bonnet that is tied at the chin. "How is the wagon moving?" she asks. Lorita explains that two shiny brown horses are running in tandem and shows the image of the wagon growing as it comes toward her. "What do you think Caleb and Anna look like when they see the wagon?" Jeremy hops up and demonstrates excitement, looking off to the distance and looking back at his imaginary big sister standing next to him.

CASE VIGNETTE 6.3.

Mr. Royce's Summarizing Activity

Mr. Royce is a high school English teacher at a residential school for the deaf. His class is reading *The Pearl* by John Steinbeck through independent reading and discussion. After students read a few paragraphs describing the scene in which the scorpion falls from the rope and into the baby's bed, Mr. Royce asks the students to tell him what they think is important from the paragraphs. Daniel volunteers the difference in the position of the scorpion's tail from flat behind it to arched over its back. "Why is this detail important?" Mr. Royce asks. They discuss how this action signifies that the scorpion may hurt the baby. "What is the next important detail?" The students point out how Juana sucks the baby's wound, identifying that the baby might be poisoned from the sting. After they have reviewed the relevant details from the paragraphs, Mr. Royce asks Daniel to summarize the paragraphs. The students continue reading, identifying the important details, and summarizing sections of the story.

Table 6.5. *Common Reading Strategies*

Strategy	Description
Activating prior knowledge through brainstorm maps	This process involves drawing a primary circle with lines extending to a set of secondary circles. There are many different ways to determine what should be in the secondary circles. Consider antonyms, synonyms, literal meanings, abstract meanings, or any other way to encourage students to extend their knowledge of the primary concept.
	Point out the words they suggested as you are reading. This process occurs prior to and during reading.
Activating prior knowledge through anticipation charts	The teacher and students set a purpose for reading, make predictions, and focus on important concepts prior to reading text by answering true/false statements based on the main idea and supporting details for the text.
Prior activities	Watch a video, ask an expert, read related trade books, reference books, maps, CDs, etc.

(Continued)

Table 6.5. *(Continued)*

Discuss purpose for reading	Why are students reading the material? What are they expected to do afterward?
Discuss type of material	Is the material a textbook, narrative story, letter, recipe, instructional manual, etc.?
Develop questions about the story	Discuss questions printed at the end of chapters, if available, or create your own with or without student assistance.
Review nonprint sources of information	What can we learn from the title? Do we know anything about the author? Do we have any clues about the structure of the story? Captions? Pictures?
Use self-assessment and self-monitoring	See example in Chapter 3: Assessment
Reciprocal Questioning (ReQuest)	Teachers and students alternate asking questions about the content they are reading (Manzo, 1969).
Survey-Question-Read--Recite-Review (SQ3R)	a. Survey—Skim the pages, noticing the title, pictures, captions, headings, boldfaced or italicized words, and any other indicators that give clues to the text.
	b. Question—If there are questions at the end of the reading material, read them. If not, the teacher and students brainstorm questions that they might want to answer based on the information provided.
	c. Read—Read one section at a time, reflecting on the questions and relating what students have learned to the information they gathered before reading.
	d. Recite—Answer the questions that were generated. Get group input from other students if the student is unable to answer the questions. If possible, generate some new questions based on the information they have gathered.
	e. (Repeat c and d with each new section.)
	f. Review—After completing the text, review questions and answers for the entire text.

(Continued)

Table 6.5. *(Continued)*

Making inferences	Readers go beyond the text to access deeper meaning by creating relationships based on prediction, prior knowledge, and personal experience (Walker, Munro, & Rickards, 1998).
Discuss organization of expository text	a. Temporal sequence—describes or lists events in their order of occurrence
	b. Explanation—explains such things as causes, effects, and enabling circumstances
	c. Comparison/contrast—compares or contrasts two events or concepts
	d. Problem/solution explains the development of a problem(s) and suggests a solution(s)
	e. Process description—describes the parts of a process
	f. Classification—explains how concepts are classified
Extending knowledge	Incorporate additional related sources of information or real-life experiences into instruction and discussion with students.

Sources: Edmonds et al., 2009; McAnally, Rose, & Quigley, 1999; Miller & Veatch, 2010.

Table 6.6. *Process for Teaching a Strategy*

Step	Substeps
Choose an authentic strategy	Teach strategies that successful readers (typically hearing and DHH) use.
	Teach strategies appropriate for the student's present level of performance based on his or her instructional level on a basic reading inventory.
	Teach only one strategy at a time.
Choose authentic materials that support the strategy	Choose materials that will support the strategy.
	Choose materials that are appropriate for the individual learner.
	Choose materials from a variety of types: narratives, documents, instructions, notes, etc.

(Continued)

Table 6.5 *(Continued)*

Step	Substeps
Demonstrate use of the strategy	Orient student to the strategy and its purpose: In what context should the student apply the strategy?
	Answer questions about the strategy: What is it? How do we apply it? When do we use it? Why do we use it rather than another strategy?
	Provide a list of the steps involved in using the strategy.
	Demonstrate your thought processes as you apply the strategy: use self-talk or think aloud to model application of the strategy for students.
	Explain why you made the decisions you made.
	Review how you applied the strategy for students.
Guide use of the strategy	a. Move from direct instruction to guidance and feedback to independent use.
	b. Follow a collaborative, team, or cooperative learning model.
	c. Give students appropriate materials that will allow them to apply the strategy with ease.
	d. Guide students through the steps one at a time.
	e. Provide for immediate success.
	f. Explain, answer questions, and reinforce student applications of the strategy.
	g. Give students a second opportunity to apply the strategy with direct assistance.
	h. Give students new material that provides a good fit with the strategy and have students talk themselves through the steps (one student is the "leader" for each step; other students are active participants) with the teacher providing feedback.
	i. Ask each student to demonstrate to you how s/he has applied the strategy to a novel piece of material.
	j. Assist students in determining which strategies to apply in specific areas and types of reading materials.
	k. Help students apply strategies across the curriculum and content areas.

(Continued)

Table 6.5. *(Continued)*

Step	Substeps
Reinforce use of the strategy	Move from best fit to worst fit.
	Provide a variety of materials that have a good fit with the strategy for students to develop the strategy to an automatic level.
	Provide other materials where the fit might not be as good.
	Provide materials where the strategy might not be effective and discuss why students might choose a different strategy for this material.
Assess its use	Use assessment rubrics to document progress (ongoing progress monitoring) of the student's mastery of skills and strategies.

Sources: Gersten, Fuchs, Williams, & Baker, 2001; Luckner & Handley, 2008; Pressley, 1998.

ONGOING PROBLEM: THE READING GAP

Despite support from the emerging research base and Causal Factors available for multiple literacy practices with DHH students, teachers and practitioners may still struggle to meet the literacy needs of their students. There is incontrovertible evidence that many DHH students face what can feel like an insurmountable gap between their ability to read and the reading demands of the classroom. It is not at all unusual for a student's reading skills to lag behind the skills expected based on grade placement (Holt, Traxler, & Allen, 1997; Karchmer & Mitchell, 2003; Kyle & Harris, 2010a; Wilbur, 2000), and the ability/expectation gap increases over time (Allen, 1986; Kyle & Harris, 2010a). Information surrounding this gap that we do not have is this: What ability/expectation gap is surmountable by modifications and adaptations? At what degree of gap will it be absolutely impossible for a student to handle the reading demands of the general education classroom? As more DHH students attend general education programs, this becomes a crucial question requiring study.

SUMMARY OF RECOMMENDED PRACTICES

To be good readers, DHH students, whether they use spoken language or some form of sign language, must have explicit instruction in grammar and text comprehension skills and strategies. They must possess the characteristics of good comprehenders presented in this chapter. Effective teachers facilitate these characteristics via explicit instruction (i.e., mediation, student imitation, teacher scaffolding, and feedback) with multiple opportunities for student practice and mastery in a language-rich environment that promotes incorporation of students' personal experiences, shared classroom experiences (e.g., language experience activities, read-alouds), and visual support. Effective teachers also "think aloud" during instruction to model metacognitive strategies (e.g., prediction, questioning, imagery, connecting to personal experiences, summarizing, and visualization) so that students can experience the connection between printed text and their own comprehension of the information provided. Through modeling and explicit instruction, teachers and students can create toolboxes full of text comprehension strategies and select appropriate strategies across various reading materials.

RESOURCES

AG Bell Association: www.agbell.org
This association's online publications site lists several language curriculums, including SMILE, a multisensory curriculum for speech, language, and reading for DHH children.
Butte Publications: www.buttepublications.com
This company publishes learning materials designed specifically for DHH students and includes language and literacy materials.
Laureate Learning: www.laureatelearning.com
Cannon et al. (2010) identified that when used with teacher mediation, Laureate Learning's *Language Links* program improved DHH students' morphosyntactic skills.

Moog, J. S., Stein, K. K., Biedenstein, J. J., & Gustus, C. H. (2003). *Teaching activities for children who are deaf and hard of hearing: A practical guide for teachers*. St. Louis, MO: The Moog Center for Deaf Education. This book provides instruction in how to develop children's language, including development through language experience stories and charts.

7 Fluency

PURPOSE

In this chapter we present an overview of fluency and two approaches to fluency instruction based on the two subpopulations found within the larger DHH population. The first approach is appropriate for the 52 percent of learners who use speech only (Gallaudet Research Institute, 2008) and who express fluency through spoken language alone. Second is an approach appropriate for the 11.4 percent of learners who express fluency through sign language alone. For the remaining 36.6 percent who use some hybrid form of speech and sign, be it sign-supported speech[1] or speech-supported sign, the teacher or education practitioner should consider addressing fluency from both perspectives.

[1.] In sign-supported speech, the communicator supports his or her spoken language with signs, but the spoken language has primacy in conveying the message. In speech-supported sign, signs have primacy in conveying the message and are accompanied by the individual's best approximation of the spoken counterpart of the sign. Depending on the individual's skills and the communicative demands of the situation, a signer may use speech-supported sign in one situation and sign-supported speech in another.

The National Reading Panel (NPR) defined fluency as "… the ability to read text quickly, accurately, and with proper expression" (National Institute of Child Health and Human Development, 2000, pp. 3–5). Traditionally, educators of hearing children have measured spoken fluency by counting the number of words read out loud correctly per minute (Carnine, Silbert, Kame'enui, & Tarver, 2004). Unfortunately, fluency may be the most misunderstood skill in reading instruction (Chard & Kame'enui, 2000; NPR, 2000) because its role is unclear. Does fluency contribute to better reading outcomes or does better reading promote the ability to read fluently? Fluency does improve when the material the individual is reading is easier than when it is harder (O'Connor, Swanson, & Geraghty, 2010), but under what other conditions does it improve? We have information about how fluency correlates with different conditions, but we have no research to date on what factors might cause improved fluency in DHH children.

When a reader uses spoken language alone or in conjunction with some sign support, the traditional measure of words correct per minute may be a sufficient measure of the reader's fluency. But when the reader renders printed text in ASL or in hybrid signs, teachers should consider alternatives to a simple word count per minute. This chapter explores effective assessments and practices for the development of fluency across languages and modalities. Because there is a limited evidence base for instruction in fluency with DHH learners, effective teachers will closely follow the literature and will consider new practices carefully.

CURRENT PERSPECTIVES ON FLUENCY

To be proficient readers, students must master all of the elements of reading, including fluency. As students proceed through the grades, informational reading passages increase and narratives decrease. For example, 55 percent of eighth-grade and 70 percent of twelfth-grade reading material is informational (National Assessment Governing Board, 2008). Students are expected to read text quickly and accurately and understand the information provided on the page. Because students are expected to glean an increasing amount of content during reading as they progress through elementary grades, students must have fluent reading abilities early to succeed. At the sentence level, fluency has been associated with 60 to 80 percent of the variance (individual child differences) in skills and abilities in hearing children who are struggling to read (O'Connor, Swanson, & Geraghty, 2010).

Fluency has been called "a bridge between word recognition and comprehension" (Schirmer, Therrien, Schaffer, & Schirmer, 2009, p. 168). This summarizes the importance of fluency within the reading process and allows us to move beyond the NPR's definition above. Like the compartmentalizing of the five big pieces of reading (i.e., phonemic awareness, alphabetic principle, fluency, vocabulary, and comprehension), looking at fluency as a separate, discrete skill misses the fact that these pieces must work together seamlessly for students to be fluent readers.

DEFINITIONS

Before proceeding with a discussion of fluency as a bridge between word recognition and comprehension, we begin with a brief definition of each of the pieces that the child must learn to weave seamlessly in order to present a fluent rendering of a printed passage. By *rendering* of a story, we refer to the process of looking at the printed word and reading it face-to-face to another person, whether through spoken English, signed English, ASL, or a hybrid form of sign. *Speed* refers to how many words a student reads per minute, or how many words he or she reads correctly per minute (Carnine, Silbert, Kame'enui, & Tarver, 2004). *Accuracy* means accurate decoding and understanding of reading content at the word, phrase, sentence, and discourse levels and is assessed by *miscue analysis* (Johns, 2004). *Proper expression* may be one of the more important aspects of fluency in DHH readers and is most assuredly the least well understood. Proper expression includes not only speed and accuracy but also the component of prosody (Kuhn & Stahl, 2003; Wise et al., 2010). *Prosody* refers to the use of intonation, pitch, stress, timing, and reading of phrases rather than reading of single words. Reading phrase-by-phrase instead of word-by-word is important because meaning comes from phrases and clauses (see Chapter 6), and the ability to unlock meaning is measured while reading large blocks of text versus single sentences or words (Kuhn & Stahl, 2004; Meisinger, Bloom, & Hynd, 2010). *Automaticity* means that the student immediately recognizes words, bypassing the decoding process (Kelly, 2003). All of these elements work together to create fluency in readers using spoken language. Gregory (Case Vignette 7.1) may fall under the category of "slow word caller" (as described in Chapter 5) because he lacks prosody and automaticity of word recognition. Although he has had many years of phonics instruction that his IEP team thought would be sufficient, and although he is a very fast decoder of single words, his fluency, prosody, and comprehension are very poor.

CASE VIGNETTE 7.1.

Gregory, a Slow Word Caller

Gregory is a quiet fourth grader with a severe unilateral hearing loss who spends most of his school day with his fourth-grade peers. He uses spoken language. Because he doesn't like attention focused on him, he frequently avoids wearing his hearing aid and often slides the aid into his desk when the teacher is not looking. He has good phonological decoding skills but often reads very slowly, without expression, and has difficulty with individual word meanings. His slow word calling affects his comprehension skills. Gregory's IEP team decides that his itinerant teacher, Mrs. Ritz, will model word-learning and comprehension strategies through shared reading of books that Gregory selects from the school library during the school's daily breakfast time. Gregory brings *James and the Giant Peach* to Mrs. Ritz's class. After discussing the title, cover, and what the story might be about, Mrs. Ritz begins reading the first paragraph. "Guardians. Hmm. I wonder what that word means. It says James lives with his aunts and they are his guardians." Through discussion, Mrs. Ritz and Gregory agree that "guardians" must be similar to people who take care of James. "How do you know?" Mrs. Ritz asks Gregory. "Because it said his parents are dead," he replies. Mrs. Ritz and Gregory continue reading the book every day, alternating turns and discussing vocabulary. Mrs. Ritz continues to model thinking-aloud strategies, using contextual clues and discussion to decipher new vocabulary words and the plot of the story. When Gregory finishes a paragraph, Mrs. Ritz asks, "Were there any words you weren't sure about?" After they discuss these words using the surrounding words in the sentence and thinking aloud, Mrs. Ritz prompts him to retell what he read in his own words.

RELATION TO LANGUAGF

While fluency skills are somewhat dependent upon decoding skills, they are equally dependent on a student's underlying knowledge and use of the grammar of language. Printed words, phrases, and sentences represent language. If a child does not understand the language he is reading, then his fluency is seriously limited. Therefore, fluency is a language skill, not just a skill of decoding speed. Manual coding of English does not necessarily unlock fluency. Deaf children do not learn signed English systems as easily as hearing children learn spoken languages (Livingston, 1983; Schick & Moeller, 1992; Supalla, 1991). Even with consistent signed English input, many deaf children make numerous errors in English syntax, have vocabularies that are smaller than their hearing peers, and demonstrate a "high degree of variability in their ability to use the bound morphology of English" (Schick, 2003, p. 122).

Recall the discussion in Chapter 6 of sentence parsing. Sentence parsing is dependent upon the way the child carves meaning from the words on the page. Consider this string of words that one of the authors learned when she was in sixth-grade English class. Punctuation is intentionally left out to make our point: *John where Tom had had had had had had had had had had had the teacher's approval.* Read it out loud. Now read it again and try to punctuate it in a manner that makes sense. The words are easy enough to read. One can read it word for word, much like a word caller would do, and one can even learn to read it quickly (17 easy words in 5 or 6 quick seconds!), but that does not mean that it will make sense. This simulates what reading might feel like to the word caller or the poor sentence parser. The following scenario will assist in proper parsing. Imagine that an English teacher is looking at a paper that John wrote and a paper that Tom wrote. Both students wrote about the same topic. In one location, John chose to use the past perfect tense and so he wrote "had had"; however, Tom chose to use the simple past tense and so he wrote "had." With the background relationship and the grammar explained, sentence parsing and, hence, fluency improve. Here is the sentence again with punctuation to guide the reader in fluent parsing of the example: *John, where Tom had had "had," had had "had had." "Had had"*

had had the teacher's approval. Fluency, then, is not only the fast rendering of words but also the meaningful organization of those words by phrasal relationship.

MEMORY PROCESSING AND AUTOMATICITY

Reading is a complex process that can exceed a child's processing, organization, and memory skills rapidly. Imagine someone is cleaning a garage. First he must open all of the drawers and cabinets to see where everything goes. He opens and shuts, moves things around, sorts and stacks, put things here and there. Readers engage in a similar process. Reading requires one to access and use mentally stored words and meanings (from various cabinets and drawers in our memory) and connect them to prior knowledge (drawers of older stuff), combine it all together (sort and stack), and then draw an inference about the passage. Not only must the reader access and process words, but he must also coordinate these processes within a limited time frame to maintain the message gleaned from the text (Kuhn, Schwanenflugel, & Meisinger, 2010). Students must be able to allocate attention to the individual components of reading while saving enough attention to decipher the meaning of unknown words and sentences within the reading passage. If too much attention is spent on lower-level reading skills such as decoding words or parsing phrases, then fluency and comprehension will suffer. This is why teachers strive for their students to develop basic decoding at the level of automaticity. Once a student can recognize words automatically, the decoding process is no longer a conscious focus during reading. A lack of conscious awareness of decoding words differentiates fluent readers from dysfluent readers (Logan, 1997). Students who read word-for-word instead of reading with proper expression overburden their memory capacities and struggle to make sense of what they have read (LaBerge & Samuels, 1974). In contrast, improving lower-level skills (e.g., letter–sound relationships) frees more attention to focus on higher-level skills, such as forming images from text for comprehension (O'Connor et al., 2010). In addition to divisions of his attention, the student must also monitor his overall reading process through multiple components of metacognition (i.e., knowing when he comprehends; knowing what he comprehends; knowing what else he needs to acquire to comprehend; and knowing how to use strategies to aid comprehension; Schirmer & McGough, 2005) to assess his understanding of the text and identify when comprehension breaks down. Clearly, reading is a complex challenge for all learners.

PROSODY

Recent research into the role of prosody (i.e., expression) in reading suggests that it plays a key role in fluency and therefore comprehension (Daane, Campbell, Grigg, Goodman, & Oranje, 2005; Hudson, Lane, & Pullen, 2005). Some researchers have shown that prosody had a causal effect on reading comprehension (i.e., correct expression leads to reading comprehension) in some hearing children (Reutzel & Hollingsworth, 1993), while others argued that the relationship between prosody and reading comprehension is bidirectional (i.e., prosody and reading comprehension are intertwined; Klauda & Guthrie, 2008). Members of the *National Assessment of Education Progress* created an assessment scale for fluency that took earlier definitions of speed and accuracy to a new level, reframing assessment to include grammar (Daane et al., 2005). For example, fluent readers in this rating scale were expected to read in meaningful phrase groups with few repetitions, preserve the syntax of the sentence, and read with expression. In addition, Hudson et al. (2005) suggested a rating system that includes an examination of prosody in fluent reading. In this rating, students were expected, for example, to use vocal emphasis and a rising and falling tone of voice, to include correct expression for a character's mental states (e.g., excitement, fear), and to honor syntactic boundaries such as phrasing, subject–verb divisions, and conjunctions. Taken together, these two scales provide a more complete understanding of what is involved in presenting a fluent rendering of text. One obvious outcome of this broader definition is that we must assess and then teach fluency through expressive reading and not through silent reading (Hasbrouck, 2006).

RESEARCH ON FLUENCY IN HEARING CHILDREN

Based on research with hearing children, fluency problems can occur alone or in combination with other issues. Recall the discussion of word callers in Chapter 5. Struggling readers can read 12 to 45 words per minute in second grade and 20 to 80 words per minute in fourth grade (O'Connor et al., 2010). Good readers in fourth grade read about three times more words per minute than poor readers (Jenkins, Fuchs, van den Broek, Espin, & Deno, 2003a). Poor readers' fluency rate grows at about half the rate of average readers (Speece & Richey, 2005), and the gap between good and poor readers widens with grade level (O'Connor et al., 2010). However, struggles with reading fluency are not related to specific ages (Meisinger et al., 2010). Laborious reading rates contribute to an overload in working memory, leaving the child with little attention for the creation of meaning from the reading passage, let alone for the integration of ideas across paragraphs within a reading passage (O'Connor et al., 2010).

The components of fluency, speed, accuracy, and automaticity are positively correlated with reading comprehension for hearing children (Jenkins et al., 2003a; Jenkins, Fuchs, van den Broek, Espin, & Deno, 2003b; Swanson & Howell, 2001; Wise et al., 2010), and dysfluent reading is a predictor of poor reading comprehension (Hudson et al., 2005; Stanovich, 1986; Meisinger et al., 2010). Of these components, automaticity of word identification is the largest contributor to reading comprehension (Kuhn & Stahl, 2003), allowing students to focus on the meanings of words instead of the decoding and identification of words (Therrien, 2004). Of course, without accurate word identification, comprehension is impossible, but accuracy alone is not enough to yield reading comprehension (Wise et al., 2010). If a child can "word call" every word on a page, she still may have no idea what she just read (Albertini & Mayer, 2011). Even after accounting for accurate word reading, fluency makes unique contributions to comprehension (Jenkins et al., 2003a; Meisinger, Schwanenflugel, & Woo, 2009). Direct instruction in fluency resulted in reading comprehension improvements for many poor readers (Mercer, Campbell, Miller, Mercer, & Lane, 2000). However, improvements in reading fluency are more difficult to obtain than improvements in decoding, word identification skills, and comprehension (Lyon &

Moats, 1997; Meyer & Felton, 1999; Torgesen, Rashotte, & Alexander, 2001). Again, the relationship between fluency and reading comprehension is unclear. Is it unidirectional, in that fluency leads to reading comprehension, or bidirectional, in that fluency and reading comprehension are inseparable? The important point to consider is that once a reader has mastered basic reading skills, effective teachers do not just stop instruction; they continue encouraging the student to become a highly fluent and expressive reader because that leads to increased interest in what is being read and increased comprehension, and thus to increased ability to learn from print.

RESEARCH ON FLUENCY IN DHH CHILDREN

Many factors influence the fluency of DHH readers. These include but are not limited to the reader's ability to reread, substitute a familiar word for an unfamiliar word, and check it against context clues for correct meaning; activate prior knowledge; create inferences for understanding the text; use prior experience as a reference; translate text to sign; create mental imagery and visualize the text; and make personal connections with the text based on personal interest (Banner & Wang, 2010). Naturally, DHH students vary in these factors and their resulting abilities to read fluently.

DHH children appear to have greater difficulty making gains in fluency in comparison to other areas of literacy (Charlesworth, Charlesworth, Raban, & Rickards, 2006). This is important to take into consideration, especially when we know that fluent renderings of English print correlated with reading comprehension in middle-school-aged DHH children (Easterbrooks & Huston, 2008). Again, we are still unclear as to whether fluent rendering of a reading passage causes better reading comprehension, if better comprehension allows the student to read more fluently, or if there is a bidirectional relationship.

DHH students frequently have impoverished vocabularies when compared to their hearing peers, resulting in fewer familiar words from which to pull when reading text. Without automatic word recognition, students must give more mental attention to decoding and deciphering the meanings of individual words, instead of complete chunks of meaningful text

(Moores & Meadow-Orlans, 1990). DHH readers, whether they use signs, speech, or a combination of both, may also substitute familiar words for unknown words, which may work in the case of synonyms (e.g., I was sleepy/tired) but not for orthographically similar words (e.g., I was tried/ tired) (Banner & Wang, 2010). If a student lacks the metacognitive skills to realize that a chosen substitution doesn't make sense within the context of the sentence, comprehension breakdowns are not repaired. Recall the example of "poked the car" versus "parked the car" in Chapter 5. In contrast, those students who successfully substitute a semantically equivalent word for an unknown word use a minimal amount of attention for decoding, leaving more attention for comprehension and better fluency.

ASSESSING FLUENCY

Fluency is measured by oral reading in most children, hearing or deaf. When a child has access to sound, it makes sense to use the tools and strategies that we use with hearing children, with modifications as needed. When the child does not have access, alternative forms of assessment are needed. Fluency can also be measured for DHH children who render text in sign language (Easterbrooks & Huston, 2008) and for the large portion of the population who uses speech and signs in combination. Variation within reading styles of DHH students makes it necessary for teachers to consider a variety of options for adequate assessment.

ASSESSING FLUENCY IN CHILDREN WHO USE SPOKEN LANGUAGE

Because even children who use their listening skills well may struggle with the fluency tasks that are assessed through traditional spoken language means (Geers, 2003; Geers, Tobey, Moog, & Brenner, 2008), the effective teacher should consider a three-pronged approach to assessment: assessing fluent rendering of grammar, assessing fluent use of prosody, and words correct per minute (WCPM) (see Hasbrouck & Tindal, 2006). Taken together, these assessment categories and their associated tools and checklists will give the teacher of children who rely on spoken language, with or without signs, a clear picture of the components that are causing a child to struggle to gain fluency. The teacher might also consider the graduated rubric found in basic reading inventories used in the local schools, which provides 1–4 Likert-type scales across rate, expression, phrasing, and punctuation. DHH students who use spoken language tend to omit some words and change word endings (e.g., -ing, -ed, etc.) during reading. These errors are usually identified during the assessment process of miscue analysis (discussed in Chapter 3), but the teacher may want to note these omissions within the context of a fluency rating, as they influence the student's fluency as well as overall comprehension.

For hearing second graders, real-world oral fluency measures, as opposed to nonsense words or connected text, most strongly related to reading comprehension, and the relationship was stronger for those students with better oral reading fluency skills (Wise et al., 2010). However, Meisinger and colleagues (2010) reported that student identification of single, isolated words did not identify students' difficulty with reading fluency for 24 percent of their students with reading disabilities. Therefore, an additional format for assessing oral fluency is through the use of monthly running records, such as those found in *Running Records for Classroom Teachers* (Clay, 2000) or the *Basic Reading Inventory* (Johns, 2008) described previously in Chapter 3. Another format for assessing fluency that is used with both hearing and deaf students is the use of a maze. A maze involves deletion of every sixth or seventh word within a reading passage, with three options presented from which the child must pick the correct word (L. S. Fuchs, Fuchs, Hosp, & Jenkins, 2001b). Mazes are included in several computer-based assessments commonly used with hearing children (e.g., Pearson's AIMSweb) and are easily accessible, as computers and the Internet are a driving force in various areas of education in the 21st century.

ASSESSING FLUENCY IN CHILDREN WHO USE SIGN LANGUAGE

For students who use sign language, with or without speech, reading fluency involves the automatic rendering of print into signed form

(Chrosniak, 1993). Although many of the children in local school systems will have some access to sound (Easterbrooks, Lederberg, Miller, Bergeron, & Connor, 2008), the 11 percent of sign-only users in local schools and schools for the deaf will need an alternative to a spoken rendering of fluent reading because they are reading one language (e.g., printed English) and rendering it face-to-face in another language (i.e., ASL or signed English). When a child does not have fluent verbal speech, we cannot reliably assess fluency through spoken means alone. Fluency is related to students' abilities to read above the third-grade level, so teachers must address this skill with their DHH students.

We assess the fluency of a child who primarily uses sign language, with or without speech, differently from a child who primarily uses spoken language, with or without sign. Timed measures of fluency are an invalid tool because the rate of simultaneous articulation of signs and spoken words is "nearly double the rate of articulation … when the two languages [ASL and English] are produced separately" (Bellugi & Fischer, 1972, p. 198). Further, there is a mismatch between word length when saying or signing English words because signed English "requires separate signs for morphological markers, making words longer via more components than their spoken versions (ex: cats v. cat+s)" (Wilbur, 2000, p. 98). Therefore, fluency assessments that focus on words per minute are an inappropriate measure of a signing student's reading fluency.

Having the child sign graded word lists is also a problem because many words beyond (or even within) the Dolch word list level have no equivalents in sign (e.g., the fourth-grade word *essential* could be signed as "important" or "must"; *shabby* could be signed as "messy" or "old"). Often children will fingerspell these words, but that gives the teacher no information as to whether or not the child understands what he or she is fingerspelling (and is a reason that teachers should use multiple assessments of a student's reading fluency). In an effort to remedy these issues, Rose, McAnally, Barkmeier, Vernig, and Long (2006) developed a process for rating silent fluent reading of DHH students. They developed the *Test of Silent Word Reading Fluency* (Pro-Ed, Inc.) to assess the general reading ability of struggling readers ages 6 years 6 months to 17 years 11 months. Students are presented with rows of contiguous text (i.e., no spaces in between the words) for a period of three minutes and must insert slash lines within the text to identify separate words. Students' raw scores are converted to standard scores using the manual. This assessment can also be used to monitor reading progress. Rose and colleagues found that this fluency tool correlated with reading comprehension scores, providing additional support for the importance of addressing fluency in DHH readers who use sign language in some manner. Assessing silent reading is an alternative to assessing spoken or signed face-to-face fluency. However, no research has been conducted yet on whether silent fluent reading or face-to-face fluent reading has better predictive value with DHH children or if either type has predictive value at all. Research is needed to determine which measure or combination of measures is more effective with which child; that is, when we should use face-to-face fluency assessment, when we should use silent fluent reading, and whether one process is more appropriate depending on whether the child uses spoken English, a signed form of English, or ASL.

One way we might measure reading fluency in signing deaf children who use English signs, ASL signs, or a combination thereof is to conduct a miscue analysis, which is a process to determine the errors a child makes while reading that limit his or her fluency. To conduct a miscue analysis with DHH students, teachers should videotape the students' performances on running records, paying attention to the various ways they incorporate signing into their rendering of print. For example, students may incorporate fingerspelling when they come across unknown words (Chaleff & Ritter, 2001). Deaf college students with reading levels at the fourth- to eighth-grade level sometimes attempted to translate what they thought words meant as opposed to signing the actual words on the page (Albertini & Mayer, 2011). When a student presents a sign that represents multiple words, such as the sign for "cook" or "kitchen," the teacher or education practitioner may need to review the videotaped reading to determine if the student presented the mouth movement for the correct English word as a measure of fluency. Gennaoui and Chaleff (2000) added the following categories to miscue analysis when analyzing the reading of DHH students: word segmentation (e.g., signing familiar, smaller words within larger, unfamiliar words, such as "close" for the word "closet"), initialization (e.g., the student signs only the first letter of a word in lieu of the correct sign or correctly indicates a name sign), sign choice (e.g., conceptual accuracy), phrase chunking (e.g., presenting one sign for a phrase, such as "wake up"), and insertions (e.g., adding "girl" after signing "she"). Teachers might incorporate these areas when conducting a miscue analysis with their signing students.

For a complete picture of both reading fluency and comprehension, teachers should ask students to retell the reading passage upon completion of the running record. They should include a discussion of the miscue analysis errors students make in their signed renderings (Luft, 2009). Case Vignette 7.2 presents how one teacher used miscue analysis and running records with his students. Case Vignette 7.3 describes the experiences of a struggling word caller whose lack of experience has caused him to exhibit poor decoding and fluency skills but with evidence of good comprehension.

CASE VIGNETTE 7.2.

Use of a Running Record for Data Collection, Miscue Analysis, and Instruction

Mr. Porter, a resource teacher for DHH students at the elementary level, gave a reading fluency measure to two of his students: Nicole, a third-grade student with a severe hearing loss who just transferred into the school district and uses spoken language, and Amber, a fourth-grade student who uses a combination of speech and sign while reading.

Nicole is 10 years of age, and Mr. Porter knows very little of her reading abilities, so he began with a primer-level reading passage and sequentially selected harder reading passages as she mastered easier passages. Nicole read the presented passages and answered the accompanying comprehension questions. Mr. Porter used the running record form to note when Nicole made word errors, substitutions, and hesitated at unfamiliar words. He noticed that Nicole had difficulty with phrasing, often substituting words of similar print form for words with multiple meanings. Mr. Porter scored the running record and comprehension questions and determined Nicole's independent and instructional reading levels. Mr. Porter also selected some of the phrases with which Nicole had difficulty for future instruction and supplemented these with

(Continued)

(Continued)

subsets of words with multiple meanings. Finally, Mr. Porter used her running record results to select reading materials that matched Nicole's instructional level to guide his instruction.

To guide Amber's reading instruction, Mr. Porter decided to use miscue analysis. After Amber selected a reading passage on her reading level and agreed to be videotaped, she read the passage independently using sign and voice. After school, Mr. Porter typed the reading passage and left enough space between the lines to make comments on Amber's sign and voice choices as he watched Amber's reading video. The following chart is Mr. Porter's miscue analysis of Amber's reading. Listed in the left column are words for which Amber made errors. Immediately to the right are the descriptions of Amber's errors for words in the text.

Word	Omission	Substitution	Finger-spelled; Appropriate?	Repetition	Self-corrected	Comments
scare		cars			no	
stairway		stair, way (initialized)			no	focus on conceptual phrasing
should		shoulder			yes	
jumped	-ed, out				no	focus on conceptual phrasing and past-tense marker
was			yes			
dare			no			
wouldn't	n't				no	focus on contractions

Based on her errors, Mr. Porter decides to first focus on conceptual phrasing and word endings, such as tense markers and contractions, during reading instruction. The use of frequent miscue analysis guides his instruction based on Amber's reading needs and documents the effects of his instruction across time.

CASE VIGNETTE 7.3.

Makouika, a Struggling Word Caller with Poor Fluency Skills

Makouika is an 11-year-old student with a moderately severe hearing loss who recently immigrated to the United States. His parents do not use spoken English in the home, and he did not attend school in his former war-torn country. He has been at the school for the deaf for one year and is still struggling with the challenge of making sense out of the sounds he is receiving through the hearing aids he acquired only six months ago. Consequently, his decoding skills are very poor, and he has limited vocabulary and grammar in both spoken and signed modes of English and his home language. These limitations result in lower scores on all measures of fluency. One bright spot in his profile is that he is learning lexical items (nouns, verbs, adjectives, adverbs) at a rapid pace even though his functional vocabulary (articles, connectors, prepositions) is severely limited. His teacher, Mrs. Reeves, has to provide him with only limited exposure to a word and he grasps the meaning. This has caused her to suspect that Makouika is a struggling word caller who may have the potential to improve his reading comprehension fairly rapidly. For this reason she pairs him with a younger student, Carlos, who has a better vocabulary than Makouika but not necessarily for his age. She has assigned them to watch DVDs of signed stories from the AlphaKids series, alternating between their instructional and independent levels as measured by the BRI (Johns, 2008). In this manner, Carlos has the opportunity to receive repeated viewings, Makouika acts out various explanations, and Carlos provides new vocabulary to Makouika, who rapidly integrates these words into his lexicon.

Another option for students who read text through sign language is the *Signed Reading Fluency Rubric for Deaf Children* (Easterbrooks & Huston, 2008), a rubric for assessing the fluency of signed renderings of stories (referred to hereafter as the *Signed Fluency Rubric*). In a study of 29 middle-school-aged delayed DHH readers, Easterbrooks and Huston identified a positive correlation between students' signed reading fluency and their comprehension of reading passages. We will explain this assessment in detail in the next section, as it also has implications for instruction. Signed reading fluency is defined as containing three components: accuracy, fluency envelope, and visual grammar. *Accuracy* is "the ability of the signer to render the concepts in English print text into a signed format that has equivalent conceptual meaning" (Easterbrooks & Huston, 2008, p. 42). The *fluency envelope* is "the overall visual appearance of an individual who is signing while reading, with or without voice, which gives the visual impression that he or she is a good reader or not a good reader" (Easterbrooks & Huston, 2008, p. 42). Fluency envelope includes those elements of visual prosody that convey mood (emotional state), intention (purpose or end goal), and affect (feeling), conveying the pragmatic (contextually appropriate) aspects of literacy. Prosody is often demonstrated by the temporal relationship, or the smooth production of handshapes, movements, and locations within a sign (Morgan, 2006b). The traits associated with fluency envelope are speed, facial expression, body movement, sign space, sign movement, and fingerspelling. *Visual grammar* refers to "key elements of signing, whether in an English-like mode or ASL, which demonstrate to the observer that the reader is visualizing the meaning of the story, conveying syntactic aspects of literacy" (Easterbrooks & Huston, 2008, p. 42). The traits associated with visual grammar are use of space, role taking, eye gaze, negation, directionality, use of classifiers, and pronominalization. Visual grammar is an important feature of a signed reading fluency examination because signing deaf children render printed English into visual grammar along a continuum of more English-like signing to more ASL-like signing. This provides a commonality with measures of spoken English grammar fluency. See Table 7.1 for a description of each of the 13 indicators included in the Signed Fluency Rubric.

The rubric in Table 7.2 is designed to provide a qualitative review of a signing child's fluency rather than a quantitative view. In order to administer this fluency assessment, the teacher chooses a reading passage that is at the student's independent reading level, as measured by a reading inventory (e.g., Johns' BRI, 2008). It is important to use reading material at the first achieved independent level to prevent the possibility that comprehension issues overshadow a student's fluency skills. The teacher videotapes the student as he or she reads the story and reviews it as many times as needed to fill in the assessment rubric. Case Vignette 7.4 explains how Mrs. Cortez used the Signed Fluency Rubric to collect fluency data with her students.

Table 7.1. *Guiding Questions Defining Fluency Rubric Aspects*

Terminology	Definition
Fluency envelope	
Speed	Does the student's speed of signing enhance or detract from the visual presentation of meaning?
Facial expression	Do the student's facial expressions match the affect of the characters and mood of the text?
Body movement	Do the student's body movements give a clear picture of the movements of the people, places, and things in the text?
Sign space	Does the student's sign space accurately represent the mood and content of the text—neither too small nor too large?
Sign movement	Does the student produce signs on the hands in a steady, relaxed, smooth manner that provides a fluid, flowing picture that enhances visualization of the story?
Fingerspelling	Does the student incorporate fingerspelling intelligibly, accurately, and appropriately? Note: Fingerspelling used as a placeholder is counted as a miscue.
Visual grammar	
Use of space	Does the student set up the scene spatially in a logical manner and then use this space when reading "aloud"?
Role taking	Does the student demonstrate relationships of the characters in space as well as interactions among characters?
Eye gaze	Does the student's eye gaze represent that which would be associated with the people, places, and things in the text?
Negation	Does the student use headshake and/or body language to indicate negation?
Directionality	Does the student move signs in a manner that presents an accurate picture of the actions within the story?
Use of classifiers	Does the student use classifiers accurately and appropriately for the text?
Pronominalization	Does the student relate pronouns to people, places, and things using appropriate forms such as indexing? (This is not an examination of invented English signs for he, she, them, their, etc., but an examination of visual grammar.)

Source: Easterbrooks & Huston, 2008, p. 43.

Table 7.2. *Signed Reading Fluency Rubric for Deaf Children*

Huston and Easterbooks

Reader's Name: DOB: Date of Tape:

Evaluator: CA: Date Tape Analyzed:

PART I FLUENCY ENVELOPE

To analyze *fluency envelope*, videotape the student reading a narrative text at his/her independent reading level and rate the performance using the rubric below. List points for each trait in the far right column. Calculate total points and indicate rating using the scale below the rubric.

General Description of Column	Not Observed (0)	Emerging (1)	Beginning (2)	Developing (3)	Mature/Fluent (4)	Points for row
		Poor attempts; laden with problems of clarity, correctness, and consistency	**Fair attempts; problems with clarity, correctness, and consistency**	**Clear attempts; may be incorrect or inconsistent**	**Clear, correct, consistent**	
Speed	Meaning unintelligible due to speed (too slow/fast)	Too slow/fast; some text meaning may be obscured due to inappropriate speed	Attempts to vary speed based on story content; most signs not obscured by speed	Speed of signing usually matches story content and does not impact intelligibility	Speed of signing consistently fits story context	
Facial expression	No affect or expression associated with story	Used as personal response, not to convey information to others	Attempts made to relate facial expression to text; may be stilled	Attempts are appropriate but may be inconsistent	Appropriate, consistent facial expression conveys content	

Body movement	No body movement associated with story	Attempts are made but are not related to the story well	Attempts are fair; some may interfere with flow of story	Good use of body movement; usually conveys content	Clear, correct, and consistent use of trait to convey content
Sign space	No awareness of sign space	Attempts are made but are inaccurate	Attempts are fair; trait interferes with story flow	Good use of space; minor errors	Sign space used accurately at all times
Sign movement	Story unintelligible due to bouncy/ stiff/jerky sign movement	Poor control; signs are primarily bouncy/stiff/jerky	Attempts to control; inappropriate movement interferes with story flow	Presentation is steady/relaxed/ smooth	Consistently steady/relaxed/ smooth with appropriate follow
Fingerspelling	Unintelligible; consistently inappropriate placement	Poor placement and control (stiff/ bouncy/jerky)	Some problems with fingerspelling placement and fluency	Primarily appropriate placement and minimal problems with fluency	Consistently appropriate placement; consistently intelligible and fluid (relaxed/ steady/smooth)

Points earned/Points possible ___ /**24** = ___ %

Fluency Envelope Rating _____

Fluency Envelope Rubric Analysis: Poor = 0%–24%; Emerging = 25%–49%; Beginning = 50%–74%; Developing = 75%–90%; Mature = 90%–100%

(continued)

Table 7.2. (Continued)

PART II VISUAL GRAMMAR

Videotape the student reading a narrative text. To analyze syntactic aspects, watch tape and rate student performance using the rubric below. List points for each trait in the right-hand column. Calculate total points and indicate rating using the scale below the rubric.

Aspect observed	Not observed (0)	Emerging (1)	Beginning (2)	Developing (3)	Mature/Fluent (4)	Points for row
Used of space	No indication of spatial awareness; people, places, and things are "layered" or randomly organized	Minimal use of space; a few people, places, and/or things are logically placed	Logical use of space is evident during only 50 percent of the read-aloud	People, places, and/ or things are placed appropriately during most of the read–aloud; makes a picture most of the time	Placement of people, places, and/or things shows evidence of reader's consistent visualization of text	
Role taking	No character interactions are identifiable	Minimal character interactions are evident through role shift	At least 50 percent of character interactions are evident through role shift	The majority of character interactions are evident through role shift	All characters are clearly and easily identifiable due to appropriate body shift/role taking	
Eye gaze	None evident; shows no evidence of text visualization	Evident during less than 30 percent of appropriate instances	Clear and appropriate during at least 50 percent of the reading	Present during most of the text rendering; promotes viewer visualization of text	Consistently appropriate and promotes visualization throughout the text	

Category				
Negation	No appropriate negative headshake observed	Present in less than 30 percent of appropriate instances	Present in at least 50 percent of appropriate instances	Present in most instances, but not all	Present in all appropriate instances
Directionality	No directionality indicated for any signs	Observed in less than 30 percent of appropriate instances	Present in at least 50 percent of appropriate instances; uses directionality inherent in sign but not between signs	Present in most instances, but not all	Directionality of signs is clear and consistent throughout the text; observer can visualize action
Use of classifiers	No use of classifiers	Minimal use of classifiers (one to two instances)	Uses classifiers in approximately 50 percent of allowable instances (for animal movements, etc)	Uses classifiers to represent concepts most of the time	Uses classifiers accurately to portray text content and support visualization
Pronominalization	No use of indexing for pronouns	Use of indexing for pronouns is unclear or minimally present	Use of indexing for pronouns is present and clear during at least 50 percent of appropriate opportunities	Use of indexing for pronouns is present and reference is clear in most appropriate instances	Use of indexing is used consistently in all appropriate opportunities and reference is clear

Points earned/Points possible _____/28 = _____ percent

Visual Grammar Rating _____

Visual Grammar Rubric Analysis: Poor = 0%–24%; Emerging = 25%–49%; Beginning = 50%–74% Developing = 75%–90%; Mature = 90%–100%

CASE VIGNETTE 7.4.

Use of the Signed Reading Fluency Rubric for Deaf Children to Determine Instructional Goals

Mrs. Cortez works on reading assessment with Vera and Anderson. Because they use varying amounts of sign language, she wants to see how well they are code-switching from English to ASL during the reading process. She uses the Signed Reading Fluency Rubric as her assessment. She chooses a book that is on each child's independent reading level and sets up her video camera because she will want to watch the children's renderings of the story several times. She gives *Snake's Dinner* to Vera and *Washing Our Dog* to Anderson because they match the children's independent reading levels. She allows them to look at the pictures in the books and ask general questions about the pictures. Next, she videotapes each child reading in sign to the camera. After school that day, with a copy of the Signed Reading Fluency Rubric in hand, she views each student's videotaped reading and compares the performance on the video to indicators on the rubric. She discovers that Vera has good use of space, facial expression, and body movement but uses no classifiers when their appropriate use is indicated in the story and has choppy sign movements and fingerspelling. Anderson has good sign speed, good body movement, and clear fingerspelling but shows no facial expression or classifiers when reading his story. Because both children are at the beginning level on many indicators, Mrs. Cortez decides to focus instruction on fluid sign movement and fingerspelling for Vera, appropriate facial expression for Anderson, and use of classifiers for both students.

Based on the combination of issues referenced above, teachers and other education practitioners will want to consider assessing reading fluency through multiple means to guide instruction. The use of only one measure may result in misleading conclusions regarding students' instructional needs (Meisinger et al., 2010).

INSTRUCTIONAL PRACTICES FOR TEACHING FLUENCY

We present the information in this section in three segments. The first segment addresses general fluency instruction practices for all students, whether users of spoken English, a signed version of English, or ASL. The second segment focuses on children with access to auditory information, whether English signers or those using spoken language. The third segment focuses on children who primarily use ASL because they do not have access to sound. Recall from Chapter 1 that a Causal Factor is a good teaching practice that causes positive learning outcomes but is not necessarily a method or material. If direct evidence from research is not available on a curriculum or strategy, then an alternative for evaluating that curriculum or strategy is to decide if positive Causal Factors are inherent in the product or practice. Good teaching practices that correlate with positive learning outcomes are 1) promotion of higher-order language and critical thinking; 2) a good match between teacher/child communication; 3) visual representation of ideas, concepts, and processes; 4) explicit instruction; and 5) scaffolding and mediation by a more knowledgeable person.

GENERAL FLUENCY INSTRUCTION PRACTICES FOR ALL STUDENTS

Time on Task. To develop reading fluency, students must master the individual skills that underlie fluency, including word decoding and recognition (Meisinger et al., 2010). Teachers who frequently read textbooks to students provide a fluent model, but they must also provide time for students to interact with text on their own (Ogle & Correa-Kovtun, 2010). Students need multiple opportunities to read if they are going to learn to read; evidence is clear that students do not have enough actual face time with books (Limbrick, McNaughton, & Clay, 1992). In fact, teachers may overestimate how much time they devote to reading instruction. In an investigation of 24 DHH students across 17 teachers in multiple service options within multiple schools, Donne and Zigmond (2008) found that teachers, on average, reported spending 103 minutes in reading instruction daily; in reality they spent 77 minutes daily during which the students spent only 15.9 percent of that time (12.3 minutes) actually reading, silently or aloud.

Indeed, it is conventional wisdom that "the more we read, the better we read." If this is true for hearing students (Taylor, Frye, & Maruyama,

1990), then we must consider its importance for DHH students. They also must have ample face time with connected text to practice these skills in an integrated, not isolated, manner to generalize both decoding and fluency skills. Krammer (2007) provided support for the importance of time spent reading when she compared hearing ($N = 10$), hard-of-hearing ($N = 5$), and deaf ($N = 5$) students' improvement in fluency under two conditions (i.e., repeated readings, described below, and listening to or watching a story). Although preliminary, results indicated improvement in fluency from pre- to post-testing but no differences between conditions, thus indicating that sheer time spent on reading was important, no matter the intervention. A drawback of this study was the low number of participants and the need for replication with sufficient numbers to demonstrate adequate power.

Repeated Readings. Related to time on task, the process of repeated readings shows favorable results (Chard, Vaughn, & Tyler, 2002; Dowhower, 1987; Samuels, 1979; Speece & Ritchey, 2005; Therrien, 2004). Repeated reading is an instructional strategy in which a student reads the same passage multiple times with teacher feedback after each reading until specified reading rates and accuracy levels are achieved by the student (Samuels, 1979; Rasinski & Padak, 2008; Wolf & Katzir-Cohen, 2001). Accuracy rates of 93–97 percent are a guideline for fluency within repeated readings (Burns, 2002). As automaticity of word identification increases, more attention is freed to focus on comprehension of the text (Markell & Deno, 1997). Automaticity results from seeing the same words over and over. Repeated reading interventions are more effective when the teacher provides feedback to the student than those in which students receive feedback only from peers (Therrien, 2004). Teacher interaction also provides scaffolding for student reading comprehension (Dowhower, 1987; Koskinen & Blum, 1984; Ensor & Koller, 1997) because it allows the teacher and student to scaffold and mediate meaning to deeper and deeper levels of comprehension (Causal Factor 5).

Repeated readings provided important support to students diagnosed with learning disabilities and influenced their reading acquisition (Rashotte & Torgeson, 1988). Strategies for repeated readings include choral reading, in which all students read the selected text at the same time; paired reading, in which two students alternate rereading the passage to each other (Schirmer & Schaffer, 2010), engaging in dialogue through role-playing; practicing scripts and performing short plays (e.g., Reader's Theater; Prescott & Lewis, 2003); and multiple readings of a story through such well-organized practices as shared reading (Luetke-Stahlman, Hayes, & Nielsen; 1996; Schleper, 1998) and dialogic reading (Fung, Chow, & McBride-Chang, 2005; Justice & Pullen, 2003; Whitehurst et al., 1994). In a study of teachers in oral schools, Shandilya (2010) found that 59 percent reported using choral reading, 47 percent used modeling and imitation, and 35 percent reported the use of repeated readings and read-alouds.

Although research in repeated readings is limited for DHH students, some researchers reported that DHH students improved their reading skills after engaging in rereading activities (Ensor & Koller, 1997; Schirmer, Therrien, Schaffer, & Schirmer, 2009). Using the repeated reading passages from Reread-Adapt and Answer-Comprehend (RAAC), Therrien, Gormley, and Kubina (2006) reported gains in reading fluency for four students with severe to profound hearing losses in second grade through supplemental instruction at students' individual reading levels. Word reading errors and reading times decreased through repeated readings. However, to aid reading comprehension, the authors suggested the addition of explicit instruction (Causal Factor 4) in comprehension monitoring strategies for deaf students.

Other Practices That Encourage Time on Task. Shared reading, guided reading, and independent reading (described in Chapter 2) are all ways in which we might engage DHH students in interactions with print. Repeated interactions with materials at a student's independent level are more important than reading at the instructional level for increasing reading fluency because this level allows the reader to scaffold his or her own knowledge (Causal Factor 5). Another factor contributing to children's time with books is the availability of options that are highly motivating and interesting (Anken & Holmes, 1977; Ewoldt, Israelite, & Dodds, 1992). Effective teachers select books, or permit students to select their own books, that are both at the students' independent level and in their areas of interest. Many teachers choose an array of books with various themes, authors, and genres at each child's independent level and encourage a student to choose from this array, thus addressing both his or her interests and level.

Another source of face time with print is the use of personal digital assistants (PDAs), smartphones, instant messaging, and Internet social networking websites. These are now ubiquitous among all students, whether hearing or deaf, and we are only beginning to understand their place in the literacy process. On the one hand, technology assures us that students are getting more face time with print, and print-based communication is the norm. On the other hand, we have very few studies of the influence of the short message standard (SMS) communication protocol on the overall literacy process. For example, a student may understand that the message "BRB" means that her phone partner has stepped away from the conversation temporarily, but she might not know that the message translates to "be right back" or how to spell out the acronym. We describe this in more detail in Chapter 8. Teachers will want to monitor the literature on the use of texting and its influence on language and literacy acquisition.

Explicit Instruction. Many DHH students will require direct and explicit instruction (i.e., teacher modeling, mediation, student imitation, teacher scaffolding, and feedback) in reading fluency strategies (e.g., phrasing and prosody, mood and expression, accurate parsing, correct expression of clauses, role taking, correct tone for negation, pausing, accurate reflection of punctuation, etc.) to increase the rate with which they apply their accurate reading skills (Oakes, Mathur, & Lane, 2010). Students need adequate time for practice and specific feedback on their reading (Allington, 2006; Hudson et al., 2005; National Reading Panel, 2000). This is especially true for DHH students who enter school with language delays that result in literacy delays. Many researchers reported that extensive practice in reading fluency with connected text improved reading rates for average readers in the primary grades (National Research Council, 1998; National Reading Panel, 2000; Reutzel & Hollingsworth, 1993) and for older students with reading difficulties (Lovett & Steinbach, 1997; O'Connor et al., 2002; Shany & Biemiller, 1995). Fluency practice in general appears more important than the specific type of fluency practice. Shany and Biemiller compared reading aloud to adult partners versus reading along with tape-recorded passages for third- and fourth-grade hearing students with poor reading abilities and found that both treatment groups gained about three words per minute per week in fluency. To make the connection between fluency and comprehension, students also need specific instruction in reading comprehension. Although students increased their reading fluency across a 20-week fluency intervention, O'Connor and colleagues (2010) reported that comprehension outcomes for students with reading difficulties were still below average. One promising practice that makes use of explicit instruction of a skill set to link fluency with comprehension is that of visualizing and verbalizing, described in Chapter 6. Although limited in direct evidence, it does incorporate all five of the Causal Factors. Case Vignette 7.5 describes how one teacher used visualizing and verbalizing in her fluency and comprehension lessons.

CASE VIGNETTE 7.5.

Visualizing and Verbalizing

Ms. Rousseau teaches a group of fifth-grade students who use sign language at a residential school. She recently completed training for Visualizing and Verbalizing (Bell, 1991) and decided to implement the first stage, picture to picture, with her students. She offers a handful of pictures, face down, to the students, and they select one as a group. She explains the process to her students in sign: "I can't see the picture. You guys will describe the picture to me, I will make a picture in my mind using your words, and we will see if the picture in my mind and the one you are holding are the same." The students take turns giving details to Ms. Rousseau. Juan signs, "big building, bike, girl." Gracyn signs, "Red bike, table, girl sit down." Ms. Rousseau signs, "What does the building look like?" Robert outlines flat faces of the building with his hands. "Okay, the building has flat faces," Ms. Rousseau replies. Gracyn indicates that the roof is red, and Juan gestures an area in front of the building, adding "flowers, table, girl, bike." Ms. Rousseau signs, "Okay. I see a big, square building. In front of the building is a garden. Over here is a table with a girl sitting down" as she describes the scene and arranges it in her signing space.

(Continued)

206 Literacy Instruction for Students Who Are Deaf and Hard of Hearing

206 Literacy Instruction for Students Who Are Deaf and Hard of Hearing

(Continued)

"Where is the bike?" she asks. Robert repeats the scene in sign and places the bike to the left of the table. "What is the girl doing?" Ms. Rousseau asks. All three students reply "writing" in unison. Using these clues, Ms. Rousseau again explains the image in her head. "Did I miss anything?" she asks. After she and the students agree on her description, Juan presents the picture to Ms. Rousseau. "Oh, I didn't know there was water in the corner of the picture!" she exclaims. After modeling this activity, Ms. Rousseau provides time for the students to practice describing pictures while she and the other students ask questions. Using the Visualizing and Verbalizing sequence, Ms. Rousseau provides single sentences for students to visualize and interpret for the other students and points out the importance of visualizing the words on the page to understand the meaning and image behind the words when reading.

Reading Phrase Units. DHH students may also need explicit instruction (Causal Factor 4) in rendering phrases fluently within reading passages. Words with multiple meanings may inhibit reading fluency when a student cannot identify the correct meaning of the word in the context of the reading passage. Many words carry different meanings when they are combined within phrases, both literal and figurative. Consider the phrase "The two girls came up to me." In order to understand that the girls approached the subject, a DHH student must understand that the "chunk" of words "came up to me" has a literal interpretation of "approached." For a student who signs, the literal English-based signed interpretation of "came up to me" can be replaced with a classifier handshape of the index and middle finger, followed by the movement of coming toward the signer. In addition, the student must read this phrase in text, search within his or her vocabulary bank for the literal meaning, realize that the words are combined in a phrase whose meaning translates to "approached," and form the correct sign to demonstrate reading comprehension.

Idioms, a common form of figurative language, are an area of great difficulty for DHH students, not only because the meaning of these words changes when they are combined but also because the new meaning of the phrase is figurative instead of literal. Consider "knock your socks off," a phrase containing four seemingly simple words. "Knock" can be used as a verb (he knocked on the door) and a noun (she heard a knock on the door). One can also take one's socks off in a literal sense. However, when these four words are combined into this particular phrase, the literal meanings of the words change into a figurative phrase that means "shock or surprise you." In order to comprehend this phrase, a DHH student must know the literal meaning of each word, recognize the phrase as a "chunk" or group of words, acknowledge that the literal translation does not fit within the context, and decipher the figurative intent behind the phrase.

In addition to multiple meanings at the word level, figurative phrases such as idioms often carry different meanings than their literal translations. Consider the metaphors "Three strikes and you're out" and "She hit that one out of the ballpark," which stem from the American pastime of baseball (Boers, 2003). Without the knowledge that these phrases are figurative, a student might interpret them literally and lose all meaning, causing a breakdown in reading comprehension. By linking these chunks of meaning to the central concept of baseball, students' prior knowledge can be accessed in addition to expanding both semantic categories of knowledge (baseball) and figurative knowledge (metaphors). Effective teachers will familiarize students with figurative expressions from the text prior to student reading for explicit instruction of the non-meaningful literal interpretation and the figurative interpretation. After a student has mastered both the correct signed rendition and the figurative meaning, he or she should be able to render the expression fluently within connected text.

FLUENCY INSTRUCTION FOR STUDENTS WITH AUDITORY ACCESS

In addition to the practices identified for all DHH students, effective teachers consider intonation-based decoding and prosody as they prepare fluency instruction for students who use spoken language. Intonation-based decoding incorporates work on intonational patterns into fluency instruction, such as placing stress on a phrase within a sentence to show that it is understood as a chunk of meaning or on a syllable within a word to distinguish its use as a noun from its use as a verb (e.g. `con/duct–con/`duct, `con/tract–con/`tract, or `in/sult–in/`sult). The way in which a child breaks sentences into phrase chunks (e.g., *This is the dog* that chased the cat *that caught the rat* that ate the cheese …) influences both interpretation of meaning and fluent spoken production of the phrase. In signed production, different conceptual signs altogether may be used for differently chunked phrase units (see example in the next sentence). Intonation-based decoding is closely related to sentence parsing in that similar words can have different syntactic and morphologic patterns that change the way words are chunked together (e.g., She ran *up the hill* versus She *ran up* the bill). Intonation can change meaning at the word level as well as the sentence level. For example, children can learn the rule that accenting may determine whether a word is a noun or a verb. When accented on the first syllable, all of the words in the following list are nouns, and when accented on the second syllable, they are verbs: `con/tent–con/`tent, `ob/ject–ob/`ject, `per/mit–per/`mit. An adaptation that teachers might incorporate into rule instruction for ASL users would be to demonstrate that a noun is changed into a verb by altering the motion of the noun (e.g., airplane/fly). The teacher would relate syllabic emphasis in spoken language to reduplication in sign language, such as contrasting the noun (e.g., chair) with its verb (e.g., to sit). Although the words are derived from the same form, their meanings differ because of syllabic stress or reduplication. The teacher would use explicit instruction and examples from the student's native language (spoken or signed) as a discussion to scaffold the structure (i.e., location of the spoken accent or reduplication) and the rule (Causal Factors 2, 4, and 5).

INSTRUCTIONAL PRACTICES FOR STUDENTS WITHOUT A SOUND-BASED LANGUAGE

For DHH students who sign, the Signed Fluency Rubric can also be used as an ongoing instructional and progress monitoring tool. Using reading material at students' independent reading levels, the teacher can assess student performance using the rubric indicators and tailor instruction according to the indicators with which the student is struggling. For example, if a student's fluency is inhibited by failure to role shift[2] during dialogue, the teacher can focus on role shift as an area of instruction, and the student can use repeated reading of the text to build fluency for this skill. The teacher can promote generalization of role shift by presenting various texts at the student's reading level with opportunities for demonstrating role shift among characters and their dialogue. If a student's rate of rendering sign to print is choppy and dysfluent, the teacher and student can work on improving signing fluency through phrasing and fingerspelling strategies. Use of the descriptors of the Signed Fluency Rubric as components of fluency instruction is similar to the process that hearing students use when they read text, convert it to a mental image, and present it fluently through spoken language. Instead of simply word calling (or fingerspelling unknown words without any connection to meaning), students must create a mental image of text and present it expressively through spoken English, English-like signing, or ASL (Easterbrooks, 2010). Case Vignettes 7.6 and7.7 present three lesson plans that exemplify what an effective teacher might do to assist students in code-switching between English and ASL during a lesson in fluency.

CASE VIGNETTE 7.6.

Visual Fluency Lesson Plan for Negation

Carlos is a second-grade student who attends language arts in the general education setting with Mrs. White and his typically hearing peers. Carlos has a severe hearing loss, uses binaural hearing aids, and communicates with a combination of signed and spoken language. Ms. Martin, his itinerant teacher, co-teaches with Mrs. White, working with the class as a whole and providing one-on-one support for Carlos when he needs it. The class is currently working on negation in the form of contractions. Ms. Martin selects a subset of the

(Continued)

---

[2] Skilled deaf readers will change the position of their bodies to reflect the action in a story. For example, if a goat is chasing a man, the reader will read the man's dialogue while pretending to look over his shoulder and run from the goat. This adds visual clarity to the words rendered from the text.

(Continued)

contractions embedded in sentences, such as: "I didn't watch TV," "I can't find my money," and "We won't go to the game." First, she has Carlos read each sentence to himself, underlining the words he thinks are contractions. Then she asks Carlos to read each sentence, providing assistance as necessary. When Carlos stumbles on "didn't," Ms. Martin shows him how this word is formed from "did" and "not." Carlos signs both words, using the past tense marker for "did." Ms. Martin models "didn't" by signing "did" with the past tense marker and shaking her head to show negation. Carlos imitates the sign and negation when Ms. Martin points to the printed word in the sentence. Next, Carlos reads "can't" by fingerspelling the word. Ms. Martin asks, "Do you see a word you know in 'can't'?" and Carlos signs and voices "can." Ms. Martin relates the "t" to "didn't," and Carlos correctly guesses that the contraction ending means "not." "How would you sign that word?" Ms. Martin asks. Carlos signs "can" while shaking his head for negation. "Right!" Ms. Martin exclaims. She also shows him an alternate sign for "can't" while shaking her head to show negation. Finally, Carlos reads the last sentence, pausing at the word "won't" and glancing at Mrs. White's word wall. "Can you show me two ways to sign that word?" Ms. Martin asks. Carlos signs and voices "will not" while shaking his head to show negation. Ms. Martin models dropping the sign for "not" and shaking her head as she signs "will." Carlos imitates. After his peers have finished the contractions activity, Carlos models these three contractions for his classmates and shows them how to use headshake to demonstrate negation in sign language.

CASE VIGNETTE 7.7.

Visual Fluency Lesson Plan—Directionality

Mrs. Burks teaches six students in the seventh grade at a day school for the deaf. All of her students have languages other than English spoken in their homes, and all use some form of signed language in varying degrees, from primarily spoken language with sign support to primarily sign language with speech approximations. Mrs. Burks is working on directional verbs in printed text, such as "Look at me," "Come to my house," "Go to school," and "Show her your paper." Her students already know the individual high-frequency words, but the concept of directionality, or showing who did what to whom, is new for her students. Mrs. Burks demonstrates signing the following phrase written

(Continued)

(*Continued*)

on her white board: "Show her your paper." Mrs. Burks indexes a girl in sign-ing space and signs PAPER SHOW while moving the sign for "show" toward the space in which she set up the girl. After a discussion of directionality and modeling of a few more example sentences, the students select partners and a bowlful of sentence strips. Each student takes a turn choosing a sentence strip and modeling the underlined directional verb for his or her partner, and the partner writes the sentence on a sheet of paper. After each partner has completed five turns, they compare their sentence strips to their partner's writ-ten interpretation and discuss any differences in answers. After agreeing on the correct signing of each directional verb phrase, they verify their accuracy with the teacher and then select two phrases to model for their peers. Mrs. Burks follows this activity with examples from favorite stories where direc-tional verbs are used.

SUMMARY OF RECOMMENDED PRACTICES

Fluency is a multifaceted component of reading for all students. In par-ticular, DHH students approach fluent reading through various commu-nication modes and styles; assessment and instruction must match these styles. Effective teachers must consider multiple and varied options for assessment and instruction regarding reading fluency. In this chapter we suggested a three-pronged approach to assessment that includes assess-ment of students' fluent renderings of grammar, fluent use of prosody, and, for some students, correct words per minute. Teachers can identify students' current levels of fluency through the use of basic reading inven-tories that provide for miscue analysis to identify strategies that students use successfully and areas where direct strategy instruction for fluency is needed. Regarding instruction, students must have actual face time with reading materials at their independent reading levels to increase their flu-ency. While fluency practice in general appears more important than the specific type of fluency practice, the combination of repeated readings with direct instruction in comprehension strategies may result in overall reading gains. Additionally, direct instruction in phrasing and parsing of sentences with a focus on intonational patterns or conceptually accurate signs can assist students in fluent renderings of reading materials. A combination of appropriate assessments, instructional strategies, and face time with books can create fluent readers.

RESOURCES

Kuhn, M., & Stahl, S. (2000). *Fluency: A review of developmental and remedial practices.* Ann Arbor, MI: Center for the Improvement of Early Reading (CIERA).
Podcasts
Go to http://www.reading.org, the site of the International Reading Association. Download and listen to the "Rasinski on Fluency" podcast.

8 Closing Thoughts, Final Directions

PURPOSE

Our intention in this textbook was to summarize the current evidence base in reading instruction, regardless of the language or communication mode a particular student uses. We do not prescribe practices that all teachers of DHH children should adopt; rather, we defer to the expertise of the education practitioner to meet the individual needs of students based on current levels of performance and current assessment data for each student.

Teachers and other practitioners who work with DHH students must meet the instructional needs of all DHH students, as local school systems work with students who have a variety of background experiences, use a variety of languages, and benefit from a variety of communication modes. Therefore, they need to use strategies that are effective with their students to promote the acquisition of reading skills. Effective strategies are supported by a foundation of research, including an evidence base of instructional efficacy with DHH students and knowledge of Causal Factors that lead to positive learning outcomes.

In this chapter, we summarize what we can currently answer about reading instruction for DHH students and present future questions in each of the major topic areas associated with literacy. We address a looming challenge presently facing literacy instruction: Most children are now learning to read on a computer or some digital device (i.e., laptop, cell phone, iPad®, etc.), and the incoming generation of educators and researchers must find instructional models that best utilize this format to meet the needs of DHH students. We close this textbook by identifying several of the major questions that have yet to be answered regarding reading instruction and DHH students.

ANSWERS FOR TODAY AND QUESTIONS FOR TOMORROW

Around the turn of this century, various efforts to summarize the evidence base in teaching reading to DHH children demonstrated that there were many weaknesses in the knowledge base in deaf education, reflecting similar problems in the general education knowledge base. This led to increased standards of rigor in research (Odom et al., 2005) and the legal requirement (in the United States) for teachers to use evidence-based practices. In the past decade, there have been notable improvements in the quality and quantity of research in deaf education, and we know several important pieces of information. First, we know that reading problems are not just the domain of deaf individuals. Thirty-five percent of adult Americans read at or below basic levels of proficiency (U.S. Department of Education, 2009). We also know that problems associated with this statistic for hearing individuals (Baer, Kutner, Sabatini, & White, 2009) are the same problems that appear in the DHH population. We then might expect a certain portion of deaf readers to struggle with literacy, but we see far more literacy problems in the population with hearing loss than in the population without. This means that additional research is needed in the areas identified by the

National Assessment of Adult Literacy (NAAL; Baer et al., 2009), as these areas relate specifically to DHH learners. These include cognition, the structure of language, how sentences relate, dual-language coding, decoding, fluency, searching text efficiently, inferential ability, reading a spoken language if using a visual language, and applying learned skills to new tasks.

ASSESSMENT

Language and literacy are fundamentally and inextricably interconnected; readers read by unlocking the meaning of language in print form. While basic assessments of grade-level vocabulary, comprehension, and spoken fluency are sufficient to provide a reading level, we simply do not have sufficient assessments to help us figure out what a student may be doing wrong when he or she is not reading on grade level. Currently there are only limited efforts to validate assessments of language and literacy for use with DHH children. One exception is in the area of phonological awareness (Webb & Lederberg, 2012). Extensive effort is needed to determine if the most commonly given language and literacy tests are valid and reliable for DHH children.

For typically hearing children, grade-level performance in English correlated highly with grade-level performance in reading (Harlaar, Hayiou-Thomas, Dale, & Plomin, 2008). Pertinent to all children, skills in comprehension of print (i.e., successfully reading sentences) and vocabulary make an important, unique contribution to reading comprehension of expository text (Ecalle, Bouchafa, Potocki, & Magnan, 2011). DHH children learning spoken language should then also benefit from direct instruction in grammar and vocabulary. Curricula for hearing students detail the language skills that are expected of a student grade by grade. For example, some hearing children in third-grade English Language Arts (ELA) are expected to identify and infer meaning from common root words, common prefixes (e.g., un-, re-, dis-, in-), and common suffixes (e.g., -tion, -ous, -ly) (Common Core State Standards Initiative, 2010). This becomes a challenge for

DHH children because they must first learn the underlying language before they can attach meaning metalinguistically to the label of that language. For example, when a child reads "He won the race," she must understand first that "he" refers to a boy before she needs to know that "he" is a pronoun.

This issue presents another layer of greater challenge in schools where the primary lange is ASL because it is rare in schools to find Sign Language Arts (SLA). At the time of this writing, only one school for the deaf in the English-speaking world (C. Zinszer, personal communication, November 11, 2010) has published an American Sign Language curriculum. What would be the third-grade equivalent of the above ELA standard in SLA? For example, what classifiers or nonmanual markings should we expect of a third-grade student who uses sign language? When should he understand the meaning of the classifier versus the metalinguistic label "classifier"? For students using a sign system based on a native spoken language, such as Signing Exact English (SEE; Gustason & Zawolkow, 2006; Gustason, Zawolkow, & Lopez, 1993), what morphemes should we expect students to produce at the third-grade level? For students who use a combination of spoken and signed communication, how much mastery and of which elements do we expect in each mode? In all languages and modes the question is: At what age should the child comprehend meaning when someone uses the structure (e.g., "Johnny, *have you been* studying?"), and at what age should we expect the child to know the metalinguistic label for the structure (i.e., "Johnny, which of these sentences uses *present perfect progressive tense?*")? Until we know the developmental sequence of sign languages from infancy through high school, efforts to compare English and ASL side by side will be hampered. Further, at the time of this writing, there are no receptive or expressive vocabulary tests of ASL or more hybrid-like sign systems that are easily accessible to the typical teacher or parent. Further investigation of the *Signed Reading Fluency Rubric for Deaf Children* (Easterbrooks & Huston, 2008) is needed to determine test norms and examine its role in recommending interventions. Readily available tests of vocabulary and grammar for all languages and in all modes must become widely available.

PHONOLOGICAL AWARENESS AND ALPHABETICS

The examination of phonological awareness and alphabetic skills of DHH students has received much attention in the recent literature. We know that many deaf children with cochlear implants and many with severe or lesser degrees of hearing loss are able to acquire letter–sound correspondences. We also know that for some children who do not have access to sound, semantic equivalents in combination with Visual Phonics are an effective way to teach some letter–sound correspondences (Beal-Alvarez, Lederberg, & Easterbrooks, 2011). Other DHH students may learn phonemic awareness skills after they learn to read (Kyle & Harris, 2010; Goldin-Meadow & Mayberry, 2001; Musselman, 2000). Unfortunately, not all children benefit from these strategies; some fall into an additional category of *struggling learner* and present challenges above and beyond those resulting from the hearing loss. Many of the studies conducted have focused on very young children who used spoken language, although some have been conducted with signing children. We need a series of replication studies to look at the usability of associated strategies with different age groups, children from different home environments, and children with greater degrees of loss to identify appropriate modifications for children with a variety of characteristics. Clearly there is a need to differentiate those approaches that are appropriate for those with and without access to sound.

In addition to phonologically based decoding, children also learn to decode morphologically. The morpheme system develops by kindergarten in typically hearing children, and inflectional morphological awareness measured in second grade predicted children's reading comprehension in fifth grade (Deacon & Kirby, 2004). This connection between the structure of the words in sentences and the ability to read is very clear in hearing children, yet we have limited evidence of this relationship in DHH children. We know that their English morphological systems are delayed, but it has been several decades since there has been much of a research focus on morphological development; there is even less in the evidence base regarding the relationship between morphological development and reading in DHH children, whether they use spoken or signed language. Do DHH children learn morphology in the same developmental sequence as hearing children? What are effective practices for teaching morphology to DHH students? Are some strategies more effective for students based on the students' preferred mode of communication? We need research to identify instructional practices for morphology that are supported by evidence-based research or Causal Factors.

Another area that has received very little attention is how we should integrate strategies that work effectively and efficiently with deaf children in separate classes into the general education classroom. Many students presently receive instruction in a general education class and then the teacher of the deaf re-teaches the lesson either through push-in or pull-out programs. Is this an effective use of the learner's time or the teacher's time? Are there ways to adapt strategies that are successful with deaf children (e.g., preteaching, repeated readings, etc.) so the general education teacher can infuse them into her regular instruction?

VOCABULARY

It is clear from the available research that children with better vocabulary and grammar skills are better readers. It is also clear that vocabulary and grammar have a mutually supportive role in that as vocabulary increases, so does grammar; as grammar increases, so does vocabulary. One seems to scaffold the other. Yet we do not know how much vocabulary improvement is necessary to bring a child to a higher level of grammar, nor do we know how much improvement in grammar is necessary to support a child's acquisition of vocabulary. We do not have any studies that tell us the rate at which DHH children at different ages are able to master vocabulary or how many words we should expect a child to learn to read and how many exposures to that word he must have before he has mastered the word to the level of automaticity. We don't know this regarding acquisition of the word in spoken form or in ASL, and we certainly don't know it related to acquisition of the print form. We know that hearing children learn many words by over-hearing conversations, but we do not know how to help deaf children learn to overhear (in spoken or signed forms) and then master words in context. We know that storybook reading is an effective tool for helping DHH children learn to read, but we do not have a clear picture of the level of support that is needed for parents to make the most effective and efficient use of the preschool years to support language and literacy development.

The literature on hearing children tells us what a good environment in support of literacy should look like (Wolfersberger, Reutzel, Sudweeks, & Fawson, 2004). In a study of preschool classrooms for DHH children (Easterbrooks, Lederberg, & Connor, 2011), those features thought of as "good" for hearing children did not hold the same importance in "good" classrooms for DHH children. If typically good environments for hearing children are not necessarily good for DHH children, then are current approaches to vocabulary based in general education practices sufficient (e.g., word walls, word webs, etc.)? Of the major ways in which children are taught vocabulary, which way is more effective and efficient in establishing vocabulary and in accounting for transfer of vocabulary knowledge? We barely have evidence on the use-fulness of traditional methods of instruction, and we certainly do not have any intervention studies that compare instructional approaches. This is one of the most important needs regarding vocabulary. What strategy or tool or product works and for whom? What strategy (e.g., incremental rehearsal, use of visual imagery) or tool or product (e.g., Fairview Reading, Lindamood-Bell Visualizing and Verbalizing) works better than another and in which skill set? For whom does it work best? Is depth of vocabulary knowledge more important than breadth of vocabulary knowledge in enhancing thinking during reading? Is it better to teach figurative language by direct instruction of the semantic equivalent (e.g., "get in the ball game" means "pay attention and partici-pate"), or is it better to let children draw pictures of the silly meaning and then the real meaning? Which vocabulary strategies help teachers "close the gap" in vocabulary acquisition that widens over time (Kyle & Harris, 2010)?

TEXT COMPREHENSION

One thing we know about successful hearing readers is that they have little trouble parsing sentences. In the sentence "He wolfed down his dinner greedily" (approximately a grade 4.5 sentence using Flesch-Kincaid scoring), we might expect a developing reader to stumble over her inclination to parse the words "down his dinner" into a prepositional phrase, which would be an incorrect parsing. Once a student reaches third-grade reading, sentence parsing becomes more and more complex and contributes to reading problems in struggling readers. Yet little is known about how DHH children mis-parse, how this influences comprehension, and what we should do about it. Significant research is needed in this area to develop strategies to encourage more flexibility in sentence parsing. Once these strategies are identified, we need to know the best ways to teach them to students so that they can select effective strategies independently while reading text.

We have decades of research supporting the importance of helping students learn to use text comprehension strategies. Yet we have very few studies that guide us toward understanding which of the 100+ strategies available are most effective. Is there a constellation of strategies (e.g., activating prior knowledge plus prediction plus summarizing) that is particularly effective? Is there an additive value to teaching multiple strategies? For example, does the child who uses three strategies comprehend better than the child who uses five or the child who uses seven? Are 10 enough? Are 20 too many? Which ones are the most effective and efficient in influencing comprehension outcomes? This would be very useful information for teachers of the deaf, given that they must maximize the instructional time that is available to them.

FLUENCY

Perhaps the least well documented area of literacy instruction is that of fluency. As with other literacy areas, we have two uniquely distinct groups of students with two separate sets of needs: students who have sufficient access to sound to provide a base for language and literacy development and students who do not. If children fall along a continuum from primarily auditory learners (hard of hearing; successful implant users) through mixed learners (sign-supported speech or speech-supported sign) to primarily visual learners (deaf; ASL users), then are there demarcation points where we should use auditory approaches versus visual approaches? What are the modifications necessary for the children who fall along various points on the continuum of communication languages and modes?

MOTIVATION

Another question that requires additional research is this: How much time should a student spend in literacy instruction? What kind of instruction is appropriate for which reading problem? Motivation, the internal drive to read, or the student's willingness to participate and engage in literacy instruction, is another factor that the National Reading Panel (2000) deemed to be a critical element to effective reading instruction. If motivation plays an important role in the time children spend in reading, and if motivation is an inherent trait, then how can we promote motivation to read? What are the barriers to student motivation, such as frustration, that teachers can remedy? What would tempt unmotivated readers to read? Today's readers spend less and less time outside of class reading from books and more and more time reading information on a digital gadget that may or may not be written in the standard form of the printed language they are learning at school.

Although we have made notable strides in our knowledge of reading since the meta-reviews of the early part of this century, much information is still needed. Renewed efforts at high-quality research should be of primary concern to teachers, parents, researchers, and other education practitioners.

LITERACY IN THE DIGITAL AGE

Society at large is spending increasing amounts of time on social networking technology in particular; students bring their cell phones with them to class in record numbers and communicate with one another all day and all night. Wikipedia is among the most popular "go-to" source for instant information, right or wrong. *Just-in-time* (JIT) information, a term borrowed from the field of business, is making its way into educational parlance (e.g., JIT instruction, JIT parenting; Rosen, 2005). JIT focuses on making information instantaneously available it bits and bytes that will grasp the attention of the digital learner, and its concepts are worth considering. If teachers want to stay apprised of what their students are experiencing, they will need to become increasingly knowledgeable of technology such as 4G networks, avatars, blogs, Facebook®, Farmville®, Flickr®, Hulu®, online gaming, game-based learning, RSS feeds, Twitter, tweeting, YouTube®, vlogs (video logs), and a whole host of means that students use to connect with one another through the Internet. As technology advances, access to the Web is becoming less and less dependent upon desktop and laptop computers, with mini-iPads® and tablets on the market. Quite literally, it is now at the tips of our fingers, and *this* is the mechanism through which most children are gaining early exposure to reading.

Students entering schools today grew up with digital babysitters in the form of video games, Internet movies, and smartphones. Further, their parents did as well. Born after 1988, "the millennial generation" (Taylor & Keeters, 2010) is the most well-educated and ethnically and racially diverse generation to date, having had personal computers available to them their whole lives. The majority of deaf people in many countries exchange printed information via digital devices and SMS (short message standard language) on mobile phones (Akamatsu, Mayer, & Farrelly, 2006; Pilling & Barrett, 2008; D. Power, Power, & Rehling, 2007; M. R. Power, Power, & Horstmanshof, 2007) with up to 600 messages per day (M. R. Power et al., 2007). Middle and high school students use text messaging as well, although their frequency in one study was highly variable, and the authors reported that "individual students' literacy levels may influence how likely they are to use the two-way text messages in the first place" (Akamatsu et al., 2006, p. 127). However, several students reported that text messaging motivated them to improve their literacy skills (Akamatsu et al., 2006).

DHH students appear to spend the majority of their digital communication time using SMS language during text messages or instant messaging, with minimal or no syntax, absence of morphological markers, and a limited lexicon (M. R. Power & Power, 2004). Use of digital devices may be a contributing factor to the infrequency of interaction with informational or instructional language (Juel, 1988). When students frequently communicate in SMS, they are deciphering an initialized form of a spoken language, such as "LOL" for "laugh out loud." This is fine if a student knows what the abbreviation means and can spell the phrase, but whether students know the referent of an SMS code or just understand conceptually that the responder was amused has serious implications for reading and writing skills. How do students decipher and relate this abbreviated language system to a standard language system, such as printed English? Students who use spoken communication have to translate from "BTW" to "by the way" with an understanding of both the concept and the printed synonyms (e.g., "hey," "also") to effectively use this concept while reading connected text. Students who experience high-frequency hearing loss or distortion have the additional deciphering task of filling in missing sounds they may not hear in common words. Students who use a sign system must internalize the meaning for the SMS code, pair the correct sign(s) and concept, and relate these signs to print. While we know that most deaf people use SMS code for communication, we don't know how to teach the language deciphering required for literacy skills. Contrastive analysis between two languages, such as the bilingual–bicultural model, permits teachers to provide direct instruction in similarities and differences between two languages. Teachers may need to learn common codes such as *afaik* (as far as I know), *2mro* (tomorrow), and *gr8* (great) if they want to understand what their students have written. How do teachers add a third language code, SMS, to their literacy instruction? How does this instruction differ for DHH students based on their mode of communication or their first language (L1)?

DHH students may also use technology in the form of C-Print, a real-time speech-to-text transcription system that provides a printed display on a screen and a printout of the spoken material (Elliot, Stinson, McKee, Everhart, & Francis, 2001). Student use of C-Print has steadily increased across time (Stinson et al., 1999). However, because C-Print is a direct translation of spoken language to its printed format, mastery of literacy skills in the particular spoken language (i.e., English, Spanish, French, etc.) seems to be a prerequisite skill for use of C-Print (Elliot et al., 2001; Stinson et al., 1999). Participants in previous C-Print research were college students. What level of literacy skills is required for C-Print to be an effective instructional modification for DHH students in the college setting? Do younger DHH students benefit from the provision of C-Print? How can teachers facilitate the use of C-Print in their classrooms?

Email is another popular format for communication that mirrors a standard language form more closely than SMS. In 2007 (M. R. Power et al., 2007), about 85 percent of deaf adults used email to correspond with both deaf and hearing people. A mere 5 years later, young adults are emailing less and less and using real-time IM and Tweets more routinely. While DHH middle and high school students rated themselves as confident in their basic computer skills, word processing, and the Internet (Luft, Bonello, & Zirzow, 2009), they may lack sufficient literacy skills to participate in society via technological communication devices in the digital age. A final consideration is access to digital devices. Erath and Larkin (2004) noted that some DHH students may suffer from a "double digital divide," meaning that they may lack both availability and communicative access to technology. As a result, DHH students may not be aware of technology options nor have access to all of the technological devices available to them, such as captioning services in public places and relay systems, and knowledge on how to use them (Luft et al., 2009). How can teachers provide for early access to communication technology to meet the language and literacy needs of their students and reduce the "double divide"? For example, is the use of deaf email partners an acceptable practice to provide cultural models and practice in literacy skills for DHH students? How can teachers and practitioners effectively utilize technology for reading instruction both inside and outside of school hours?

Old-fashioned, hard-bound, turn-the-actual-page books are rapidly becoming less and less a source of information for all of us. *What* students are reading, *where* they are reading it, *why* they are reading it, and *when* they are reading it should be of interest to all educational practitioners.

Teachers will want to tap into the stream of information that is engaging their students to use this as a means of motivating learners to increase their literacy skills. All of the technologies mentioned above will become obsolete within the decade after publication of this book as the major companies (Apple, Amazon, Google, and Microsoft) vie for the education dollar.

SUMMARY OF RECOMMENDED PRACTICES

Many DHH students remain behind their hearing peers in reading abilities at the end of high school (Allen, 1986). However, teachers and practitioners have the means to prevent this in most students with hearing loss through the use of documented, evidence-based instructional practices. The field of deaf education is accumulating a collection of research-based evidence that supports a constellation of practices, materials, strategies, and interventions for use in literacy instruction. The evidence base has improved dramatically in the past decade, and modern options (technology, early hearing detection and intervention, recognition of ASL, just-in-time learning) have opened new opportunities for many students. This is not necessarily true for all students, though, as there are those with additional intrapersonal challenges (e.g., intellectual disabilities, limited English proficiency) or interpersonal challenges (e.g., recent immigrants who enter the educational system without an established first language). The current growth spurt in the availability of evidence-based practices must continue, and we must find answers to the questions raised in this chapter to increase the literacy skills of DHH students. Early intervention, early access to language and literacy development, and better technology (e.g., Universal Newborn Hearing Screening, cochlear implants, digital hearing aids) are improving the chances that a child will start his or her school years with the necessary background and skills to learn to read. The field has a clearer perspective on what constitutes a sufficient evidence base, and various reviews of that evidence base are leading researchers to seek answers. We have attempted to highlight some key areas for investigation above. However, teachers are still faced daily with the challenge of teaching reading to children with limited language and limited prerequisite skills. In order to compensate for students' gaps in language and experience, teachers must employ the use of verified curricula that support syntactic, morphological, semantic, and pragmatic language as they relate to reading instruction in an appropriate developmental sequence. Teachers must choose instructional strategies that are based in sound teaching practices that focus on helping students to master the skills necessary to understand text. This must be done with motivating materials. Teachers must model fluent language, regardless of mode, for their students during instruction. But the researchers cannot work alone. Administrators and teachers must work together to establish and sustain students' current levels of literacy skills via valid assessments. Teachers and practitioners must use evidence-based strategies and document effective instructional strategies for individual students. It will take all of us working together to sustain improvements in literacy instruction and ensure that each deaf or hard-of-hearing student experiences success in literacy development.

REFERENCES

AIMSweb. (2010). *Assessment and data management for RTI.* Retrieved from http://www.aimsweb.com

Akamatsu, C. T. (1988). Instruction in text structure: Metacognitive strategy instruction for literacy development in deaf students. *ACEHI/ACEDA, 14,* 13–32.

Akamatsu, C. T., & Andrews, J. F. (1993). It takes two to be literate: Literacy interactions between parent and child. *Sign Language Studies, 81,* 333–360.

Akamatsu, C. T., Mayer, C., & Farrelly, S. (2006). An investigation of two-way text messaging use with deaf students at the secondary level. *Journal of Deaf Studies and Deaf Education, 11*(1), 120–131. doi:10.1093/deafed/enj013

Akamatsu, C. T., Mayer, C., & Hardy-Braz, S. (2008). Why considerations of verbal aptitude are important in educating deaf and hard-of-hearing students. In M. Marschark & P. C. Hauser (Eds.), *Deaf cognition: Foundations and outcomes* (pp. 131–169). New York, NY: Oxford University Press.

Akhtar, N., & Tomasello, M. (1997). Young children's productivity with word order and verb morphology. *Developmental Psychology, 33*(6), 952–965.

Albertini, J. (1993). Critical literacy, whole language, and teaching of writing to deaf students: Who should dictate to whom? *TESOL, 27*(1), 59–73.

Albertini, J., & Mayer, C. (2011). Using miscue analysis to assess comprehension in deaf college readers. *Journal of Deaf Studies and Deaf Education, 16*(1), 35–46. doi:10.1093/deafed/enq017

Alegria, J., Leybaert, J., Charlier, B., & Hage, C. (1992). On the origin of phonological representations in the deaf: Hearing lips and hands. In J. Alegria, D. Holender, J. Morais, & M. Radeau (Eds.), *Analytic approaches to human cognition* (pp. 107–132). Amsterdam, The Netherlands: North-Holland.

Allen, T. (1986). Patterns of academic achievement among hearing impaired students: 1974 and 1983. In A. Schildroth & M. Karchmer (Eds.), *Deaf children in America* (pp. 161–206). Boston, MA: College-Hill Press.

Allington, R. L. (2006). Fluency: Still waiting after all these years. In S. J. Samuels & A. E. Farstrup (Eds.), *What research has to say about reading fluency* (pp. 94–105). Newark, DE: International Reading Association.

Anderson, D., & Reilly, J. S. (2002). The MacArthur Communicative Development Inventory: Normative data for American Sign Language. *Journal of Deaf Studies and Deaf Education, 7*(2), 83–106.

Anderson, M., Noren, N. J., Kilgore, J., Howard, W., & Krohn, E. (1999). *The apple tree curriculum for developing written language.* Austin, TX: PRO-ED.

Andrews, J. (1988). Deaf children's acquisition of prereading skills using the reciprocal teaching procedure. *Exceptional Children, 54*(4), 349–355.

Andrews, S., Miller, B., & Rayner, K. (2004). Eye movements and morphological segmentation of compound words: There is a mouse in mousetrap. *European Journal of Cognitive Psychology, 16*(1/2), 285–311.

Anglin, J. M. (1993). Vocabulary development: A morphological analysis. *Monographs of the Society for Research in Child Development, Serial No. 238, 58*(10), 1–165.

Anken, J. R., & Holmes, D. W. (1977). Use of adapted "classics" in a reading program for deaf students. *American Annals of the Deaf, 122*(1), 8–14.

Anthony, J. L., & Lonigan, C. J. (2004). The nature of phonological awareness: Converging evidence from four studies of preschool and early grade school children. *Journal of Educational Psychology, 96*, 43–55.

Aram, D., Most, T., & Mayafit, H. (2006, July). Contributions of mother-child storybook telling and joint writing to literacy development in kindergarteners with hearing loss. *Language, Speech, and Hearing Services in Schools, 37*, 1–15. doi:0161-1461/06/3703-0001

Arnold, D. H., Lonigan, C. J., Whitehurst, G. J., & Epstein, J. N. (1994). Accelerating language development though picture book reading: Replication and extension to a videotape training format. *Journal of Educational Psychology, 86*(2), 235–243.

Ausbrooks-Rusher, M., Schimmel, C., & Edwards, S. (2012). Utilizing Fairview as a bilingual response to intervention (RTI): Comprehensive curriculum review with supporting data. *Theory and Practice in Language Studies, 7,* 1317–1329.

Baddeley, A., Gathercole, S., & Papagno, C. (1998). The phonological loop as a language learning device. *Psychological Review, 105*(1), 158–173.

Baer, J., Kutner, M., Sabatini, J., & White, S. (2009, February). *Basic reading skills and the literacy of America's least literate adults: Results from the 2003 National Assessment of Adult Literacy (NAAL) supplemental studies.* National Center for Education Statistics, Institute of Educational Sciences. Retrieved July 20, 2011, from http://nces.ed.gov/pubs2009/2009481.pdf

Bailes, C., Searls, S., Slobodzian, J., & Staton, J. (1986). *It's your turn now: Using dialogue journals with deaf students.* Washington, DC: Gallaudet University, Laurent Clerc National Deaf Education Center.

Balch, W. R. (2007). Effects of test expectation on multiple-choice performance and subjective ratings. *Teaching of Psychology, 34*(4), 219–225.

Banks, J., Gray, C., & Fyfe, R. (1990). The written recall of printed stories by severely deaf children. *British Journal of Educational Psychology, 60*(2), 192–206.

Banner, A., & Wang, Y. (2010). An analysis of the reading strategies used by adult and student deaf readers. *Journal of Deaf Studies and Deaf Education, 16*(1), 2–23. doi:10.1093/deafed/enq027

Baumann, J. F., Edwards, E. C., Boland, E. M., Olejnik, S., & Kame'enui, E . (2003). Vocabulary tricks: Effects of instruction in morphology and context on fifth-grade students' ability to derive and infer word meanings. *American Educational Research Journal, 40*(2), 447–494.

Beal-Alvarez, J. S., & Easterbrooks, S. R. (2012). Increasing children's ASL classifier production: A multi-component intervention. Manuscript submitted for publication.

Beal-Alvarez, J. S., Lederberg, A. R., & Easterbrooks, S. R. (2011). Grapheme-phoneme acquisition of deaf preschoolers. *Journal of Deaf Studies and Deaf Education, 17*(1), 39–60. doi:10.1093/deafed/enr030

Beck, I. L., McKeown, M. G., & Kucan, L. (2002). *Bringing words to life: Robust vocabulary instruction.* New York, NY: Guilford.

Bell, N. (1991). Gestalt imagery: A critical factor in language comprehension. *Annals of Dyslexia, 41,* 246–260.

Bell, N. (2007). *Visualizing and verbalizing for language comprehension and thinking.* San Luis Obispo, CA: Gander Publishing.

Bellugi, U., & Fischer, S. (1972). A comparison of sign language and spoken language: Rate and grammatical mechanisms. *Cognition, 1,* 173–200.

Bergeron, J. P., Lederberg, A. L., Easterbrooks, S. R., Miller, E. M., & Connor, C. M. (2009). Building the alphabetic principle in young children who are deaf or hard of hearing. *The Volta Review, 109*(2–3), 87–119.

Berko, J. (1958). The child's learning of English morphology. *Word, 14*, 150–177.

Berninger, V. W., Abbott, R. D., Nagy, W., & Carlisle, J. (2010). Growth in phonological, orthographic, and morphological awareness in grades 1 to 6. *Journal of Psycholinguistic Research, 39*, 141–163.

Biemiller, A. (2005). Size and sequence in vocabulary development: Implications for choosing words for primary grade vocabulary instruction. In E. H. Heivert & M. L. Kamil (Eds.), *Teaching and learning vocabulary: Bringing research to practice* (pp. 232–242). Mahwah, NJ: Erlbaum.

Biemiller, A., & Boote, C. (2006). An effective method of building meaning vocabulary in primary grades. *Journal of Educational Psychology, 98*(1), 44–62.

Biemiller, A., & Slonim, N. (2001). Estimating root word vocabulary growth in normative advantaged populations: Evidence for a common sequence of vocabulary acquisition. *Journal of Educational Psychology, 93*(3), 498–520.

Boers, F. (2003). Applied linguistics perspectives on cross-cultural variation in conceptual metaphor. *Metaphor and Symbol, 18*(4), 231–238.

Bonvillian, J. D. (1983). Effects of signability and imagery on word recall of deaf and hearing students. *Perceptual Motor Skills, 56*, 775–791.

Boothroyd, A., Geers, A., & Moog, J. (1991). Practical implications of cochlear implants in children. *Ear and Hearing, 12*(Suppl), 81–89.

Bos, C. S., & Anders, P. L. (1990). Effects of interactive vocabulary instruction on the vocabulary learning and reading comprehension of junior-high learning disabled students. *Learning Disability Quarterly, 13*, 31–42.

Bourne, R. (2006–2007, Winter). Teaching activities that expand the "known" in a primary grade classroom: Phonemic awareness, phonics, and word wall words and read and respond (R & R). *Illinois Reading Council Journal, 35*(1), 14–21.

Boutin, D. (2008). Persistence in postsecondary environments of students with hearing impairments. *Journal of Rehabilitation, 74*, 25–31. Retrieved from http://www.redorbit.com/news/education/1354454/persistence_in_postsecondary_environments_of_students_with_hearing_impairments/

Bow, C. P., Blamey, P. J., Paatsch, L. E., & Sarant, J. Z. (2004). The effects of phonological and morphological training on speech perception scores, and grammatical judgments in deaf and hard-of-hearing children. *Journal of Deaf Studies and Deaf Education, 9*, 305–314.

Bowe, F. G. (2002). Enhancing reading ability to prevent students from becoming "low-functioning deaf" as adults. *American Annals of the Deaf, 147*(5), 22–27.

Brabham, E. G., & Villaume, S. K. (2001). Building walls of words. *The Reading Teacher, 54*(7), 700–702.

Brackenbury, T., Burroughs, E., & Hewitt, L. E. (2008). A qualitative examination of current guidelines for evidence-based practice in child language intervention. *Language, Speech, and Hearing Services in Schools, 39*(1), 78–88.

Brackenbury, T., Ryan, T., & Messenheimer, T. (2006). Incidental word learning in a hearing child of deaf adults. *Journal of Deaf Studies and Deaf Education, 11*, 76–93.

Brandão, A. C., & Oakhill, J. (2005). How do you know this answer? Children's use of text data and general knowledge in story comprehension. *Reading and Writing, 18*, 687–713.

Brigham, M., & Hartman, H. (2010). What is your prediction? Teaching the metacognitive skill of prediction to a class of sixth- and seventh-grade students who are deaf. *American Annals of the Deaf, 155*(2), 137–142. doi:10.1353/aad.2010.0004

Brown, P. M., & Brewer, L. C. (1996). Cognitive processes of deaf and hearing skilled and less skilled readers. *Journal of Deaf Studies and Deaf Education, 1*(4), 263–269.

Brown, R. (1973). *A first language: The early stages*. Cambridge, MA: Harvard University Press.

Brown, V. L., Hammill, D. D., & Wiederholt, J. L. (2008). *Test of Reading Comprehension (TCR)* (4th ed.). Austin, TX: PRO-ED.

Brownell, R. (2000a). *Receptive One-Word Picture Vocabulary Test* (4th ed.). Austin, TX: PRO-ED.

Brownell, R. (2000b). *Expressive One-Word Picture Vocabulary Test* (4th ed.). Austin, TX: PRO-ED.

Bruner, J. (1973). *Going beyond the information given*. New York, NY: Norton.

Bruner, J., Goodnow, J., & Austin, A. (1956). *A study of thinking*. New York, NY: Wiley.

Bryant, P., Nunes, T., & Bindman, M. (1997). Children's understanding of the connection between grammar and spelling. In B. Blachman (Ed.), *Foundations of reading acquisition and dyslexia* (pp. 219–240). Mahwah, NJ: Erlbaum.

Burns, M. K. (2002). Utilizing a comprehensive system of assessment to intervention using curriculum-based assessments. *Intervention in School and Clinic, 38*, 8–13.

Burns, M. K., Dean, V. J., & Foley, S. (2004). Preteaching unknown key words with incremental rehearsal to improve reading fluency and comprehension with children identified as reading disabled. *Journal of School Psychology, 42*, 303–314.

Button, K., Johnson, M. J., & Furgerson, P. (1996). Interactive writing in a primary classroom. *The Reading Teacher, 49*(6), 446–454.

Byrnes, B. (2001). *Cognitive development and learning in instructional contexts* (2nd ed.). Needham Heights, MA: Allyn & Bacon.

Cain, K. (2007). Deriving word meanings from context: Does explanation facilitate contextual analysis? *Journal of Research in Reading, 30*(4), 347–359.

Cain, K., Oakhill, J., & Lemmon, K. (2004). Individual differences in the inference of word meanings from context: The influence of reading comprehension, vocabulary knowledge, and memory capacity. *Journal of Educational Psychology, 96*(4), 671–681.

Calkin, L. (1994). *The art of teaching writing.* Portsmouth, NH: Heinemann.

Calvert, D. R. (1981). EPIC (Experimental project in instructional concentration): Report of a study of the influence on intensifying instruction for elementary-school age deaf children. *American Annals of the Deaf, 126*(8), 865–984.

Campbell, R., Burden, V., & Wright, H. (1992). Spelling and speaking in pre-lingual deafness: unexpected role for isolated "alphabetic" spelling skills. In C. M. Sterling & C. Robson (Eds.), *Psychology, spelling, and education* (pp. 185–199). Philadelphia, PA: Multilingual Matters.

Campbell, R., & Wright, H. (1988). Deafness, spelling, and rhyme. *Quarterly Journal of Experimental Psychology, 40A,* 771–788.

Cannon, J., Fredrick, L., & Easterbrooks, S. (2010). Vocabulary instruction through books read in American Sign Language for English-language learners with hearing loss. *Communication Disorders Quarterly, 31*(2), 98–112.

Carlisle, J. F. (1995). Morphological awareness and early reading achievement. In L. Feldman (Ed.), *Morphological aspects of language processing* (pp. 189–209). Hillsdale, NJ: Erlbaum.

Carlisle, J. F., & Nomanbhoy, D. M. (1993). Phonological and morphological awareness in first graders. *Applied Psycholinguistics, 14,* 177–195.

Carnine, D. W., Silbert, J., Kame'enui, E. J., & Tarver, S. G. (2004). *Direct instruction reading* (4th ed). Upper Saddle River, NJ: Pearson Education.

Carrow-Woolfolk, E. (1996). *Oral and Written Language Scales (OWLS).* Circle Pines, MN: American Guidance Service.

Carrow-Woolfolk, E. (1999). *Test for Auditory Comprehension of Language (TACL)* (3rd ed.). Austin, TX: PRO-ED.

Case, B. J. (2005). *Policy report: Accommodations to improve instruction and assessment of students who are deaf or hard of hearing.* Pearson Education. Retrieved from http://www.pearsonassessments.com/NR/rdonlyres/318B76 DB-853A-449F-A02E-CC53C8CFD1DB/0/Deaf.pdf

Cawthon, S. W. (2007). Hidden benefits and unintended consequences of No Child Left Behind policies for students who are deaf or hard of hearing. *American Educational Research Journal, 44*(3), 460–492. doi:10.3102/0002831207306760

Cawthon, S. W., & The Online Research Lab. (2007). Accommodations use for statewide standardized assessments: Prevalence and recommendations for students who are deaf or hard of hearing. *Journal of Deaf Studies and Deaf Education, 13*(1), 55–76. doi:10.1093/deafed/enm029

Cawthon, S. W., & Wurtz, K. A. (2008). Alternate assessment use with students who are deaf or hard of hearing: An exploratory mixed-methods analysis of portfolio, checklists, and out-of-level test formats. *Journal of Deaf Studies and Deaf Education, 14*(2), 155–178. doi:10.1093/deafed/enn027

Chaleff, C. D., & Ritter, M. H. (2001). The use of miscue analysis with deaf readers. *The Reading Teacher, 55*(2), 190–200.

Chall, J. S., & Dale, E. (1995). *Readability revisited: The new Dale-Chall readability formula.* Brookline, MA: Brookline Books.

Chamberlain, C., & Mayberry, R. (2000). Theorizing about the relation between American Sign Language and reading. In C. Chamberlain, J. Morford, & R. Mayberry (Eds.), *Language acquisition by eye* (pp. 221–259). Mahwah, NJ: Erlbaum.

Chapman, C., Laird, J., & KewalRamani, A. (2010, December). *Trends in high school dropout and completion rates in the United States: 1972–2008. Compendium report.* Retrieved July 20, 2011, from http://nces.ed.gov/pubs2011/2011012.pdf

Chapman, W. (1998). *Curriculum compacting.* Retrieved from http://www.metagifted.org/topics/gifted/curriculum/compacting/

Chard, D. J., & Kame'enui, E. J . (2000). Struggling first-grade readers: The frequency and progress of their reading. *Journal of Special Education, 34*(1), 28–38.

Chard, D., Vaughn, S., & Tyler, B. J. (2002). A synthesis of research on effective interventions for building reading fluency with elementary students with learning disabilities. *Journal of Learning Disabilities 36*(5), 386–406.

Charlesworth, A., Charlesworth, R., Raban, B., & Rickards, F. (2006). Reading recovery for children with hearing loss. *The Volta Review, 106*(1), 29–51.

Charlier, B. L., & Leybaert, J. (2000). The rhyming skills of deaf children educated with phonologically augmented speechreading. *Quarterly Journal of Experimental Psychology, 53A,* 349–375.

Cheng, C. (2008). The bilingual acquisition of compound words and its relation to reading skills. *Dissertation Abstracts International Section A: Humanities and Social Sciences, 69*(5-A), 1717.

Chern, C. (1993) Chinese students' word-solving strategies in reading in English. In T. Huckin, M. Haynes, & J. Coady (Eds.), *Second language reading and vocabulary learning* (pp. 67–82). Norwood, NJ: Ablex Publishing.

Chomsky, N. (1995). *The minimalist program.* Cambridge, MA: MIT Press.

Chrosniak, P. (1993). Reading in English as a translation task: Fluent deaf young adults. In D. J. Leu (Ed.), *Examining central issues in literacy research, theory, and practice.* Forty-Second Yearbook of the National Reading Conference. Chicago, IL: National Reading Conference.

Clark, D. M., Gilbert, G., & Anderson, M. L. (2011). Morphological knowledge and decoding skills of deaf readers. *Psychology, 2*(2), 109–116. doi:10.4236/psych.2011.22018

Clarke, J. (1991). Using visual organizers to focus on thinking. *Journal of Reading, 34*(7), 536–34.

Clay, M. (1972). *Reading: The patterning of complex behavior.* Auckland, New Zealand: Heinemann.

Clay, M. (1975). *What did I write?* Portsmouth, NH: Heinemann.

Clay, M. (1993). *Reading Recovery: A guidebook for teachers in training.* Portsmouth, NH: Heinemann.

Clay, M. (2000). *Running records for classroom teachers.* Portsmouth, NH: Heinemann.

Clifton, C., & Duffy, S. (2001). Sentence comprehension: Roles of linguistic structure. *Annual Review of Psychology, 52,* 167–196.

Colin, S., Magnan, A., Ecalle, J., & Leybaert, J. (2007). Relation between deaf children's phonological skills in kindergarten and word recognition performance in first grade. *Journal of Child Psychology and Psychiatry, and Allied Disciplines, 48*(2), 139–46.

Common Core State Standards Initiative. (2010). Common core state standards for English language arts and literacy in History/special studies, science, and technical studies. Retrieved from http://www.corestandards.org/assets/CCSSI_ELA%20Standards.pdf

Conference of Educational Administrators of Schools and Programs for the Deaf. (2006). *Assessment, equity, and access for deaf and hard of hearing children: Demonstrating student progress under the No Child Left Behind Act.* Retrieved from http://www.ceasd.org/acrobat/CEASD_assessment_equity.pdf

Connor, C. M., Craig, H., Raudenbush, S. W., Heavner, K., & Zwolan, T. A. (2006). The age at which young deaf children receive cochlear implants and their vocabulary and speech-production growth: Is there an added value for early implantation? *Ear & Hearing, 27*(6), 628–644.

Connor, C. M., Hieber, S., Arts, H. A., & Zwolan, T. A. (2000). Speech, vocabulary, and the education of children using cochlear implants: Oral or total communication? *Journal of Speech, Language, and Hearing Research, 43*(5), 1185–1204.

Connor, C. M., & Zwolan, T. A. (2004). Examining multiple sources of influence on the reading comprehension skills of children who use cochlear implants. *Journal of Speech, Language, and Hearing Research, 47*(3), 509–526.

Cooper, D. J. (2000). *Literacy: Helping children construct meaning* (4th ed.). New York, NY: Houghton Mifflin.

Cornett, R. O. (1967). Cued Speech. *American Annals of the Deaf, 112*, 3–13.

Council for Exceptional Children. (2009). *Student progress monitoring.* Retrieved from http://www.cec.sped.org/AM/Template.cfm?Section=Progress_Monitoring_Curriculum_Based_Measurement&Template=/TaggedPage/TaggedPageDisplay.cfm&TPLID=36&ContentID=5535

Coxhead, A. (2000). A new academic word list. *TESOL Quarterly, 34*, 213–238.

Crosson, J., & Geers, A. (2001). Analysis of narrative ability in children with cochlear implants. *Ear & Hearing, 22*(5), 381–394.

Cummins, J. (1984). *Bilingualism and special education: Issues in assessment and pedagogy.* San Diego, CA: College Hill Press.

Cummins, J. (2000). *Language, power, and pedagogy: Bilingual children in the crossfire.* Clevedon, England: Multilingual Matters.

Cunningham, A. E., & Stanovich, K, E . (1997). Early reading acquisition and its relation to reading experience and ability 10 years later. *Developmental Psychology, 33*, 934–945.

Cunningham, A. E., & Stanovich, K. E. (1998). What reading does for the mind. *American Evaluator, 22*, 8–15.

Daane, M. C., Campbell, J. R., Grigg, W. S., Goodman, M. J., & Oranje, A. (2005). Fourth-grade students reading aloud: NAEP 2002 special study of oral reading (NCES 2006-469). U.S. Department of Education. Institute of Education Sciences, National Center for Education Statistics. Washington, DC: Government Printing Office.

Daneman, M., & Hannon, B. (2001). Using working memory theory to investigate the construct validity of multiple-choice reading comprehension tests such as the SAT. *Journal of Experimental Psychology: General, 130*, 208–223.

Deacon, S. H., & Kirby, J. R. (2004). Morphological awareness: Just "more phonological"? The roles of morphological and phonological awareness in reading development. *Applied Psycholinguistics, 25*, 223–238.

DesJardin, J. L., Ambrose, S. E., & Eisenberg, L. S. (2008). Literacy skills in children with cochlear implants: The importance of early oral language and joint storybook reading. *Journal of Deaf Studies and Deaf Education*, *14*(1), 22–43.

DesJardin, J. L., & Eisenberg, L. S. (2007). Maternal contributions: Supporting language development in children with cochlear implants. *Ear and Hearing*, *28*, 456–469.

deVilliers, J. G., & deVilliers, P. A. (1973). A cross-sectional study of the acquisition of grammatical morphemes in child speech. *Journal of Psycholinguistic Research*, *2*, 267–278.

deVilliers, P. A., & Pomerantz, S. B. (1992). Hearing-impaired students learning new words from written context. *Applied Psycholinguistics*, *13*, 409–431. doi:10.1017/S0142716400005749

Dimino, J. A., Taylor, R. M., & Gersten, R. M. (1995). Synthesis of the research on story grammar as a means to increase comprehension. *Reading & Writing Quarterly: Overcoming Learning Difficulties*, *11*(1), 53–72.

Dixon, M., & Rossi, J. (1995). Directors of their own learning: A reading strategy for students with learning disabilities. *Teaching Exceptional Children*, *27*(2), 10–14.

Dohm, A., & Wyatt, I. (2002, Fall). College at work: Outlook and earnings for college graduates, 2000–10. *Occupational Outlook Quarterly*, *46*(3), 3–15.

Dolch, E. W. (1948). *Problems in reading*. Champaign IL: The Garrard Press.

Donne, V., & Zigmond, N. (2008). Engagement during reading instruction for students who are deaf or hard of hearing in public schools. *American Annals of the Deaf*, *153*(3), 294–303.

Dowhower, S. L. (1987). Effects of repeated reading on second-grade transitional readers' fluency and comprehension. *Reading Research Quarterly*, *22*, 389–406.

Dry, E., & Earle, P. T. (1988). Can Johnny have time to read? *American Annals of the Deaf*, *133*(3), 219–222.

Duncan, J. (1999). Conversational skills of children with hearing loss and children with normal hearing in an integrated setting. *The Volta Review*, *101*(4), 193–203.

Dunn, L. M., & Dunn, L. M. (2007). *Peabody Picture Vocabulary Test-3rd Ed. (PPVT-III)*. San Antonio, TX: Pearson.

Dunst, C. J., Herter, S., Shields, H., & Bennis, L. (2001). Mapping community-based natural learning opportunities. *Young Exceptional Children*, *4*(4), 16–24.

Dynarski, M., Agodini, R., Heaviside, S., Novak, T., Carey, N., Campuzano, L.,…& Sussex, W. (2007). *Effectiveness of reading and mathematics software products: Findings from the first student cohort*. Washington, DC: U.S. Department of Education, Institute of Education Sciences.

Easterbrooks, S. R. (1983). Literal and metaphoric understanding of four pairs of polar adjectives across four domains by hearing and hearing impaired children at two age levels. *Dissertation Abstracts International, 44*(8), 2437A. (UMI No. DA 8326396)

Easterbrooks, S. R. (1985, November/December). On prepositions. *Perspectives for Teachers of the Hearing Impaired, 4*(2), 15–17.

Easterbrooks, S. R. (2010). Evidence-based curricula and practices that support development of reading skills. In M. Marschark & P. E. Spencer (Eds.), *Evidence-based curricula and practices* (pp. 111–126). New York, NY: Oxford University Press.

Easterbrooks, S. R., & Baker, S. (2002). *Language learning in children who are deaf and hard of hearing: Multiple pathways.* Boston, MA: Allyn & Bacon.

Easterbrooks, S. R., & Beal-Alvarez, J. (2012). States' reading outcomes of students who are d/deaf or hard of hearing. *American Annals of the Deaf, 157*(1), 27–40.

Easterbrooks, S. R., & Estes, E. (2007). *Helping deaf and hard of hearing students to use spoken language.* Thousand Oaks, CA: Corwin Press.

Easterbrooks, S. R., & Huston, S. (2008). The signed reading fluency of students who are deaf/hard of hearing. *Journal of Deaf Studies and Deaf Education, 13*, 37–54.

Easterbrooks, S. R., Lederberg, A. R., & Connor, C. M. (2011). Contributions of the emergent literacy environment to literacy outcomes for young children who are deaf. *American Annals of the Deaf, 155*(4), 467–480.

Easterbrooks, S. R., Lederberg, A. R., Miller, E. M., Bergeron, J. P., & Connor, C. M. (2008). Emergent literacy skills during early childhood in children with hearing loss: Strengths and weaknesses. *The Volta Review, 108*(2), 91–114.

Easterbrooks, S. R., & Putney, L. L. (2008). Development of initial and advanced standards of knowledge and skills for teachers of children who are deaf or hard of hearing. *Communication Disorders Quarterly, 30*(1), 5–11.

Easterbrooks, S. R., & Stephenson, B. (2006). An examination of twenty literacy, science, and mathematics practices used to educate students who are deaf or hard of hearing. *American Annals of the Deaf, 151*(4), 385–397.

Ebbers, S., & Denton, C. (2008). A root awakening: Vocabulary instruction for older students with reading difficulties. *Learning Disabilities Research and Practice, 23*(2), 90–102.

Ecalle, J., Bouchafa, H., Potocki, A., & Magnan, A. (2011). Comprehension of written sentences as a core component of children's reading comprehension. *Journal of Research in Reading.* doi:10.1111/j.1467-9817.2011.01491.x

Edmonds, M., Vaughn, S., Wexler, J., Reutebuch, C., Cable, A., Tackett, K., & Schnakenberg, J. (2009). A synthesis of reading interventions and effects on reading comprehension outcomes for older struggling readers. *Review of Educational Research, 79*(1), 262–300.

Egan, M. (1999). Reflections on effective use of graphic organizers. *Journal of Adolescent and Adult Literacy, 42*(8), 641–645.

Elliot, L. B., Stinson, M. S., McKee, B. G., Everhart, V. S., & Francis, P. J. (2001). College students' perceptions of the C-Print speech-to-text transcription system. *Journal of Deaf Studies and Deaf Education, 6*(4), 285–298.

Engen, E., & Engen, T. (1983). *Rhode Island Test of Language Structure (RITLS).* Austin, TX: PRO-ED.

Englert, C. S., Berry, R., & Dunsmore, K. (2001). A case study of the apprenticeship process: Another perspective on the apprentice and the scaffolding metaphor. *Journal of Learning Disabilities, 34*(2), 152–171.

Englert, C. S., & Dunsmore, K. (2002). A diversity of teaching and learning paths: Teaching writing in situated activity. In J. Brophy (Ed.), *Social constructivist teaching: Affordances and constraints* (pp. 81–130). Boston, MA: JAI.

Enns, C., Hall, R., Isaac, B., & MacDonald, P. (2007). Process and product: Creating stories with deaf students. *TESL Canada Journal/Revue TESL du Canada, 25*(1), 1–22.

Enns, C., & Zimmer, K. (2009). *Research study: Adapting the British Sign Language Receptive Skills Test into American Sign Language. Summary Report.* Retrieved from http://home.cc.umanitoba.ca/~ennscj/ASLtestsummary.pdf

Ensor, A. D. I., & Koller, J. R . (1997). The effect of the method of repeated readings on the reading rate and word recognition accuracy of deaf adolescents. *Journal of Deaf Studies and Deaf Education, 2*(2), 61–70.

Erath, A. S., & Larkin, V. M. (2004). Making distance education accessible for students who are deaf and hard-of-hearing. *Assistive Technology, 16*(2), 116–123.

Erting, L., & Pfau, J. (1997). *Becoming bilingual: Facilitating English literacy development using ASL in preschool.* Washington, DC: Gallaudet University Pre-College National Mission Programs.

Ewoldt, C., Israelite, N., & Dodds, R. (1992). The ability of deaf students to understand text: A comparison of the perceptions of teachers and students. *American Annals of the Deaf, 137*, 351–361.

Fairview Learning Network. (2010). *Tools for literacy—A new way of thinking.* Retrieved from http://www.fairviewlearning.com

Farkas, G., & Beron, K. (2004). The detailed age trajectory of oral vocabulary knowledge: Differences by class and race. *Social Science Research, 33*(3), 464–497.

Farrington, P. (2007, June). Using context cues: Children as reading detectives. *Literacy Today*, 8–9.

Fenson, L., Dale, P. S., Reznick, J. S., Bates, E., Thal, D. J., & Pethick, S. J. (1994). Variability in early communicative development. *Monographs of the Society for Research in Child Development, 59*(5) (Serial No. 242), 1–173.

Feuerstein, R., Hoffman, M., & Miller, R. (1980). *Instrumental enrichment: An intervention program for cognitive modifiability.* Baltimore, MD: University Park Press.

Fisher, B. (1995). Writing workshop in a first grade classroom. *Teaching PreK-8, 26*, 66–68.

Fitzgerald, E. (1929). *Straight language for the deaf.* Staunton, VA: McClure Company.

Flesch, R. (1948). A new readability yardstick. *Journal of Applied Psychology, 32*, 221–233.

Flesch, R. (1955). *Why Johnny can't read.* New York, NY: Harper and Row.

Florida Literacy Coalition. (n.d.). *Literacy and corrections.* Retrieved from http://www.floridaliteracy.org/refguide/corrections.pdf

Fountas, I. C., & Pinnell, G. S. (1996). *Guided reading: Good first teaching for all children.* Portsmouth, NH: Heinemann.

Fountas, I. C., & Pinnell, G. S. (2001). *Guiding readers and writers. Grades 3–6. Teaching comprehension, genre, and content literacy.* Portsmouth, NH: Heinemann.

Fountas, I. C., & Pinnell, G. S. (2005). *Leveled books K-8: Matching texts to readers for effective teaching.* Portsmouth, NH: Heinemann.

Fountas, I., & Pinnell, G. S. (2009). *Leveled books: K-8* [curriculum materials]. Retrieved from http://www.fountasandpinnellleveledbooks.com/default.aspx

Fowler, A., & Liberman, I. (1995). The role of phonology and orthography in morphological awareness. In L. Feldman (Ed.), *Morphological aspects of language processing* (pp. 157–188). Hillsdale, NJ: Erlbaum.

Frase, L. (2008). Guided writing. *Effective Teaching Solutions.* Retrieved from http://www.effectiveteachingsolutions.com/guidedwritingpdf.pdf

French, M. (1999a). *Starting with assessment: A developmental approach to deaf children's literacy.* Washington, DC: Laurent Clerc National Deaf Education Center.

French, M. (1999b). *The toolkit: Appendices for starting the assessment.* Washington, DC: Gallaudet University, Pre-College National Mission Programs.

French, M. M., Hallau, M. G., & Ewoldt, C. (1985). *Kendall demonstration elementary school language arts curriculum guide* (2nd ed.). Washington, DC: Pre-College Programs, Gallaudet University.

Freyd, P., & Baron, J. (1982). Individual differences in acquisition of derivational morphology. *Journal of Verbal Learning and Verbal Behavior, 21*, 282–296.

Fritchmann, N. S., Deshler, D. D., & Schumaker, J. B. (2007). The effects of instruction in an inference strategy on the reading comprehension skills of adolescents with disabilities. *Learning Disability Quarterly, 30*(4), 245–262.

Fry, E. G. (1989). Reading formulas—maligned but valid. *Journal of Reading, 32,* 292–297.

Fuchs, L. S., Fuchs, D., Hosp, M. K., & Jenkins, J. R. (2001b). Text fluency as an indicator of reading competence: A theoretical, empirical, and historical analysis. *Scientific Studies of Reading, 5*(3), 239–256.

Fukkink, R. G., & de Glopper, K. (1998). Effects of instruction in deriving word meanings from context: A meta-analysis. *Review of Educational Research, 68,* 450–469.

Fung, P. C., Chow, B. W., & McBride-Chang, C. (2005). The impact of a dialogic reading program on deaf and hard-of-hearing kindergarten and early primary school-aged students in Hong Kong. *Journal of Deaf Studies and Deaf Education, 10*(1), 82–95.

Gabig, C. (2008). Verbal working memory and story retelling in school-age children with autism. *Language, Speech, and Hearing Services in Schools, 39*(4), 498–511.

Gallaudet Research Institute. (2005). *Regional and national summary report of data from the 2003-2004 Annual Survey of Deaf and Hard of Hearing Children and Youth.* Washington, DC: Gallaudet University.

Gallaudet Research Institute. (2008, November). *Regional and national summary report of data from the 2007-2008 Annual Survey of Deaf and Hard of Hearing Children and Youth.* Washington, DC: Gallaudet University. Retrieved June 23, 2009, from http://research.gallaudet.edu/Demographics/2008_National_Summary.pdf

Garate, M. (2000, Spring). Reading to children…guided reading and writing…shared reading and writing…independent reading: Program modifications for ESL students. *Odyssey, 1*(2), 7–10.

Gathercole, S. E., Hitch, G. J., Service, E., & Martin, A. J. (1997). Phonological short-term memory and new word learning in children. *Developmental Psychology, 33,* 966–979.

Gaustad, M. G., & Kelly, R. (2004). The relationship between reading achievement and morphological word analysis in deaf and hearing students matched for reading level. *Journal of Deaf Studies and Deaf Education, 9,* 269–285.

Gaustad, M. G., Kelly, R. R., Payne, J. A., & Lylak, E. (2002). Deaf and hearing students' morphological knowledge applied to printed English. *American Annals of the Deaf, 147*(5), 5–21.

Gaustad, M., & Kelly, R. (2004). The relationship between reading achievement and morphological word analysis in deaf and hearing students matched for reading level. *Journal of Deaf Studies and Deaf Education, 9,* 269–285.

Geers, A. (2002). Factors affecting the development of speech, language, and literacy in children with early cochlear implantation. *Language, Speech, and Hearing Services in Schools, 33*(3), 172–183.

Geers, A. E. (2003). Predictors of reading skill development in children with early cochlear implantation. *Ear and Hearing, 24*(Suppl. 1), 59S–68S.

Geers, A. E., Moog, J. S., Biedenstein, J., Brenner, C., & Hayes, H. (2009). Spoken language scores of children using cochlear implants compared to hearing age-mates at school entry. *Journal of Deaf Studies and Deaf Education, 14*(3), 371–385.

Geers, A. E., Tobey, E. A., Moog, J., & Brenner, C. (2008). Long-term outcomes of cochlear implantation in the preschool years: From elementary grades to high school. *International Journal of Audiology, 27*(Suppl. 2), 21–30.

Geers, A., & Hayes, H. (2011). Reading, writing, and phonological processing skills of adolescents with 10 or more years of cochlear implant experience. *Ear and Hearing, 32*, 49S–59S.

Gennaoui, M., & Chaleff, C. (2000). Miscue analysis for deaf readers. *Odyssey, 2*, 28–33.

Gentry, M. M., Chinn, K. C., & Moulton, R. D. (2004). Effectiveness of multimedia reading materials used with children who are deaf. *American Annals of the Deaf, 149*(5), 394–403.

Georgia Department of Education. (2011). *Georgia Performance Standards.* Retrieved from https://www.georgiastandards.org/Standards/Pages/Browse Standards/BrowseGPS.aspx

Gersten, R., Fuchs, L., Williams, J., & Baker, S. (2001). Teaching reading comprehension to students with learning disabilities: A review of research. *Review of Educational Research, 71*, 279–320.

Gibson, S. A. (2008). Guided writing lessons: Second-grade students' development of strategic behavior. *Reading Horizons, 48*(2), 111–132.

Gibson, S. A. (2009). An effective framework for primary-grade guided writing instruction. *The Reading Teacher, 62*(4), 324–335.

Glass, L., Clause, C., & Kreiner, D. (2007). Effect of test-expectancy and word bank availability on test performance. *College Student Journal, 41*(2), 342–351.

Goldin-Meadow, S., & Mayberry, R. I. (2001). How do profoundly deaf children learn to read? *Learning Disabilities Research & Practice, 16*, 222–229.

Goldin-Meadow, S., & Mylander, C. (1984). Gestural communication in deaf children: The effects and noneffects of parental input on early language development. *Monographs for the Society for Research in Child Development, 49*(3–4), 1–151.

Goldstein, G., & Behko, J. M. (2003). The profile of multiple language proficiencies: A measure for evaluating language samples of deaf children. *Journal of Deaf Studies and Deaf Education, 8*(4), 452–463. doi:10.1093/deafed/eng027

Good, R. H., & Kaminski, R. A. (Eds.). (2007). *Dynamic indicators of basic early literacy skills* (6th ed.). Eugene, OR: Institute for the Development of Educational Achievement. Retrieved from http://dibels.uoregon.edu/

Goodman, C. A. (2006). Teaching manual communication to preservice teachers of the deaf in an accredited comprehensive undergraduate teacher preparation program. *American Annals of the Deaf, 151*(1), 5–15.

Goodman, K. S. (1986). *What's whole in whole language?* Portsmouth, NH: Heinemann.

Gottfried, A. E. (1985). Academic intrinsic motivation in elementary and junior high school students. *Journal of Educational Psychology, 77,* 631–645.

Gottfried, A. E. (1990). Academic intrinsic motivation in young elementary school children. *Journal of Educational Psychology, 82,* 525–538.

Gough, P. B. (1984). Word recognition. In P. D. Pearson, R. Barr, M. Kamil, & P. Mosenthal (Eds.), *Handbook of reading research* (pp. 225–253). New York, NY: Longman.

Graham, S. (2005). Preview [Editorial]. *Exceptional Children, 7*(2), 135.

Griffith, P. L., & Ripich, D. N. (1988). Story structure recall in hearing-impaired, learning-disabled and nondisabled children. *American Annals of the Deaf, 133,* 43–50.

Griffith, P., Ripich, D., & Dastoli, S. (1990). Narrative abilities in hearing impaired children: Propositions and Cohesion, *American Annals of the Deaf,* 14–21.

Grosjean, F. (2008). *Studying bilinguals.* Oxford, England: Oxford University Press.

Guarino, D. (1989). *Is your mama a llama?* New York, NY: Scholastic.

Gunn, T. M. (2008). The effects of questioning on text processing. *Reading Psychology, 29*(5), 405–442.

Gustason, G., & Zawolkow, E. (2006). *Signing Exact English.* Los Alamitos, CA: Modern Signs Press.

Gustason, G., Zawolkow, E., & Lopez, L. (1993). *Signing Exact English.* Los Alamitos, CA: Modern Signs Press.

Guthrie, J. T., Van Meter, P., McCann, A. D., Wigfield, A., Bennett, L., Poundstone, C. C…Mitchell, A. M. (1996). Growth of literacy engagement: Changes in motivations and strategies during concept-oriented reading instruction. *Reading Research Quarterly, 31*(3), 306–332.

Hage, C., & Leybaert, J. (2006). The effect of Cued Speech on the development of spoken language. In P. E. Spencer & M. Marschark (Eds.), *Advances in the spoken language development of deaf and hard-of-hearing children* (pp. 193–211). New York, NY: Oxford University Press.

Hall, T. (2002). *Explicit instruction.* Wakefield, MA: National Center on Accessing the General Curriculum. Retrieved from http://www.cast.org/publications/ncac/ncac_explicit.html

Hammill, D. D., Wiederholt, J. L., & Allen, E. A. (2006). *Test of Silent Contextual Reading Fluency (TSCRF).* Austin, TX: PRO-ED.

Hanson, V. L., Shankweiler, D., & Fischer, F. W. (1983). Determinants of spelling ability in deaf and hearing adults: Access to linguistic structure. *Cognition, 14,* 323–344.

Haptonstall-Nykaza, T. S. (2004). *The transition from fingerspelling to English print: Facilitating English decoding* (Unpublished master's thesis). University of Colorado, Boulder, CO.

Haptonstall-Nykaza, T. S., & Schick, B. (2007). The transition from fingerspelling to English print: Facilitating English decoding. *Journal of Deaf Studies and Deaf Education, 12*(2), 172–183.

Harlaar, N., Hayiou-Thomas, M. E., Dale, P. S., & Plomin, R. (2008). Why do preschool language abilities correlate with later reading? A twin study. *Journal of Speech, Language, and Hearing Research, 51,* 688–705. doi:10.1044/1092-4388(2008/049)

Harmon, J. M., Wood, K. D., Hedrick, W. B., Vintinner, J., & Willeford, T. (2009). Interactive word walls: More than just reading the writing on the walls. *Journal of Adolescent & Adult Literacy, 52*(5), 398–408. doi:10.1598/JAAL.52.5.4

Harris, M. (1992). *Language experience and early language development: From input to uptake.* Hove, England: Erlbaum.

Harris, M., & Moreno, C. (2004). Deaf children's use of phonological coding: Evidence from reading, spelling, and working memory. *Journal of Deaf Studies and Deaf Education, 9*(3), 253–268.

Harris, M., & Moreno, C. (2006). Speech reading and learning to read: A comparison of 8-year-old profoundly deaf children with good and poor reading ability. *Journal of Deaf Studies and Deaf Education, 11*(2), 189–201. doi:10.1093/deafed/enj021

Hart, B., & Risley, R. T. (1995). *Meaningful differences in the everyday experience of young American children.* Baltimore, MD: Paul H. Brookes.

Hartman, M. (1996). Thinking and learning in classroom discourse. *The Volta Review, 98,* 93–106.

Hasbrouck, J. (2006). For students who are not yet fluent, silent reading is not the best use of classroom time. *American Educator, 30*(2). Retrieved from http://www.aft.org/newspubs/periodicals/ae/summer2006/hasbrouck.cfm

Hasbrouck, J., & Tindal, G. A. (2006). Oral reading fluency norms: A valuable assessment tool for reading teachers. *The Reading Teacher, 59*(7), 636–644.

Hauser, P., Lukomski, J., & Hillman, T. (2008). Development of deaf and hard-of-hearing students' executive function. In M. Marschark & P. Hauser (Eds.), *Deaf cognition: Foundations and outcomes* (pp. 286–309). Cary, NC: Oxford University Press.

Hayes, H., Geers, A., Treiman, R., & Moog, J. (2009). Receptive vocabulary development in deaf children with cochlear implants: Achievement in an intensive auditory-oral educational setting. *Ear & Hearing, 30,* 128–135.

Heenan, R. A. (2007). Literacy and deafness: A qualitative analysis into the efficacy of an adapted reading recovery program. *Dissertation Abstracts International Section A: Humanities and Social Sciences, 67*(10-A), 3711.

Heift, T. (2004). Corrective feedback and learner uptake in CALL. *ReCALL, 6*(2), 416–431. doi.10.1017/S0958344004001120

Helms, L. L., & Schleper, D. R. (2000, Summer). Fun projects after school including writing. *Odyssey, 1*(3), 13–16.

Henderson, E. (1985). *Teaching spelling.* Boston, MA: Houghton Mifflin.

Hermans, D., Knoors, H., Ormel, E., & Verhoeven, L. (2008a). Modeling reading vocabulary learning in deaf children in bilingual education programs. *Journal of Deaf Studies and Deaf Education, 13*(1), 1–20.

Heubert, J. P., & Hauser, R. M. (1999). *High stakes: Testing for tracking, promotion, and graduation.* Washington, DC: National Academy Press.

Hibbing, A. N., & Rankin-Erikson, J. L. (2003). A picture is worth a thousand words: Using visual images to improve comprehension for the middle school struggling readers. *Reading Teacher, 56,* 758–770.

Hirsh-Pasek, K. (1987). The metalinguistics of fingerspelling: An alternative way to increase vocabulary in congenitally deaf readers. *Reading Research Quarterly, 22,* 455–474.

Hirvonen, R., Georgiou, G., & Lerkkanen, M.-K. (2010). Task-focused behavior and literacy development: A reciprocal relationship. *Journal of Research in Reading, 33*(3), 302–319.

Hollenbeck, K., Tindal, G., & Almond, P. (1999). Teachers' knowledge of accommodations as a validity issue in high-stakes testing. *The Journal of Special Education, 32*(3), 175–183.

Holmes, V. L., & Moulton, M. R. (1997). Dialogue journals as an ESL learning strategy. *Journal of Adolescent & Adult Literacy, 40*(8), 616–621.

Holt, J. A., Traxler, C. B., & Allen, T. E. (1997). Interpreting the scores: A user's guide to the 9th edition Stanford Achievement Test for educators of deaf and hard-of-hearing students. *Gallaudet Research Institute Technical Report 97-1.* Washington, DC: Gallaudet University.

Horton, S. V., Lovitt, T. C., & Bergerund, D. (1990). The effectiveness of graphic organizers for three classifications of secondary students in content area classes. *Journal of Learning Disabilities, 23,* 12–22.

Hu, M., & Nation, I. S. P. (2000). Vocabulary density and reading comprehension. *Reading in a Foreign Language, 13,* 403–430.

Hudson, R. F., Lane, H. B., & Pullen, P. C. (2005). Reading fluency assessment and instruction: What, why, and how? *Reading Teacher, 58,* 702–714.

Huttenlocher, J., Haight, W., Bryk, A., Sletzer, M., & Lyons, T. (1991). Early vocabulary growth: Relation to input and gender. *Developmental Psychology, 27*(23), 236–248.

Hyerle, D. (2009). *Visual tools for transforming information into knowledge* (2nd ed). Thousand Oaks, CA: Corwin Press.

Individuals with Disabilities Education Improvement Act of 2004, 20 U. S. C. 33 § 1400 et seq. (2004). Reauthorization of the Individuals with Disabilities Education Act of 1990.

International Communication Learning Institute. (2008). *See-the-sound: Visual Phonics.* Retrieved from http://seethesound.org/visual_phonics.html

International Reading Association. (1999). High-stakes assessment in reading: A position statement of the International Reading Association. *The Reading Teacher, 53*(3), 257–264.

Jenkins, J. R., Fuchs, L. S., van den Broek, P., Espin, C., & Deno, S. (2003a). Sources of individual differences in reading comprehension and reading fluency. *Journal of Educational Psychology, 95,* 719–729.

Jenkins, J. R., Fuchs, L. S., van den Broek, P., Epsin, C., & Deno, S. L. (2003b). Accuracy and fluency in list and context reading of skilled and RD groups: Absolute and relative performance levels. *Learning Disabilities Research and Practice, 18,* 237–245.

Johns, J. (2004). *Basic reading inventory: Pre-primer through grade 12—Revised* (9th ed.). New York, NY: Kendall Hunt.

Johns, J. (2008). *Basic Reading Inventory: Pre-primer through grade 12—Revised* (10th ed.). New York, NY: Kendall Hunt.

Johnson-Glenberg, M. (2000). Training reading comprehension in adequate decoders/poor comprehenders: Verbal and visual strategies. *Journal of Educational Psychology, 92*(4), 772–782.

Jones, P. (1991). The various benefits of dialogue journals. In J. K. Peyton & J. Staton (Eds.), *Writing our lives: Reflections on dialogue journal writing with adults learning English* (pp. 102–126). Englewood Cliffs, NJ: Prentice Hall Regents.

Juel, C. (1988). Learning to read and write: A longitudinal study of 54 children from first through fourth grades. *Journal of Educational Psychology, 80,* 437–447.

Justice, L. M., & Pullen, P. C. (2003). Promising interventions for promoting emergent literacy skills: Three evidence-based approaches. *Topics in Early Childhood Special Education, 23*(3), 99–113.

Kaderavek, J., & Pakulski, L. (2007a). Facilitating literacy development in young children with hearing loss. *Seminars in Speech & Language, 28*(1), 69–78.

Kaderavek, J., & Pakulski, L. (2007b). Mother-child story book interactions: Literacy orientation of pre-schoolers with hearing impairment. *Journal of Early Childhood Literacy, 7*, 49–72.

Karchmer, M. A., & Mitchell, R. E. (2003). Demographic and achievement characteristics of deaf and hard of hearing students. In M. Marschark & P. E. Spencer (Eds.), *Oxford handbook of deaf studies, language, and education* (pp. 21–37). New York, NY: Oxford University Press.

Kelly, L. (1996). The interaction of syntactic competence and vocabulary during reading by deaf students. *Journal of Deaf Studies and Deaf Education, 1*(1), 75–90.

Kelly, L. (2003). The importance of processing automaticity and temporary storage capacity to the differences in comprehension between skilled and less skilled college-age deaf readers. *Journal of Deaf Studies and Deaf Education, 8*, 230–249.

Kelly, R. R., & Gaustad, M. G. (2007). Deaf college students' mathematical skills relative to morphological knowledge, reading level, and language proficiency. *Journal of Deaf Studies and Deaf Education, 12*, 25–37.

Kiese-Himmel, C., & Reeh, M. (2006). Assessment of expressive vocabulary outcomes in hearing-impaired children with hearing aids: Do bilaterally hearing-impaired children catch up? *The Journal of Laryngology & Otology, 120*, 619–626.

King-Sears, M. E., & Bowman-Kruhm, M. (2010). Attending to specialized reading instruction for adolescents with mild disabilities. *Teaching Exceptional Children, 42*(4), 30–40.

Klauda, S. L., & Guthrie, J. T. (2008). Relationship of three components of reading fluency to reading comprehension. *Journal of Educational Psychology, 100*(2), 310–321.

Klecan-Aker J., & Blondeau, R. (1990). An examination of the written stories of hearing impaired school-aged children. *The Volta Review, 92*, 275–282.

Koskinen, P. S., & Blum, I. H. (1984). Repeated oral reading and the acquisition of fluency. In J. Niles & L. Harris (Eds.), *Changing perspectives on research and in reading/language processing and instruction, 33rd Yearbook of the National Reading Conference* (pp. 183–187). Rochester, NY: National Reading Conference.

Kozulin, A., & Presseisen, B. Z. (1995). Mediated learning experience and psychological tools: Vygotsky's and Feuerstein's perspectives in a study of student learning. *Educational Psychologist, 30*(2), 67–75.

Kraemer, J., Kramer, S., Koch, H., Madigan, K., & Steely, D. (2001). Using direct instruction programs to teach comprehension and language skills to deaf and hard of hearing students. *Direct Instruction News, 1*(1–2), 23–31. ED467298.

Krammer, C. D. (2007). The effect of the methods of repeated and assisted reading on the reading fluency and comprehension of deaf and hard of hearing students. *Dissertation Abstracts International Section A: Humanities and Social Sciences, 68*(3-A), 954.

Kuhn, M. R., & Stahl, S. A. (2003). Fluency: A review of developmental and remedial practices. *Journal of Educational Psychology, 95*, 3–21.

Kuhn, M. R., Schwanenflugel, P. J., & Meisinger, E. B. (2010, April/May/June). Review of research: Aligning theory and assessment of reading fluency: Automaticity, prosody, and definitions of fluency. *Reading Research Quarterly, 45*(2), 230–251. doi:10.1598/RRQ.45.2.4

Kuhn, M., & Stahl, S. (2000). *Fluency: A review of developmental and remedial practices.* Ann Arbor, MI: Center for the Improvement of Early Reading (CIERA).

Kyle, F. E., & Harris, M. (2006). Concurrent correlates and predictors of reading and spelling achievement in deaf and hearing school children. *Journal of Deaf Studies and Deaf Education, 11*, 273–288. doi:10.1093/deafed/enj037

Kyle, F. E., & Harris, M. (2010a). Predictors of reading development in deaf children: A 3-year longitudinal study. *Journal of Experimental Child Psychology, 107*(3), 229–243.

Kyle, F. E., & Harris, M. (2010b). Concurrent correlates and predictors of reading and spelling achievement in deaf and hearing school children. *Journal of Deaf Studies and Deaf Education, 11*(3), 273–288.

Laberge, D., & Samuels, S. (1974). Toward a theory of automatic information processing in reading. *Cognitive Psychology, 6*, 293–323.

Lamb, H. A. (1986). The effects of a read-aloud program with language interaction. *Dissertation Abstracts International, 47*(5-A). (UMI No. 8616894)

Lane, H., Hoffmeister, R., & Bahan, B. (1996). *A journey into the deaf-world.* San Diego, CA: Dawn Sign Press.

Lang, H. G., & Albertini, J. A. (2001). Construction of meaning in the authentic science writing of deaf students. *Journal of Deaf Studies and Deaf Education, 6*, 258–284.

Lang, H. G., & Lewis, R. C. (n.d.). Promoting literacy in the classroom through writing-to-learn strategies: Guided-free write. Retrieved from http://www.deafed.net/ContentResources/Science/WTLGuidedFree.ppt

Lang, H., & Pagliaro, C. (2007). Factors predicting recall of mathematics terms by deaf students: Implications for teaching. *Journal of Deaf Studies and Deaf Education, 12*(4), 449–460.

LaSasso, C. L., Crain, K., & Leybaert, J. (2003). Rhyme generation in deaf students: The effect of exposure to Cued Speech. *Journal of Deaf Studies and Deaf Education, 8,* 250–270 LaSasso, C., & Metzger, M. (1998). An alternate route for preparing deaf children for bi-bi programs: The home language as L1 and Cued Speech for conveying traditionally spoken languages. *Journal of Deaf Studies and Deaf Education, 3*(4), 265–289.

LaSasso, C., & Mobley, R. (1997). National survey of reading instruction for deaf and hard of hearing students in the U.S. *The Volta Review, 99*(1), 31–60.

Laurent Clerc National Deaf Education Center. (n.d.). *Programs and projects: Leading from behind: Language experience in action.* Retrieved from http://www.gallaudet.edu/clerc_center/information_and_resources/info_to_go/language_and_literacy/literacy_at_the_clerc_center/literacy-it_all_connects/leading_from_behind_language_experience_in_action.html

Laurent Clerc National Deaf Education Center. (n.d.). *Portfolios for student growth.* Retrieved from http://clerccenter2.gallaudet.edu/products/?id=217

Laurent Clerc National Deaf Education Center. (2010a). *Shared reading and writing.* Retrieved from http://library.gallaudet.edu/Clerc_Center/Information_and_Resources/Info_to_Go/Language_and_Literacy/Literacy_at_the_Clerc_Center/Literacy-It_All_Connects/Shared_Reading_and_Writing.html

Laurent Clerc National Deaf Education Center. (2010b). *Writer's workshop.* Retrieved from http://library.gallaudet.edu/Clerc_Center/Information_and_Resources/Info_to_Go/Language_and_Literacy/Literacy_at_the_Clerc_Center/Literacy-It_All_Connects/Writers_Workshop.html

Laurent Clerc National Deaf Education Center. (2010c). *Research reading and writing.* Retrieved from http://library.gallaudet.edu/Clerc_Center/Information_and_Resources/Info_to_Go/Language_and_Literacy/Literacy_at_the_Clerc_Center/Literacy-It_All_Connects/Research_Reading_and_Writing.html

Laurent Clerc National Deaf Education Center. (2010d). *Journals and logs.* Retrieved from http://library.gallaudet.edu/Clerc_Center/Information_and_Resources/Info_to_Go/Language_and_Literacy/Literacy_at_the_Clerc_Center/Literacy-It_All_Connects/Journals_and_Logs.html

Lederberg, A. R., & Beal-Alvarez, J. S. (2011). Expressing meaning: From communicative intent to building vocabulary. In P. E. Spencer & M. Marschark (Eds.), *Oxford handbook of deaf studies, language, and education* (2nd ed., pp. 258–275). New York, NY: Oxford University Press.

Lederberg, A. R., & Everhart, V. S. (1998). Communication between deaf children and their hearing mothers: The role of language, gesture, and vocalizations. *Journal of Speech, Language, and Hearing Research, 41*, 887–899.

Lederberg, A. R., Miller, E. M, Easterbrooks, S. R., & Connor, C. M. (2011). *Foundations for literacy*. Unpublished curriculum. Atlanta, GA: Georgia State University.

Lederberg, A. R., & Mobley, C. E. (1990). The effect of hearing impairment on the quality of attachment and mother-toddler interaction. *Child Development, 61*, 1596–1604.

Lederberg, A. R., Prezbindowski, A. K., & Spencer, P. E. (2000). Word-learning skills of deaf preschoolers: The development of novel mapping and rapid word-learning strategies. *Child Development, 71*(6), 1571–1585.

Levy, J., Rodriguez, R., & Wubbels, T. (1993). Teacher communication style and instruction. In D. Fisher (Ed.), *The study of learning environments* (Vol. 7, pp. 11–19). Perth, Australia: Curtin University of Technology Press.

Leybaert, J. (1993). Reading ability in the deaf: The roles of phonological codes. In M. Marschark & D. Clark (Eds.), *Psychological perspectives on deafness* (pp. 269–309). Hillsdale, NJ: Earlbaum.

Leybaert, J. (2000). Phonology acquired through the eyes and spelling in deaf children. *Journal of Experimental Child Psychology, 75*(4), 291–318.

Leybaert, J., & Alegria, J. (1995). Spelling development in deaf and hearing children: Evidence for use of morphological regularities in French. *Reading and Writing: An Interdisciplinary Journal, 7*, 89–109.

Leybaert, J., & Charlier, B. (1996). Visual speech in the head: The effect of Cued-Speech on rhyming, remembering, and spelling. *Journal of Deaf Studies and Deaf Education, 1*(4), 234–248.

Liberman, I. Y., & Shankweiler, D. (1985). Phonology and the problems of learning to read and write. *Remedial and Special Education, 6*(6), 8–17.

Limbrick, E. A., McNaughton, S., & Clay, M. M. (1992). Time engaged in reading: A critical factor in reading achievement. *American Annals of the Deaf, 137*, 309–314.

Ling, D. (2002). *Speech and the hearing-impaired child: Theory and practice* (2nd ed.). Washington, DC: Alexander Graham Bell Association for the Deaf and Hard-of-Hearing.

Livingston, S. (1983). Levels of development in the language of deaf children: ASL grammatical processes, signed English structures, and semantic features. *Sign Language Studies, 40*, 193–286.

Loeterman, M., Paul, P. V., & Donahue, S. (2002, February). Reading and deaf children. *Reading Online, 5*(6). Retrieved from http://www.readingonline.org/articles/art_index.asp?HREF=loeterman/index.html

Logan, G. D. (1997) Automaticity and reading: Perspectives from the instance theory of automatization. *Reading & Writing Quarterly, 13*(2), 123–146. doi:10.1080/1057356970130203

Lonigan, C. J., Burgess, S. R., & Anthony, J. L. (2000). Development of emergent literacy and early reading skills in preschool children: Evidence from a latent-variable longitudinal study. *Developmental Psychology, 36,* 596–613.

Lovett, M. W., & Steinbach, K. A. (1997). The effectiveness of remedial programs for reading disabled children of different ages: Does the benefit decrease for older children? *Learning Disabilities Quarterly, 20,* 189–210.

Lucas, C., Bayley, R., & Valli, C. (2001). *Sociolinguistic variation in American Sign Language.* Washington, DC: Gallaudet University Press.

Luckner, J. L., & Bowen, S. (2006). Assessment practices of professionals serving students who are deaf or hard of hearing: An initial investigation. *American Annals of the Deaf, 151*(4), 410–417.

Luckner, J. L., Bowen, S., & Carter, K. (2001). Visual teaching strategies for students who are deaf or hard of hearing. *Teaching Exceptional Children, 33*(3), 38–44.

Luckner, J. L., & Cooke, C. (2010). A summary of the vocabulary research with students who are deaf or hard of hearing. *American Annals of the Deaf, 155*(1), 38–67.

Luckner, J., & Handley, C. (2008). A summary of the reading comprehension research undertaken with students who are deaf or hard of hearing. *American Annals of the Deaf, 153*(1), 6–36.

Luckner, J., Sebald, A., Cooney, J., Young, J., & Muir, S. (2005/2006). An examination of the evidence-based literacy research in deaf education. *American Annals of the Deaf, 150*(5), 443–454.

Luetke-Stahlman, B. (1989). Documenting syntactically and semantically incomplete bimodal input to hearing-impaired participants. *American Annals of the Deaf, 133,* 230–234.

Luetke-Stahlman, B. (1998). *Language issues in deaf education.* Hillsboro, OR: Butte Publications.

Luetke-Stahlman, B., Hayes, P. L., & Nielsen, D. (1996). Essential practice as adults read to meet the needs of deaf and hard of hearing students. *American Annals of the Deaf, 141*(1), 309–329.

Luetke-Stahlman, B., & Moeller, M. P. (1990). Enhancing parents' use of SEE-2: Progress and retention. *American Annals of the Deaf, 135,* 371–378.

Luetke-Stahlman, B., & Nielsen, D. (2002). Phonological awareness: One key to the reading proficiency of deaf children. *American Annals of the Deaf, 147,* 11–17.

Luetke-Stahlman, B., & Nielsen, D. C. (2003). The contribution of phonological awareness and receptive and expressive English to the reading ability of deaf students with varying degrees of exposure to accurate English. *Journal of Deaf Studies and Deaf Education, 8*(4), 464–484.

Luft, P. (2009). Miscues: Meaningful assessment aids instruction. *Odyssey, 10,* 7–11.

Luft, P., Bonello, M., & Zirzow, N. K. (2009). Technology skill assessment for deaf and hard of hearing students in secondary school. *American Annals of the Deaf, 154*(4), 389–399.

Lyon, G. R., & Moats, L. C. (1997). Critical conceptual and methodological considerations in reading intervention research. *Journal of Learning Disabilities, 30,* 578–588.

MacGregor, S. K., & Thomas, L. B. (1988). A computer-mediated text system to develop communication skills for hearing-impaired students. *American Annals of the Deaf, 133*(4), 280–284.

Malone, N., Baluja, K. F., Costanzo, J. M., & Davis, S. J. (2003, December). The foreign-born population: 2000. *Census 2000 Brief.* Retrieved from http://www.census.gov/prod/2003pubs/c2kbr-34.pdf

Mann, V. (2003). Language processes: Keys to reading disability. In H. L. Swanson, K. R. Harris, & S. Graham (Eds.), *Handbook of learning disabilities* (pp. 213–228). New York, NY: The Guilford Press.

Manzo, A.V. (1969). The ReQuest procedure. *Journal of Reading, 12,* 123–126.

Mariage, T. V. (1996). The construction and reconstruction of two discourse spaces in a special education classroom: A sociolinguistic examination of Sharing Chair and Morning Message (Doctoral dissertation, Michigan State University). *Dissertation Abstracts International, 58,* 133.

Mariage, T. V. (2001). Features of an interactive writing discourse: Conversational involvement, conventional knowledge, and internalization in "Morning Message." *Journal of Learning Disabilities, 34*(2), 172–196.

Markell, M. A., & Deno, S. L. (1997). Effects of increasing oral reading: Generalization across reading tasks. *Journal of Special Education, 31,* 233–250.

Marschark, M., & Hauser, P. (2008). Cognitive underpinnings of learning by deaf and hard- of-hearing students. In M. Marschark & P. Hauser (Eds.), *Deaf cognition: Foundations and outcomes* (pp. 3–23). Cary, NC: Oxford University Press.

Marschark, M., Lang, H., & Albertini, J. (2002). *Educating deaf students: From research to practice.* New York, NY: Oxford University Press.

Marschark, M., Spencer, P. E., & Nathan, P. E. (2011). *Oxford handbook of deaf studies, language, and education* (Vol. 1, 2nd ed.). New York, NY: Oxford University Press.

Marschark, M., & Wauters, L. (2008). Language comprehension and learning by deaf students. In M. Marschark & P. Hauser (Eds.), *Deaf cognition:*

Foundations and outcomes (pp. 309–350). Cary, NC: Oxford University Press.

Marschark, M., West, S., Nall, L., & Everhart, V. (1986). Development of creative language devices in signed and oral production. *Journal of Experimental Child Psychology, 41*(3), 543–550. doi:10.1016/0022-0965(86)90008-1

Martin, D. S., & Jonas, B. S. (1986). Cognitive modifiability in the deaf adolescent. Washington, DC: Gallaudet University. ERIC Document Reproduction Service No. ED276159.

Martinez, M., & Roser, N. (1985). Read it again: The value of repeated readings during storytime. *The Reading Teacher, 62,* 485–490.

Mather, N., Hammill, D. D., Allen, E. A., & Roberts, R. (2004). *Test of Silent Word Reading Fluency (TOSWRF).* Austin, TX: PRO-ED.

Mautte, L. A. (1991). The effects of adult-interactive behaviors within the context of repeated storybook readings upon the language development and selected prereading skills of prekindergarten at-risk students. *Dissertation Abstracts International, 52*(1), 122A. (UMI No. 9115887)

Maxwell, M., & Bernstein, M. (1985). The synergy of sign and speech in Simultaneous Communication. *Applied Psycholinguistics, 6,* 63–81.

Mayberry, R. I. & Waters, G. S. (1991). Children's memory for sign and fingerspelling in relation to production rate and sign language input. In P. Siple & S. Fischer (Eds.), *Theoretical issues in sign language research: Volume II, Psychology* (pp. 211–229). Chicago, IL: The University of Chicago Press.

Mayer, C., & Akamatsu, C. T. (2000). Deaf children creating written texts: Contributions of American Sign Language and signed forms of English. *American Annals of the Deaf, 145*(5), 394–403.

Mayer, C., & Lowenbraun, S. (1990). Total communication use among elementary teachers of hearing impaired children. *American Annals of the Deaf, 135,* 257–263.

Mayer, C., & Wells, G. (1996). Can the linguistic interdependence theory support a bilingual-bicultural model of literacy education for deaf students? *Journal of Deaf Studies and Deaf Education, 1*(2), 93–107.

Mayne, A. M., Yoshinaga-Itano, C., Sedey, A. L., & Carey, A. (2000). Expressive vocabulary development of infants and toddlers who are deaf or hard of hearing. *The Volta Review, 100*(5), 1–28.

McAnally, P. L., Rose, S., & Quigley, S. P. (1999). *Reading practices with deaf learners.* Austin, TX: PRO-ED.

McBride-Chang, C., Wagner, R. K., Muse, A., Chow, B. W.-Y., & Shu, H. (2005). The role of morphological awareness in children's vocabulary acquisition in English. *Applied Psycholinguistics, 26,* 415–435.

McCormick, C. E., & Mason, J. M. (1989). Fostering reading for Head Start children with Little Books. In J. Allen & J. M. Mason (Eds.), *Risk makers, risk takers, risk breakers: Reducing the risks for young literacy learners* (pp. 154–177). Portsmouth, NH: Heinemann.

McKee, D., & Kennedy, G. (2006). The distribution of signs in New Zealand Sign Language. *Sign Language Studies, 6*(4), 372–390.

McKenna, M. C., & Kear, D. J. (1990). Measuring attitude toward reading: A new tool for teachers. *The Reading Teacher, 43*, 626–639.

McKeown, M. G., Beck, I. L., Omanson, R. C., & Pople, M. T. (1985). Some effects of the nature and frequency of vocabulary instruction on the knowledge and use of words. *Reading Research Quarterly, 20*, 522–535.

Meisinger, E. B., Bloom, J. S., & Hynd, G. W. (2010). Reading fluency: Implications for the assessment of children with reading disabilities. *Annals of Dyslexia, 60*, 1–17. doi:10.1007/s11881-009-0031-z

Meisinger, E. B., Schwanenflugel, P. J., & Woo, D. (2009). *The contribution of text reading fluency to reading comprehension in the elementary grades.* Unpublished manuscript. University of Georgia, Athens, GA.

Mercer, C. D., Campbell, K. U., Miller, M. D., Mercer, K. D., & Lane, H. B. (2000). Effects of a reading fluency intervention for middle schoolers with specific learning disabilities. *Learning Disabilities Research, 15*(4), 177–187.

Meyer, M. R., & Felton, R. H. (1999). Repeated reading to enhance fluency: Old approaches and new directions. *Annals of Dyslexia, 49*, 283–306.

Miles, J., & Stelmack, R. M. (1994). Learning disability subtypes and the effects of auditory and visual priming on visual event-related potentials to words. *Journal of Clinical and Experimental Neuropsychology, S16*(1), 43–64. doi:10.1080/01688639408402616

Miller, C., Rose, S., & Hooper, C. (2011). *AvenueDHH—Design and development of a literacy e-progress monitoring environment for deaf and hard of hearing learners.* Washington, DC: USDOE-OSEP Project Director's Conference.

Miller, M., & Veatch, N. (2010). Teaching literacy in context: Choosing and using instructional strategies. *Reading Teacher, 64*(3), 154–165.

Miller, W. (2001). *The reading teacher's survival kit: Ready-to-use checklists, activities and materials to help all students become successful readers.* San Francisco, CA: Jossey-Bass.

Mitchell, R. E., & Karchmer, M. A. (2004). Chasing the mythical ten percent: Parental hearing status of deaf and hard of hearing students in the United States. *Sign Language Studies, 4*(2), 138–163.

Moeller, M. P. (2000). Early intervention and language development in children who are deaf and hard of hearing. *Pediatrics, 106*(3), 41–49.

Moog, J. S., & Biedenstein, J. (1998). *Teacher Assessment of Spoken Language (TASL)*. St. Louis, MO: Moog Center for Deaf Education.

Moog, J. S., & Geers, A. E. (1990). *Early speech perception test for profoundly hearing-impaired children*. St. Louis, MO: Central Institute for the Deaf.

Moog, J., Stein, K., Biedenstein, J., & Gustus, C. (2003). *Teaching activities for children who are deaf and hard of hearing: A practical guide for teachers*. St. Louis, MO: Moog Center for Deaf Education.

Moog, J. S., Stein, K. K., Biedenstein, J. J., & Gustus, C. H. (2003). *Teaching activities for children who are deaf and hard of hearing: A practical guide for teachers*. St. Louis, MO: Moog Center for Deaf Education.

Moores, D., & Meadow-Orlans, K. (Eds.). (1990). *Educational and developmental aspects of deafness*. Washington, DC: Gallaudet University Press.

Morgan, G. (2006a). The development of narrative skills in British Sign Language. In B. Schick, M. Marschark, & P. E. Spencer (Eds.), *Advances in the sign language development of deaf children* (pp. 314–343). New York, NY: Oxford University Press.

Morgan, G. (2006b). "Children are just lingual": The development of phonology in British Sign Language (BSL). *Lingua, 116*, 1507–1523.

Morrison, D., Trezek, B. J., & Paul, P. V. (2008, Spring). Can you see that sound? A rationale for a multisensory intervention tool for struggling readers. *Balanced Reading Instruction, 15(1),* 11–26.

Mousley, K., & Kelly, R. (1998). Problem-solving strategies for teaching mathematics to deaf students. *American Annals of the Deaf, 143*(4), 325–446.

Mueller, J. (2010). *Authentic assessment toolbox*. Retrieved from http://jonathan.mueller.faculty.noctrl.edu/toolbox/whatisit.htm#definitions

Musselman, C. (2000). How do children who can't hear learn to read an alphabetic script? A review of the literature on reading and deafness. *Journal of Deaf Studies and Deaf Education, 5*, 9–31.

Musselman, C., & Akamatsu, C. T. (1999). Interpersonal communication skills of deaf adolescents and their relationship to communication history. *Journal of Deaf Studies and Deaf Education, 4*(4), 305–320.

Musselman, C., & Kircaali-Iftar, G. (1996). The development of spoken language in deaf children: Explaining the unexplained variance. *Journal of Deaf Studies and Deaf Education, 1*(2), 108–121.

Nagy, W., & Anderson, R. C. (1984). How many words are there in printed school English? *Reading Research Quarterly, 19*, 304–330.

Nagy, W., Anderson, R. C., & Herman, P. (1987). Learning word meanings from context during normal reading. *American Educational Research Journal, 24*, 237–270.

Nagy, W., Berninger, V., Abbott, R. D., Vaughan, K., & Vermeulen, K. (2003). Relationship of morphology and other language skills to literacy skills in at-risk second-grade readers and at-risk fourth-grade writers. *Journal of Educational Psychology, 95*, 730–742.

Nagy, W., Diakidoy, I., & Anderson, R. C. (1993). The acquisition of morphology: Learning the contribution of suffixes to the meanings of derivatives. *Journal of Reading Behavior, 25*, 155–170.

Nagy, W. E. (1988). *Teaching vocabulary to improve reading comprehension.* Newark, DE: International Reading Association.

Nagy, W. E., & Herman, P. A. (1987). Breadth and depth of vocabulary knowledge: Implications for acquisition and instruction. In M. McKeown & M. Curtis (Eds.), *The nature of vocabulary acquisition* (pp. 19–35). Hillsdale, NJ: Erlbaum.

Nagy, W., & Scott, J. A. (1990). Word schemas: Expectations about the form and meaning of new words. *Cognition and Instruction, 7*, 105–127.

National Academy of Education's Commission on Reading. (1985). *Becoming a nation of readers: The report of the commission on reading.* Champaign, IL: University of Illinois.

National Assessment Governing Board. (2008). *Reading framework for the 2009 NAEP.* Washington, DC: U.S. Government Printing Office.

National Association of State Directors of Special Education. (2006). *Meeting the needs of students who are deaf or hard of hearing: Educational services guidelines.* Alexandria, VA: Author.

National Center for Education Statistics. (2009). *The Nation's Report Card: Reading 2009* (NCES 2010–458). Washington, DC: Institute of Education Sciences, U.S. Department of Education.

National Center on Response to Intervention. (2010). *Essential components of RTI—A closer look at Response to Intervention.* Washington, DC: U.S. Department of Education. Retrieved from http://www.rti4success.org

National Institute of Child Health and Human Development (NICHHD). (2000). Report of the National Reading Panel. *Teaching children to read: An evidence-based assessment of the scientific research on reading and its implications for reading instruction* (NIH Publication No. 00-4734). Washington, DC: U.S. Government Printing Office.

National Reading Panel. (2000b). *Report of the National Reading Panel: Teaching children to read.* Washington, DC: U.S. Department of Health and Human Services.

National Reading Panel. (n.d.). *Teaching children to read: An evidence-based assessment of the scientific research literature on reading and its implications for reading instruction.* Retrieved from http://www.nichd.nih.gov/publications/nrp/smallbook.cfm

National Research Council. (1998). *Preventing reading difficulties in young child ren.* Washington, DC: National Academy Press.

Neely, J. (1991). Semantic priming effects in visual word recognition: A selective review of current findings and theory. In D. Besner & G. Humphreys (Eds.), *Basic processes in reading: Visual word recognition* (pp.264–336). Hillsdale, NJ: Erlbaum.

Neidle, C., Kegl, J., MacLaughlin, D., Bahan, B., & Lee, R. G. (2000). *The syntax of American Sign Language: Functional categories and hierarchical structure.* Cambridge, MA: MIT Press.

Nelson, K. E. (1998). Toward a differentiated account of facilitators of literacy development and ASL in deaf children. *Topics in Language Disorders, 18*(4), 73–88.

Neuman, S. B. (2004). The effect of print-rich classroom environments on early literacy growth. *The Reading Teacher, 58*(1), 89–91.

Neuman, S. B., & Celano, D. (2001). Access to print in low-income and middle-income communities: An ecological study of four neighborhoods. *Reading Research Quarterly, 36*(1), 8–26. doi:10.1598/RRQ.36.1.1

Newcomer, P., & Barenbaum, E. (2003). *Test of Phonological Awareness Skills (TOPAS).* Austin, TX: PRO-ED.

Nicholas, J. G. (2000). Age differences in the use of informative/heuristic communicative functions in young children with and without hearing loss who are learning spoken language. *Journal of Speech, Language, and Hearing Research, 43*, 380–394.

Nicholas, J. G., & Geers, A. E. (2003). Hearing status, language modality, and young children's communicative and linguistic behavior. *Journal of Deaf Studies and Deaf Education, 8*(4), 422–437.

Nicholls, G., & Ling, D. (1982). Cued speech and the reception of spoken language. *Journal of Speech and Hearing Research, 25*, 262–269.

Nicholson, T. (1991). Do children read words better in context or in lists? A classic study revisited. *Journal of Educational Psychology, 83*(4), 444–450.

No Child Left Behind. (2007). Modified academic achievement standards: Non-regulatory guidance. Retrieved from http://www2.ed.gov/policy/speced/guid/modachieve-summary.html

No Child Let Behind Act of 2001, 20 U. S. C. 70 § 6301 et seq. (2002).

Nover, S., Andrews, J. F., Baker, S., Everhart, V. S., & Bradford, M. (2002). *Star schools' USDLC Engaged Learning Project No. 5, ASL/English bilingual instruction for deaf students: Evaluation and impact study, final report 1997–2002.* New Mexico School for the Deaf, Santa Fe, NM.

Nover, S. M., Christensen, K. M., & Cheng, I. (1998). Development of ASL and English competence for learners who are deaf. *Topics in Language Disorders, 18*(4), 661–672.

Nunan, D. (1991). *Language teaching methodology*. Hertfordshire, England: Prentice Hall International.

Nunes, T., Burman, D., Evans, D., & Bell, D. (2010). Writing a language that you can't hear. In N. Brunswick, S. McDougal, & P. deMornay (Eds.), *Reading and dyslexia in different orthographies* (pp. 109–128). New York, NY: Psychology Press.

O'Connor, I., & Klein, P. (2004). Exploration of strategies for facilitating the reading comprehension of high-functioning students with autism spectrum disorders. *Journal of Autism and Developmental Disorders, 34*(2), 115–127.

O'Connor, R. E., Bell, K. M., Harty, K. R., Larkin, L. K., Sackor, S., & Zigmond, N. (2002). Teaching reading to poor readers in the intermediate grades: A comparison of text difficulty. *Journal of Educational Psychology, 94*, 474–485.

O'Connor, R. E., Swanson, H. L., & Geraghty, C. (2010). Improvement in reading rate under independent and difficult text levels: Influences on word and comprehension skills. *Journal of Educational Psychology, 102*(1), 1–19.

Oakes, W. P., Mathur, S. R., & Lane, K. L. (2010). Reading intervention for students with challenging behavior: A focus on fluency. *Behavioral Disorders, 35*(2), 120–139.

Odom, S. L., Brantlinger, E., Gersten, R., Horner, R. H., Thompson, B., & Harris, K. R. (2005). Research in special education: Scientific methods and evidence-based practices. *Exceptional Children, 7*(2), 137–148.

Ogle, D. (1986). K-W-L: A teaching model that develops active reading of expository text. *The Reading Teacher, 39*, 564–571.

Ogle, D., & Correa-Kovtun, A. (2010). Supporting English-language learners and struggling readers with the "partner reading and content, too" routine. *The Reading Teacher, 63*(7), 532–542.

Ozuro, Y., Best, R., Bell, C., Witherspoon, A., & McNamara, D. S. (2007). Influence of question format and text availability on the assessment of expository text comprehension. *Cognition and Instruction, 25*(4), 399–438.

Paatsch, L., Blamey, P., Sarant, J., & Bow, C. (2006). The effects of speech production and vocabulary training on different components of spoken-language performance. *Journal of Deaf Studies and Deaf Education, 11*(1), 39–55.

Padden, C., & Ramsey, C. (1998). Reading ability in signing deaf children. *Topics in Language Disorders, 18*(4), 30–46.

Padden, C., & Ramsey, C. (2000). American Sign Language and reading ability in deaf children. In C. Chamberlain, J. P. Morford, & R. I. Mayberry (Eds.), *Language acquisition by eye* (pp. 165–189). Mahwah, NJ: Erlbaum.

Paivio, A. (1986). *Mental representations*. New York, NY: Oxford University Press.

Paivio, A. (1989). A dual coding perspective on imagery and the brain. In J. W. Brown (Ed.), *Neuropsychology of visual perception* (pp. 203–216). Hillsdale, NJ: Erlbaum.

Paivio, A. (1991). Dual coding theory: Retrospect and current status. *Canadian Journal of Psychology, 45,* 255–287.

Paivio, A. (2008). How children learn and retain information: The dual coding theory. In S. B. Neuman (Ed.), *Educating the other America* (pp. 227–242). Baltimore, MD: Paul H. Brookes.

Pajares, F., & Miller, M. D. (1997). Mathematics self-efficacy and mathematical problem solving: Implications of using different forms of assessment. *The Journal of Experimental Education, 65*(3), 213–228.

Pakulski, L. A., & Kaderavek, J. N. (2001). Narrative production by children who are deaf or hard of hearing: The effect of role-play. *The Volta Review, 103*(3), 127–194.

Parault, S. J., & Williams, H. M. (2010). Reading motivation, reading amount, and text comprehension in deaf and hearing adults. *Journal of Deaf Studies and Deaf Education, 15*(2), 120–135. doi:10.1093/deafed/enp031

Partington, G., & Galloway, A. (2005/2006). Effective practices in teaching indigenous students with conductive hearing loss. *Childhood Education, 82*(2), 101–6.

Paul, P. V. (1996). Reading vocabulary knowledge and deafness. *Journal of Deaf Studies and Deaf Education, 1*(1), 3–15.

Paul, P. V. (1998). *Literacy and deafness: The development of reading, writing, and literate thought.* Needham Heights, MA: Allyn & Bacon.

Paul, P. V., Wang, Y., Trezek, B. J., & Luckner, J. L. (2009). Phonology is necessary, but not sufficient: A rejoinder. *American Annals of the Deaf, 154*(4), 346–356.

Paul, P., & Gustafson, G. (1991). Hearing-impaired students' comprehension of high-frequency multimeaning words. *Remedial and Special Education (RASE), 12*(4), 52–62.

Paul, P., & Quigley, S. (1994). *Language and deafness* (2nd ed.). San Diego, CA: Singular Publishing.

Penno, J. F., Wilkinson, I. A. G., & Moore, D. W. (2002). Vocabulary acquisition from teacher explanation and repeated listening to stories: Do they overcome the Matthew effect? *Journal of Educational Psychology, 94,* 23–33.

PEPNet. (2009, Fall). How do we improve test equity? PEPNet has some of the answers. *Perspectives.* Retrieved from http://www.pepnet.org/newsletter/2009_fall/fall09Final.pdf

PEPNet. (2009, Spring). Fair and equal testing for students who are deaf/HH. *Perspectives.* Retrieved from http://www.pepnet.org/newsletter/2009_spring/spring09Final.pdf

Perfetti, C. A., & Sandak, R. (2000). Reading optimally builds on spoken language: Implications for deaf readers. *Journal of Deaf Studies and Deaf Education, 5*(1), 32–50.

Perner, D. E. (2007). No Child Left Behind: Issues of assessing students with the most significant cognitive disabilities. *Education and Training in Developmental Disabilities, 42,* 243–251.

Petitto, L. A., Katerelos, M., Levy, B., Gauna, K., Tétrault, K., & Ferraro, V. (2001). Bilingual signed and spoken language acquisition from birth: Implications for mechanisms underlying bilingual language acquisition. *Journal of Child Language, 28*(2), 1–44.

Peyton, J., & Seyoum, M. (1988). *The effect of teacher strategies on students' interactive writing: The case of dialogue journals.* Los Angeles, CA: Center for Language Education and Research, University of California, Los Angeles. ERIC Document Reproduction Service No. ED298763.

Phelps-Teresaki, D., & Phelps-Gunn, T. (2000). *Teaching competence in written language: A systematic program for developing writing skills—Second edition.* Austin, TX: PRO-ED.

Phillips, S. E. (1994). High-stakes testing accommodations: Validity versus disabled rights. *Applied Measurement in Education, 7*(2), 93–120.

Pilling, D., & Barrett, P. (2008). Text communication preferences of deaf people in the United Kingdom. *Journal of Deaf Education and Deaf Studies, 13*(1), 92–103. doi:10.1093/deafed/enm034

Power, D., Power, M. R., & Rehling, B. (2007). German deaf people using text communication: Short message service, TTY, relay service, FAX, and e-mail. *American Annals of the Deaf, 152,* 291–301.

Power, M. R., & Power, D. (2004). Everyone here speaks TXT: Deaf people using SMS in Australia and the rest of the world. *Journal of Deaf Education and Deaf Studies, 9*(3), 333–343. doi:10.1093/deafed/enh042

Power, M. R., Power, D., & Horstmanshof, L. (2007). Deaf people communicating via SMS, TTY, relay service, fax, and computers in Australia. *Journal of Deaf Studies and Deaf Education, 12*(1), 80–92. doi:10.1093/deafed/enl01

Prescott, J. O., & Lewis, M. (2003, January). The power of Reader's Theater. *Instructor, 112*(5), 22–27.

Pressley, M. (1998). Comprehension strategies instruction. In J. Osborn & F. Lehr (Eds.), *Literacy for all: Issues in teaching and learning* (pp. 113–133). New York, NY: Guilford.

Pressman, L. J., Pipp-Siegal, S., Yoshinaga-Itano, C., & Deas, A. (1999). Maternal sensitivity predicts language gained in preschool children who are deaf and hard of hearing. *Journal of Deaf Studies and Deaf Education, 4,* 294–304.

Prinz, P. M., & Strong, M. (1998) ASL proficiency and English literacy within a bilingual deaf education model of instruction. *Topics in Language Disorders, 18*(4), 47–60.

Quigley, S. P., & King, C. M. (1980). Syntactic performance of hearing impaired and normal hearing individuals. *Applied Psycholinguistics, 1,* 329–356.

Quigley, S. P., McAnally, P., Rose, S., & King, C. (2002). *Reading Milestones* (3rd ed.). Austin, TX: PRO-Ed.

Quigley, S., McAnally, P., Rose, S., & Payne, J. (2003). *Reading Bridge.* Austin, TX: PRO-ED.

Quigley, S. P., Montanelli, D. S., & Wilbur, R. B. (1976). Some aspects of the verb system in the language of deaf students. *Journal of Speech and Hearing Research, 19,* 536–550.

Quigley, S. P., Power, D. J., & Steinkamp, M. W. (1977). The language structure of deaf children. *The Volta Review, 79,* 73–84.

Quigley, S. P., Smith, M. L., & Wilbur, R. B. (1974). Comprehension of relativized sentences by deaf students. *Journal of Speech and Hearing Research, 17,* 325–341.

Quigley, S. P., Wilbur, R. B., & Montanelli, D. S. (1976). Complement structures in the language of deaf students. *Journal of Speech and Hearing Research, 19,* 448–457.

Rangel, F. (2000, Spring). Language experience using real life—and teaching to change it. *Odyssey, 1*(2), 18–22.

Rashotte, C. A., & Torgeson, J. K. (1988). Repeated reading and reading fluency in learning disabled children. *Reading Research Quarterly 20*(2), 180–188.

Rasinski, T. (1999). Making and writing words. *Reading Online.* International Reading Association. Retrieved from http://www.readingonline.org/articles/words/rasinski.html

Rasinski, T. V., & Padak, N. D. (2008). *From phonics to fluency: Effective teaching of decoding and reading fluency in the elementary school* (2nd ed.). Boston, MA: Allyn & Bacon.

Reese, E., & Newcombe, R. (2007). Training mothers in elaborative reminiscing enhances children's autobiographical memory and narrative. *Child Development, 78*(4), 1153–1170.

Reeves, J. B., Newell, W., Holcomb, B. R., & Stinson, M. (2000). The sign language skills classroom observation: A process for describing sign language proficiency in classroom settings. *American Annals of the Deaf, 145*(4), 315–341.

Reutzel, D. R., & Hollingsworth, P. M. (1993). Effects of fluency training on second graders' reading comprehension. *Journal of Educational Research, 86,* 325–331.

Richardson, E., & DiBenedetto, B. (1985). *Decoding Skills Test (DST).* Parkton, MD: York Press.

Richardson, J., MacLeod-Gallinger, J., McKee, B. G., & Long, G. I. (2000). Approaches to studying in deaf and hearing students in higher education. *Journal of Deaf Studies and Deaf Education, 5*, 156–173.

Rief, S. (2010). The dyslexia checklist: A practical reference for parents and teachers. San Francisco, CA: Jossey-Bass.

Rittenhouse, R., & Stearns, K. (1990). Figurative language and reading comprehension in American deaf and hard of-hearing children: Textual interactions. *International Journal of Language & Communication Disorders, 25*(3), 369–374.

Robbins, N. L., & Hatcher, C. W (1981). The effects of syntax on the reading comprehension of hearing impaired children. *The Volta Review, 83*, 105–115.

Roberts, G., Torgesen, J. K., Boradman, A., & Scammacca, N. (2009). Evidence-based strategies for reading instruction of older students with learning disabilities. *Learning Disabilities Research & Practice, 23*(2), 63–69.

Robertson, L., Dow, G., & Hainzinger, S. (2006). Story retelling patterns among children with and without hearing loss: Effects of repeated practice and parent-child attunement. *The Volta Review, 106*(2), 147–170.

Rose, D. H., & Meyer, A. (2002). *Teaching every student in the digital age: Universal design for learning.* Alexandria, VA: ASCD.

Rose, D. H., & Meyer, A. (2006). *A practical reader in universal design for learning.* Cambridge, MA: Harvard Education Press.

Rose, S., & McAnally, P. (n.d.). *The Reading Milestones program, Reading Bridges series, and the No Child Left Behind Act of 2001.* Austin, TX: PRO-ED. Retrieved from http://www.proedinc.com/downloads/M10950ReadingMilestonesResearch.pdf

Rose, S., McAnally, P., Barkmeier, L., Virnig, S., & Long, J. (2006). *Technical Report #9: Silent Reading Fluency Test: Reliability, validity, and sensitivity to growth for students who are deaf and hard of hearing at the elementary, middle school, and high school levels.* Research Institute on Progress Monitoring (RIPM), University of Minnesota. Retrieved from http://www.progress-monitoring.org/Techreports/TR9dhhsrftTR.doc

Rosen, D. (2005). Just-in-time instruction: Supporting teacher education candidates developing technology skills. In C. Crawford et al. (Eds.), *Proceedings of Society for Information Technology & Teacher Education International Conference 2005* (pp. 1221–1223). Chesapeake, VA: AACE. Retrieved from http://www.editlib.org/p/19194

Routman, R. (1994). *Invitations: Changing as teachers and learners K–12.* Portsmouth, NH: Heinemann.

Rumelhart, D. E. (1985). Toward an interactive model of reading. In Singer and Ruddell (Eds.), *Theoretical models and the processes of reading* (3rd ed.). Newark, DE: International Reading Association.

Rupley, W., & Slough, S. (2010). Building prior knowledge and vocabulary in science in the intermediate grades: Creating hooks for learning. *Literacy Research and Instruction, 49*, 99–112.

Sadoski, M., & Paivio, A. (2004). A dual coding theoretical model of reading. In R. B. Ruddell & N. J. Unrau (Eds.), *Theoretical models and processes of reading* (5th ed., pp. 1329–1362). Newark, DE: International Reading Association.

Saffran, J., Newport, E., Aslin, R., Tunick, R., & Barrueco, S. (1997). Incidental language learning: Listening (and learning) out of the corner of your ear. *Psychological Science, 8*(2), 101–105.

Samuels, S. J. (1979). The method of repeated readings. *The Reading Teacher, 32*, 403–408.

Sarant, J. Z., Holt, C. M., Dowell, R. C., Rickards, F. W., & Blamey, P. J. (2009). Spoken language development in oral preschool children with permanent childhood deafness. *Journal of Deaf Studies and Deaf Education, 14*(2), 205–217.

Scarborough, H. S., & Brady, S. A. (2002). Toward a common terminology for talking about speech and reading: A glossary of the "phon" words and some related terms. *Journal of Literacy Research, 34*, 299–334.

Scherer, P. (1969). *Visual learning processes in deaf children.* Final report [microform]. Washington, DC: ERIC Clearinghouse. ERIC Document Reproduction Service No. 042298. Retrieved from http://www.eric.ed.gov/ERICWebPortal/search/detailmini.jsp?_nfpb=true&_&ERICExtSearch_SearchValue_0=ED042298&ERICExtSearch_SearchType_0=no&accno=ED042298

Schick, B. (2003). The development of American Sign Language and manually coded English systems. In M. Marschark & P. Spencer (Eds.), *Oxford handbook of deaf studies, language, and education* (pp. 219–231). New York, NY: Oxford University Press.

Schick, B., & Moeller, M. P. (1992). What is learnable in manually-coded English sign systems? *Applied Psycholinguistics, 13*, 313–340.

Schick, B., Williams, K., & Kupermintz, H. (2006). Look who's being left behind: Educational interpreters and access to education for deaf and hard-of-hearing students. *Journal of Deaf Studies and Deaf Education, 11*(1), 3–20. doi:10.1093/deafed/enj007

Schimmel, C., & Edwards, S. (2003). Literacy strategies for the classroom: Putting bi-bi theory into practice. *Odyssey, 5*, 58–63.

Schimmel, C., Edwards, S., & Prickett, H. (1999). Reading!…pah! (I got it!). *American Annals of the Deaf, 144*(4), 298–308.

Schirmer, B. R. (1993). Constructing meaning from narrative text: Cognitive processes of deaf children. *American Annals of the Deaf, 138*, 397–403.

Schirmer, B. R., Bailey, J., & Fitzgerald, S. M. (1999). Using a writing assessment rubric of writing development of children who are deaf. *Exceptional Children*, 65(3), 383–397.

Schirmer, B. R., & McGough, S. M. (2005). Teaching reading to children who are deaf: Do the conclusions of the National Reading Panel apply? *Review of Educational Research*, 75, 83–117.

Schirmer, B. R., & Schaffer, L. (2010). Guided reading approach: Teaching students who are deaf and others who struggle. *Teaching Exceptional Children*, 42(5), 52–58.

Schirmer, B. R., Therrien, W. J., Schaffer, L., & Schirmer, T. N. (2009). Repeated reading as an instructional intervention with deaf readers: Effect on fluency and reading achievement. *Reading Improvement*, 46(3), 168–177.

Schleper, D. (1995). Reading to deaf children: Learning from deaf adults. *Perspectives in Education and Deafness*, 13(4), 4–8.

Schleper, D. (2002). *Leading from behind: Language experience in action.* Washington, DC: Gallaudet University, Laurent Clerc National Deaf Education Center.

Schleper, D. R. (1998). *Read it again and again.* Washington, DC: Laurent Clerc National Deaf Education Center at Gallaudet University.

Schleper, D. R. (2000a, Spring). Dialogue journals... for students, teachers, and parents: Meeting students where they are. *Odyssey*, 1(2), 11–14.

Schleper, D. R. (2000b, Spring). Writers' workshop: I-Ching "Eugene" Shih-Brave student. *Odyssey*, 1(2), 23–26.

Schleper, D. R. (2002, Fall). SSR? DEAR? USSR? Or DIRT? No matter what you call it, independent reading is for everyone. *Odyssey*, 26–28.

Schleper, D. R. (2006, Fall/Winter). Shared reading—a history: Changing lives one family at a time. *Odyssey*, 4–11.

Sedey, A. (1995). *Fast mapping of novel fingerspelled words by profoundly deaf students* (Unpublished doctoral dissertation). University of Wisconsin, Madison.

Sénéchal, M., LeFevre, J., Thomas, E., Daley, K. (1998). Differential effects of home literacy experiences on the development of oral and written language. *Reading Research Quarterly*, 32, 96–116.

Shandilya, G. V. (2010). Evidence-based (or not!) practices used for reading instruction in oral deaf education schools. *Independent Studies and Capstones*. Paper 596. Program in Audiology and Communication Sciences, Washington University School of Medicine. Retrieved from http://digital-commons.wustl.edu/pacs_capstones/596

Shany, M. T., & Biemiller, A. (1995). Assisted reading practice: Effects on performance for poor readers in grades 3 and 4. *Reading Research Quarterly*, 30, 382–395.

Sheen, Y. (2006). Exploring the relationship between characteristics of recasts and learner uptake. *Language Teaching Research, 10*(4), 361–392. doi:10.1191/1362168806lr203oa

Shefelbine, J. L. (1990). Student factors related to variability in learning word meanings from context. *Journal of Reading Behavior, 22,* 71–97.

Shin, J., Deno, S., & Espin, C. (2000). Technical adequacy of the Maze task for curriculum-based measurement of reading growth. *Journal of Special Education, 34*(3), 164–172.

Shu, H., Anderson, R. C., & Zhang, H. (1995). Incidental learning of word meanings while reading: A Chinese and American cross-cultural study. *Reading Research Quarterly, 30*(1), 76–95.

Siegler, R. S. (1995). How does change occur: A microgenetic study of number conservation. *Cognitive Psychology, 25,* 225–273.

Singleton, J., Supalla, S., Litchfield, S., & Schley, S. (1998). From sign to word: Considering modality constraints in ASL/English bilingual education. *Topics in Language Disorders 18*(4), 16–30.

Singson, M., Mahony, D., & Mann, V. (2000). The relation between reading ability and morphological skills: Evidence from derivational suffixes. *Reading and Writing: An Interdisciplinary Journal, 12,* 219–252.

Smith, C. (2000, Spring). Letting Calvin and Hobbes teach English. *Odyssey, 1*(2), 38–40.

Smith, J. J. (2002). *The use of graphic organizers in vocabulary instruction.* Retrieved from ERIC database. (ED463556)

Snedeker, J., & Yuan, S. (2008). Effects of prosodic and lexical constraints in young children (and adults). *Journal of Memory and Language, 58*(2), 574–608. doi:10.1016/j.jml.2007.08.001

Snoddon, K. (2010). *American Sign Language and early literacy: Research as praxis* (Unpublished doctoral dissertation). University of Toronto, Toronto, Canada.

Speece, D. L., & Ritchey, K. D. (2005). A longitudinal study of the development of oral reading fluency in young children at risk for reading failure. *Journal of Learning Disabilities, 38,* 387–399.

Speer, S. R., Kjelgaard, M. M., & Dobroth, K. M. (1996). The influence of prosodic structure on the resolution of temporary syntactic closure ambiguities. *Journal of Psycholinguistic Research, 25*(2), 249–271. doi:10.1007/BF01708573

Spencer, P. E. (1993). Communication behaviors of infants with hearing loss and their hearing mothers. *Journal of Speech and Hearing Research, 36,* 311–321.

Spencer, P. E., & Marschark, M. (Eds.) (2006). *Advances in the spoken language development of deaf and hard-of-hearing children.* New York: Oxford University Press.

Stahl, S. A. (1986). Three principles of effective vocabulary instruction. *Journal of Reading, 29*, 662–668.

Stahl, S. A., & Fairbanks, M. M. (1986). The effects of vocabulary instruction: A model-based meta-analysis. *Review of Educational Research, 56*, 72–110.

Stainthorp, R. (1989). A balanced approach to the teaching of literacy. *Reading, 23*(2), 69–79.

Stanovich, K. E. (1980). Toward an interactive-compensatory model of individual differences in the development of reading fluency. *Reading Research Quarterly, 16*, 32–71.

Stanovich, K. E. (1986). Matthew effects in reading: Some consequences of individual differences in the acquisition of literacy. *Reading Research Quarterly, 21*, 360–407.

Staton, J. (1987). *Dialogue journals.* ERIC Digest ED28276. Urbana, IL: ERIC Clearinghouse on Reading and Communication Skills. Retrieved from http://www.ericdigests.org/pre-926/journals.htm

Stauffer, R. G. (1969). *Directing reading maturity as a cognitive process.* New York, NY: Harper & Row.

Stauffer, R. G. (1969). *Teaching reading as a thinking process.* New York, NY: Harper & Row.

Stebick, D., & Dain, D. (2007). *Comprehension strategies for your K-6 literacy classroom: Thinking before, during and after reading.* Thousand Oaks, CA: Corwin Press.

Stiggins, R. J. (1994). *Student-centered classroom assessment.* New York, NY: MacMillan.

Stiggins, R. J. (1998). *Classroom assessment for student success.* Washington, DC: National Education Association.

Stinson, M., Eisenberg, S., Horn, C., Larson, J., Leavitt, H., & Stuckless, R. (1999). *Real-time speech-to-text services: A report of the National Task Force on Quality of Services in the Postsecondary Education of Deaf and Hard of Hearing students.* Rochester, NY: Northeast Technical Assistance Center, Rochester Institute of Technology.

Stoner, M., & Easterbrooks, S. (2006). Using a visual tool to increase adjectives in the written language of students who are deaf or hard of hearing. *Communication Disorders Quarterly, 27*(2), 95–109.

Stoner, M., Easterbrooks, S. R., & Laughton, J. (2005). Handwritten and word-processed story retellings by school-aged students who are deaf and hard of hearing. *Journal of Special Education and Technology, 20*(3), 35–44.

Strassman, B. (1997). Metacognition and reading in children who are deaf: A review of the research. *Journal of Deaf Studies and Deaf Education, 2*, 140–149.

Strong, M. (Ed.). (1988). *Language, learning, and deafness.* Cambridge, MA: Cambridge University Press.

Sullivan, J. F. (2006). *Developing knowledge of polysemous vocabulary* (Unpublished doctoral dissertation). University of Waterloo, Ontario, Canada. Retrieved from http://uwspace.uwaterloo.ca/bitstream/10012/2637/1/Jennifer%20Sullivan%20PhD%20Dissertation%202006.pdf

Supalla, S. (1991). Manually coded English: The modality question in signed language development. In P. Siple & S. Fischer (Eds.), *Theoretical issues in sign language research* (Vol. 2, pp. 85–109). Chicago, IL: University of Chicago Press.

Swanson, H. L., & Howell, M. (2001). Working memory, short-term memory, and speech rate as predictors of children's reading. *Journal of Educational Psychology, 93*(4), 720–734.

Swanwick, R., & Watson, L. (2007). Parents sharing books with young deaf children in spoken English and in BSL: The common and diverse features of different language settings. *Journal of Deaf Studies and Deaf Education, 12*(3), 385–405. doi:10.1093/deafed/enm004

Tabors, P. (1996, December). *Predicting fourth grade reading comprehension from school age and preschool age data: A preliminary analysis.* Paper presented at the Annual Meeting of the National Reading Conference, Charleston, SC.

Tade, W. J., & Vitali, G. J. (1994). *Children's early intervention for speech-language-reading.* East Aurora, NY: Slosson Education Publications.

Tarulli, N. J. (1998). Using photography to enhance language and learning: A picture can encourage a thousand words. *Language, Speech, and Hearing Services in Schools, 29,* 54–57.

Tasker, S. L., & Schmidt, L. A. (2008). The "dual usage problem" in the explanations of "joint attention" and children's socioemotional development: A reconceptualization. *Developmental Review, 28,* 263–288. doi:10.1016/j.dr.2007.07.001

Tavil, Z. M., & Soylemez, A. S. (2008). Vocabulary teaching through storytelling to very young learners in kindergarten. *Ekev Academic Review, 12*(35), 371–382.

Taylor, B. M., Frye, B. J., & Mauyama, G. M. (1990). Time spent reading and reading growth. *American Educational Research Journal, 27*(2), 351–362.

Taylor, B. M., Pearson, P. D., Peterson, D. S., & Rodriguez, M. C. (2003). Reading growth in high-poverty classrooms: The influence of teacher practices that encourage cognitive engagement in literacy learning. *Elementary School Journal, 104,* 3–28.

Taylor, P., & Keeters, S. (Eds.) (2010, February). *Millenials—A portrait of a generation: Confident, connected, open to change.* Washington, DC: Pew Research

Center. Retrieved from http://pewsocialtrends.org/assets/pdf/millennials-c onfident-connected-open-to-change.pdf

Therrien, W. J. (2004). Fluency and comprehension gains as a result of repeated reading: A meta-analysis. *Remedial and Special Education, 25,* 252–261.

Therrien, W., Gormley, S., & Kubina, R. (2006). Boosting fluency and comprehension to improve reading achievement. *Teaching Exceptional Children, 38*(3), 22–26.

Tindal, G., Hollenbeck, K., Heath, W., & Almond, P. (1997). *The effect of using computers as an accommodation in a statewide writing test* (Technical Research Report). Eugene, OR: University of Oregon, Behavioral Research and Teaching.

Todman, J., & Seedhouse, E. (1994). Visual-action code processing by deaf and hearing children. *Language and Cognitive Processes, 9*(2), 129–141.

Tomasello, M., Akhtar, N., Dodson, K., & Rekau, L. (1997). Differential productivity in young children's use of nouns and verbs. *Journal of Child Language, 24,* 373–387.

Tomlinson, C. A. (1995). *Differentiating instruction for advanced learners in the mixed-ability middle school classroom.* Retrieved from ERIC Database. (ED443572)

Tomlinson, C. A., (2001). *How to differentiate instruction in mixed-ability classrooms* (2nd ed.) Alexandria, VA: ASCD.

Tompkins, L. B. (2000, Summer). Guided reading and writing: A role for parents in leading children to literacy. *Odyssey,* 18–21.

Topor, I. L. (2009). *Fact sheet: Functional vision assessment.* Colorado Services to Children with Deafblindness. Retrieved from http://www.cde.state.co.us/ cdesped/download/pdf/dbFuncVisionAssmt.pdf

Torgesen, J. K., Rashotte, C. A., & Alexander, A. W. (2001). Principles of fluency instruction in reading: Relationships with established empirical outcomes. In M. Wolf (Ed.), *Dyslexia, fluency, & the brain* (pp. 333–355). Parkton, MD: York Press.

Traxler, C. B. (2000). The Stanford Achievement Test, 9th ed.: National norming and performance standards for deaf and hard-of-hearing students. *Journal of Deaf Studies and Deaf Education, 5*(43), 337–348.

Treiman, R., & Cassar, M. (1996). Effects of morphology on children's spelling of final consonant clusters. *Journal of Experimental Child Psychology, 63,* 141–170.

Trezek, B. J., Gampp, T. L., Wang, Y., Paul, P. V., & Woods, D. G. (2007). Using Visual Phonics to supplement beginning reading instruction for students who are deaf or hard of hearing. *Journal of Deaf Studies and Deaf Education, 12,* 373–384.

Trezek, B. J., & Malmgren, K. W. (2005). The efficacy of utilizing a phonics treatment package with middle school deaf and hard-of-hearing students. *Journal of Deaf Studies and Deaf Education, 10*, 256–271.

Trezek, B. J., & Wang, Y. (2006). Implications of utilizing a phonics-based reading curriculum with children who are deaf or hard of hearing. *Journal of Deaf Studies and Deaf Education, 11*, 202–213.

Trezek, B. J., Wang, Y., & Paul, P. V. (2010). *Reading and deafness: Theory, research and practice.* Clifton Park, NY: Delmar Cengage Learning.

Tucker, J. A. (1989). *Basic flashcard technique when vocabulary is the goal.* Unpublished teaching materials, School of Education, University of Chattanooga, Chattanooga, TN.

Turner, J. (1995). The influence of classroom contexts on young children's motivation for literacy. *Reading Research Quarterly, 30*, 410–441.

Tyler, A., & Nagy, W. (1990). Use of derivational morphology during reading. *Cognition, 36*, 17–34.

U.S. Department of Education, Institute of Education Sciences, National Center for Education Statistics, National Assessment of Educational Progress (NAEP). (2002). *Oral Reading Study.* Retrieved from http://nces.ed.gov/nationsreportcard/studies/ors/results.asp

U.S. Department of Education, Office of Special Education and Rehabilitative Services, Office of Special Education Programs. (2009). *28th Annual Report to Congress on the Implementation of the Individuals with Disabilities Education Act, 2006*, vol. 2, Washington, D.C. Retrieved from: http://www2.ed.gov/about/reports/annual/osep/2006/parts-b-c/28th-vol-2.pdf.

U.S. Department of Education's National Commission on Excellence in Education. (1983, April). *A nation at risk: The imperative for educational reform. A report to the nation and the secretary of education, United States Department of Education by the National Commission on Excellence in Education.* Retrieved from http://reagan.procon.org/sourcefiles/a-nation-at-risk-reagan-april-1983.pdf

U.S. Department of Education. (2005, February). *No Child Left Behind Act of 2001 Annual Report to Congress.* Retrieved from http://www2.ed.gov/about/reports/annual/nclb/nclbrpt2005.pdf

U.S. Department of Education (2009, February). *Basic reading skills and the literacy of America's least literate adults.* Washington, DC: Institute for Education Sciences. Retrieved from http://nces.ed.gov/pubs2009/2009481.pdf

United Nations Educational, Scientific and Cultural Organization (UNESCO). (2008). *International literacy statistics: A review of concepts, methodology, and current data.* Montreal, Canada: UNESCO Institute for Statistics.

University of Rochester Medical Center. (2010). *Degrees of hearing loss.* Retrieved from http://www.urmc.rochester.edu/audiology/conditions/degrees.cfm

Valencia, S. W., & Buly, M. R. (2004). Behind test scores: What struggling readers really need to know. *The Reading Teacher, 56,* 520–531.

Vaughn, S., & Linan-Thompson, S. (2004). *Research-based methods of reading instruction, grades K-3.* Alexandria, VA: Association for Supervision and Curriculum Development.

Vernon, M., Rafiman, L. J., Greenberg, S. F., & Monteiror, B. (2001). Forensic pretrial police interview of deaf suspects avoiding legal pitfalls. *International Journal of Law and Psychiatry, 24*(1), 43–59.

Vogel, S. A. (1977). Morphological ability in normal and dyslexic children. *Journal of Learning Disabilities, 10,* 41–49.

Voit, M. (2009). *Do dialogue journals with recasts improve the writing skills for adult learners with limited literacy skills?* (Master's thesis). Hamline University, Saint Paul, MN. Retrieved from http://www.hamline.edu/SiteSearch.aspx?searchtext=voit

Vygotsky, L. S. (1978). *Mind and society: The development of higher mental processes.* Cambridge, MA: Harvard University Press.

Waddy-Smith, B., & Wilson, V. (2003, Fall). See that sound: Visual phonics helps deaf and hard of hearing students develop reading skills. *Odyssey,* 14–18.

Wagner, M., & Davis, M. (2006). How are we preparing students with emotional disturbances for the transition to young adulthood? National Longitudinal Transition Study 2. *Journal of Emotional and Behavioral Disorders, 14,* 86–98.

Wagner, R. K., Torgesen, J. K., & Rashotte, C. A. (1994). Development of reading-related phonological processing abilities: New evidence of bidirectional causality from a latent variable longitudinal study. *Developmental Psychology, 30,* 73–87.

Wakeman, S. Y., Browder, D. M., Meirer, I., & McColl, A. (2007). The implications of No Child Left Behind for students with developmental disabilities. *Mental Retardation and Developmental Disabilities, 13,* 143–150.

Walker, L., Munro, J., & Rickards, F. (1989a). Teaching inferential reading strategies through pictures. *The Volta Review, 100*(2), 105–120.

Walker, L., Munro, J., & Rickards, F. (1989b). Literal and inferential reading comprehension of students who are deaf or hard of hearing. *The Volta Review, 100*(2), 87–103.

Wallace, G., & Hammill, D. D. (2001). *Comprehensive Receptive and Expressive Vocabulary Test (CREVT)* (2nd ed.). Austin, TX: PRO-ED.

Waters, G. S., & Doehring, D. G. (1990). Reading acquisition in congenitally deaf children who communicate orally: Insights from an analysis of component reading, language, and memory skills. In T. H. Carr & B. A. Levy (Eds.), *Reading and its development: Component skills approaches* (pp. 323–373). San Diego, CA: Academic Press.

Weaver, B. (2006). *Formal versus informal assessments.* Retrieved from http://content.scholastic.com/browse/article.jsp?id=4452

Webb, M. L., & Lederberg, A. R. (2012). *Measuring phonological awareness in DHH children.* Manuscript submitted for publication.

Wertsch, J. V., & Sohmer, R. (1995). Vygotsky on learning and development. *Human Development, 38*(6), 332–337.

Westerveld, M., & Gillon, G. (2010). Profiling oral narrative ability in young school-aged children. *International Journal of Speech-Language Pathology, 12*(3), 178–89.

White, A. H. (2002). Assessing semantic-syntactic features of verbs from thirteen verb subsets. *American Annals of the Deaf, 147*, 65–77.

White, T., Power, M., & White, S. (1989). Morphological analysis: Implications for teaching and understanding vocabulary growth in diverse elementary schools: Decoding and word meaning. *Journal of Educational Psychology, 82*, 283–304.

Whitehurst, G. J., Epstein, J. N., Angell, A. L., Payne, A. C., Crone, D. A., & Fischel, J. E. (1994). Outcomes of an emergent literacy intervention in Head Start. *Journal of Educational Psychology, 86*(4), 542–555.

Whitesell, K., & Easterbrooks, S. (2005). *Executive summary of state-by-state reviews of content.* Retrieved from http://www.deafed.net/DeafedForums/Uploads/=46379_Exec%20Summary%20of%20States.doc

Wiederholt, J. L., & Blalock, G. (2000). *Gray Silent Reading Test (GSRT).* Austin, TX: PRO-ED.

Wilbur, R. B. (2000). The use of ASL to support the development of English and literacy. *Journal of Deaf Studies and Deaf Education, 5*(1), 81–104.

Wilkes, E. (1999). *Cottage Acquisition Scales for Listening, Language and Speech (CASLLS).* San Antonio, TX: Sunshine Cottage School for the Deaf.

Williams, C. (2011). Adapted interactive writing instruction with kindergarten children who are deaf or hard of hearing. *American Annals of the Deaf, 156*(1), 23–34.

Williams, C., Phillips-Birdsong, C., Hufnagel, K., Hungler, D., & Lundstrom, R. P. (2009). Word study instruction in the K-2 classroom. *The Reading Teacher, 62*(7), 570–578. doi:10.1598/RT.62.7.3

Wise, J. C., Sevcik, R. A., Morris, R. D., Lovett, M. W., Wolf, M., Kuhn, M.,…Schwanenflugel, P. (2010). The relationship between different measures of oral reading fluency and reading comprehension in second-grade students who evidence different oral reading fluency difficulties. *Language, Speech, and Hearing Services in Schools, 41*, 340–348.

Wolbers, K. A. (2008). Using balanced and interactive writing instruction to improve the higher order and lower order writing skills of deaf students. *Journal of Deaf Studies and Deaf Education, 13*(2), 257–277.

Wolf, M., & Katzir-Cohen, T. (2001). Reading fluency and its intervention. *Scientific Studies of Reading, 5,* 211–239.

Wolfersberger, M. E., Reutzel, D. R., Sudweeks, R., & Fawson, P. C. (2004). Developing and validating the classroom literacy environmental profile (CLEP): A tool for examining the "print richness" of early childhood and elementary classrooms. *Journal of Literacy Research, 36*(2), 211–272. doi:10.1207/ s15548430jlr3602_4

Woodcock, R. N. (1987). *Woodcock Reading Mastery Tests-Revised (WRMT-R).* Circle Pines, MN: American Guidance Services.

World-Class Instructional Design and Assessment. (2007). *ACCESS for ELLs.* Retrieved from http://www.wida.us/assessment/access/index.aspx

Yoshinaga-Itano, C., Snyder, L. S., & Mayberry, R. (1996). Can lexical/semantic skills differentiate deaf or hard of hearing readers and non-readers? *The Volta Review, 98,* 39–61.

Zheng, Y., Cheng, L., & Klinger, D. A. (2007). Do test formats in reading comprehension affect second-language students' test performance differently? *TESL Canada Journal, 25*(1), 65–80.

INDEX